Your All-in-One Resource

On the CD that accompanies this book, you'll find additional resources to extend your learning. The CD interface resembles the one shown here:

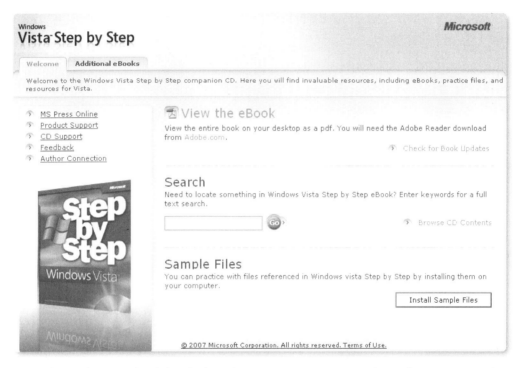

Windows
Vista Step by Step   *Microsoft*

| Welcome | **Additional eBooks** |

Welcome to the Windows Vista Step by Step companion CD. Here you will find invaluable resources, including eBooks, practice files, and resources for Vista.

MS Press Online
Product Support
CD Support
Feedback
Author Connection

View the eBook

View the entire book on your desktop as a pdf. You will need the Adobe Reader download from Adobe.com.

Check for Book Updates

Search

Need to locate something in Windows Vista Step by Step eBook? Enter keywords for a full text search.

[ ] **Go ›**   Browse CD Contents

Sample Files

You can practice with files referenced in Windows vista Step by Step by installing them on your computer.

Install Sample Files

© 2007 Microsoft Corporation. All rights reserved. Terms of Use.

From the Welcome tab of the CD interface, you can access a variety of resources on the CD or online, including the following:

- Search or view the electronic version of this book.
- Install the book's practice files.
- Check for book updates.*
- Get product support or CD support.*
- Send us feedback.

D1712645

* Requires Internet access

From the Additional eBooks tab of the CD interface, you can access electronic books and reference materials on the CD, including the following:

- *Microsoft Computer Dictionary, Fifth Edition*
- *Windows Vista Product Guide*

Microsoft

Building Web Applications with Microsoft® Office SharePoint® Designer 2007 Step by Step

John Jansen

PUBLISHED BY
Microsoft Press
A Division of Microsoft Corporation
One Microsoft Way
Redmond, Washington 98052-6399

Library of Congress Control Number: 2008940521

Printed and bound in the United States of America.

1 2 3 4 5 6 7 8 9   QWT   4 3 2 1 0 9

Distributed in Canada by H.B. Fenn and Company Ltd.

A CIP catalogue record for this book is available from the British Library.

Microsoft Press books are available through booksellers and distributors worldwide. For further information about international editions, contact your local Microsoft Corporation office or contact Microsoft Press International directly at fax (425) 936-7329. Visit our Web site at www.microsoft.com/mspress. Send comments to mspinput@microsoft.com.

Acquisitions Editor: Juliana Aldous Atkinson
Developmental Editor: Sandra Haynes
Project Editor: Valerie Woolley
Editorial Production: Online Training Solutions, Inc.
Technical Reviewer: Bob Hogan; Technical Review services provided by Content Master, a member of CM Group, Ltd.
Cover: Tom Draper Design

Body Part No. X15-28136

Contents

What do you think of this book? We want to hear from you!

Microsoft is interested in hearing your feedback so we can continually improve our books and learning resources for you. To participate in a brief online survey, please visit:

microsoft.com/learning/booksurvey

What do you think of this book? We want to hear from you!

Microsoft is interested in hearing your feedback so we can continually improve our books and learning
resources for you. To participate in a brief online survey, please visit:

microsoft.com/learning/booksurvey

Introduction

Welcome to *Building Web Applications with Microsoft Office SharePoint Designer 2007 Step by Step*. You are probably reading this book because your organization or your Internet service provider has upgraded its server and its intranet to the Microsoft Office SharePoint platform, and you need to know how to build a solution on top of that platform. SharePoint is a powerful platform with which you can create simple solutions to complex business problems. Because of its power, though, it can be somewhat overwhelming, and that makes it difficult to know where to start.

The intent of this book is to guide you to a starting point. When you are building applications on the Web (to streamline an organization's business processes, display inventory in a warehouse, or simply make Web pages look good), there are as many issues that need to be resolved as there are people to resolve to them. There is no way that one book can show you how to address all of your specific needs. However, what this book *can* give you is a fundamental understanding of the SharePoint platform and the way that Microsoft Office SharePoint Designer interacts with that platform. It can provide a description to help you understand what is going on when you perform an action or create an automated business process, and it can give you the tools and insight to modify your solution to the best of your ability.

SharePoint Designer is a complex tool. After you read this book, you will better understand that complexity and how to take advantage of all the tools that are exposed through the SharePoint Designer user interface.

Server Environments

One of the most complex aspects of working with SharePoint is that it is a server technology. SharePoint replaces the old, disparate processes with streamlined, coded solutions, but these solutions run on a server and allow client applications such as Microsoft Office Word and Microsoft Office Excel to be more powerful than they could otherwise be. Working in a server environment is new to a lot of us, and it can at times be difficult to understand why things work the way they do. To make the overall processes simpler for your users, you will need to build solutions that take into consideration the fact that the changes you make are being written to a server, that you are modifying code such as Cascading Style Sheets that is shared across numerous applications, and that you might be accessing data over which you have no control (other than the ability to display it). Before your organization switched to SharePoint, you probably saved a page to a file share and sent out an e-mail message to notify your co-workers where it was. Doing so was simple, though not very manageable; now you can save that document to a SharePoint site, and your co-workers will be notified automatically. Before, you would probably keep track of your contacts in an e-mail program or (worse) in a yellow legal pad, and now you can keep a dynamic list of contacts and actions for those contacts in a SharePoint list. In this book, I not only describe how to accomplish the above scenarios in SharePoint, but also how to use SharePoint Designer to build a rich environment that allows you to customize the notifications, the actions, the status, and the end-to-end usability of the SharePoint platform.

This book is about creating applications on the Web, so looking at what makes up an application is a good place to start. From the server perspective, there are many different ways to think about applications: application pools, Web applications, Webs, sites, site collections, and domains, to name just a few. These terms describe applications from the server administrator or site administrator level, and are therefore not relevant to the scope of this book. For the purposes of this book, an *application* is any object that reacts to input from a user to exercise server code. There are three main components in the definition that are essential: *object*, *input*, and *server code*. When you have a firm understanding of each of those essential elements, this definition will help you as you build upon the lessons in this book.

Although the definition itself is a bit complex, the *scope* of the definition is small. In fact, it can pertain to a single text box on a single page. As you work through this book, you will build several small applications that fit this definition, each of which will exist inside the same SharePoint site. Because your understanding of this definition is so important, we will take a close look at it in Chapter 1, "Working with Web Applications."

Scenarios Addressed by This Book

One of the core scenarios addressed by the SharePoint platform is that of a team that needs to collaborate on a project. In this scenario, each team member needs to be kept in the loop for ongoing activities, and all of the members need to know what is expected of them. In this book, you will build several applications that enable teams to be more productive and in sync. You will create menu controls that enable custom navigation through a Web site, ASP.NET controls that bind to data sources to render dynamic content, data views with conditional formatting and custom filters that create rich views of the data that is important to a team, and workflows that automatically generate status documents based on data entered by different team members. You will also create a rich user interface by modifying master pages, ASP.NET controls, and SharePoint controls.

These goals are applicable *specifically* to any team whose members need to supply information to others, gather information from those teammates, and collaborate with people outside the team to build a successful business. However, the goals will be presented in a way that makes them applicable to a much broader solution. For example, when you build a new menu application, you will do so in a way that applies to any Web site you see on the Internet today. When you create a new data view, you will do so in a way that is relevant to any list of data.

Expectations and Looking Ahead

This book makes some assumptions about your knowledge. It expects that you already have at least a basic knowledge of how SharePoint Designer works and that you have read *Microsoft Office SharePoint Designer 2007 Step by Step* by Penelope Coventry (Microsoft Press, 2008). This book does not spend time describing parts of the user interface that are not relevant to the immediate task at hand, so I recommend that if you have not read that book, you do so first.

SharePoint is a rich platform, and SharePoint Designer is a very powerful tool that is intimately familiar with that platform. In this book, you will jump from the browser to the designer and back to accomplish your goals, and I make it clear when and why it is best to use the browser versus when it is best to use SharePoint Designer.

Microsoft Office SharePoint Designer 2007 is a tool that was created in the Microsoft Office product group specifically for creating applications on the SharePoint platform. It began its life as Microsoft Office FrontPage and, in fact, was built by the product team that had previously released FrontPage. That same team also created Microsoft Expression Web, as well as the design surface for creating Web pages in Web Express in Microsoft Visual Studio. The primary difference between Expression Web 1.0 and SharePoint Designer 2007 is that SharePoint Designer can open sites on the SharePoint platform and then work with content specific to SharePoint, but Expression Web cannot. (However, pages created in Expression Web can be imported into a SharePoint site and then edited via SharePoint Designer.)

FrontPage was divided into these three products so that now a developer can use Visual Studio to create a layout with server controls on it, the developer can hand the layout to an Expression Web page designer who designs the look of the page, and finally the page designer hands the page to a SharePoint Designer application builder who can leverage the page to create a brand for the application. As these products move into later versions, I expect them to become more focused on their own target markets and diverge more (Expression Web 2, for example, supports PHP); however, the design surface should remain relatively consistent. For the purposes of this book, you will use SharePoint Designer for all of these tasks.

I hope that you find this book useful and applicable to your specific challenge, and that you come away with the knowledge and expertise to build rich applications on the SharePoint Platform.

Features and Conventions
of This Book

This book has been designed to lead you step by step through all the tasks you are most likely to want to perform in Microsoft Office SharePoint Designer 2007. If you start at the beginning and work your way through all the exercises, you will gain enough proficiency to be able to create complex Web sites and pages. However, each topic is self contained. If you complete all the exercises and later need help remembering how to perform a procedure, the following features of this book will help you locate specific information:

- **Detailed table of contents.** Scan this listing of the topics within each chapter to quickly find the information you want.

- **Chapter thumb tabs.** Easily locate the beginning of the chapter you want.

- **Topic-specific running heads.** Within a chapter, quickly locate the topic you want by looking at the running head of odd-numbered pages.

- **Detailed index.** Look up specific tasks and features and general concepts in the index, which has been carefully crafted with the reader in mind.

- **Companion CD.** Install the practice files needed for the step-by-step exercises, and consult a fully searchable electronic version of this book and other useful resources contained on this CD.

You can save time when you use this book by understanding how the *Step by Step* series shows special instructions, keys to press, buttons to click, and other functionality.

> **Important** You might notice that the screen shots shown in this book differ in general appearance from those that appear on your screen. The screen shots in this book were captured on a computer running Windows Server 2008 with the Windows Standard color and appearance settings, to optimize the readability of the screen shots.

Convention	Meaning
	This icon indicates a reference to the book's companion CD.
USE	This paragraph preceding a step-by-step exercise indicates the practice files or programs that you will use when working through the exercise.
BE SURE TO	This paragraph preceding or following a step-by-step exercise indicates any requirements you should attend to before beginning the exercise or actions you should take to restore your system after completing the exercise.
1 **2**	Large numbered steps guide you through hands-on exercises.
Tip	These paragraphs provide a helpful hint or shortcut that makes working through a task easier, or information about other available options.
Important	These paragraphs point out information that you need to know to complete a procedure.
Troubleshooting	These paragraphs warn you of potential missteps that might prevent you from continuing with the exercise.
See Also	These paragraphs direct you to more information about a given topic in this book or elsewhere.
Save	The first time you are told to click a button in an exercise, a picture of the button appears in the left margin.
Enter	In step-by-step exercises, keys you must press appear as they would on a keyboard.
Ctrl + Tab	A plus sign (+) between two key names means that you must hold down the first key while you press the second key. For example, "Press Ctrl + Tab" means "hold down the Ctrl key while you press the Tab key."
Program interface elements and user input	In steps, the names of program elements, such as buttons, commands, and dialog boxes, are shown in bold characters. Text that you are supposed to type is also shown in bold characters.
Paths and emphasized words	Folder paths, URLs, and emphasized words are shown in italic characters.

Using the Companion CD

The companion CD included with this book contains the practice files and sample lists you'll use as you work through the book's exercises, as well as other electronic resources that will help you learn how to use Microsoft Office SharePoint Designer 2007. For the exercises in most of the chapters, you will simply use the default Microsoft Windows SharePoint Services Web templates and lists, so those chapters do not include any practice files.

What's on the CD?

The following table lists the practice files and sample lists that are supplied on the book's CD for each exercise.

Chapter	Folder\File
Chapter 1: Working with Web Applications	None
Chapter 2: Working with SharePoint Sites in SharePoint Designer	None
Chapter 3: Accessing the Styles Behind SharePoint Pages	None
Chapter 4: Creating Layout with Cascading Style Sheets	None
Chapter 5: Working with Master Pages	MasterPages\newDefault.master
Chapter 6: Creating Custom Navigation Controls	ASPControls\newDefault.master ASPControls\tempDefault.aspx
Chapter 7: Creating Data Sources in SharePoint	None
Chapter 8: Creating Data Views	DataViews\Customers.stp DataViews\newDefault.master DataViews\tempDefault.aspx
Chapter 9: Using ASP.NET and SharePoint Controls in Data Views	DataViewControls\menu.xml DataViewControls\newDefault.master DataViewControls\tempDefault.aspx
Chapter 10: Using Parameters in a Data View	Parameters\newParameters.aspx Parameters\products.stp
Chapter 11: Customizing List Forms and Pages	None
Chapter 12: Using the Windows Workflow Foundation	None

In addition to the practice files and sample lists, the CD contains some exciting resources that will enhance your ability to get the most out of using this book and SharePoint Designer, including the following:

- *Building Web Applications with Microsoft Office SharePoint Designer 2007 Step by Step* in eBook format
- *Microsoft Computer Dictionary, Fifth Edition* eBook
- *Windows Vista Product Guide*

> **Important** The companion CD for this book does not contain the Microsoft Office SharePoint Designer 2007 software. You should purchase and install that software before using this book. You can download a trial version of the software at *www.microsoft.com/downloads/details.aspx?FamilyID=baa3ad86-bfc1-4bd4-9812-d9e710d44f42&DisplayLang=en.*

Minimum System Requirements

To perform the exercises in this book, ensure that your computer meets the requirements described in this section.

SharePoint Designer

Your computer should meet the following requirements to run SharePoint Designer:

- **Processor.** Pentium 700 megahertz (MHz) or higher; 2 gigahertz (GHz) recommended.
- **Memory.** 512 megabytes (MB) of RAM; 1 gigabyte (GB) or more recommended.
- **Hard disk.** For the eBooks and downloads, we recommend 3 GB of available hard disk space with 2 GB on the hard disk where the operating system is installed. SharePoint Designer requires a minimum of 1.5 GB of hard disk space.

> **Tip** Hard disk space requirements vary depending on configuration; custom installation choices might require more or less hard disk space.

- **Operating System.** Windows XP with Service Pack 1 (SP1), Windows Vista, Windows Server 2003, or Windows Server 2008.
- **Drive.** DVD drive.
- **Display.** Monitor with 1024 x 768 or higher screen resolution and 16-bit or higher color depth.

Windows SharePoint Services

In addition to SharePoint Designer, you might also need Windows SharePoint Services 3.0 on your computer. This would be the case if you do not yet have an Internet service provider that hosts SharePoint for you, or if your company has not yet installed it on your corporate intranet. Your computer should meet the following requirements to run Windows SharePoint Services:

- **Operating System.** Windows Server 2003 with Service Pack 1 (Windows SharePoint Services with Service Pack 1 will also install on Windows Server 2003 64-bit editions and Windows Server 2008)
- **Processor.** 2.5 gigahertz (GHz) recommended
- **Memory.** 1.0 gigabyte (GB) of RAM recommended
- **Software.** Microsoft .NET Framework 3.0

Step-by-Step Exercises

In addition to the hardware, software, and connections required to run SharePoint Designer 2007, you will need the following to successfully complete the exercises in this book:

- 1 MB of available hard disk space for the practice files

Installing the Practice Files

All exercises in *Building Web Applications with Microsoft Office SharePoint Designer 2007 Step by Step* use the blog Web site template that is included when you connect to Windows SharePoint Services 3.0 via a browser or SharePoint Designer. For some exercises, there are also practice files and sample lists that come on this book's accompanying CD.

To install the files from the CD:

1. Remove the companion CD from the envelope at the back of the book, and insert it into the CD drive of your computer.

The Step By Step Companion CD License Terms appear. Follow the on-screen directions. To use the practice files, you must accept the terms of the license agreement. After you accept the license agreement, a menu page appears.

> **Important** If the menu page does not appear, click the Start button, and then click Computer. Display the Folders list in the Navigation Pane, click the icon for your CD drive, and then in the right pane, double-click the StartCD executable file.

2. Click **Install Practice Files**.

3. Click **Next** on the first page, and then click **Next** to accept the terms of the license agreement on the next page.

4. If you want to install the practice files to a location other than the default folder (*Documents\Microsoft Press\BuildingWebAppsSBS*), click the **Change** button, select the new drive and path, and then click **OK**.

> **Important** If you install the practice files to a location other than the default, you will need to substitute that path within the exercises.

5. Click **Next** on the **Choose Destination Location** page, and then click **Install** on the **Ready to Install the Program** page to install the selected practice files.

6. After the practice files have been installed, click **Finish**.

7. Close the **Step by Step Companion CD** window, remove the companion CD from the CD drive, and return it to the envelope at the back of the book.

Using the Practice Files

When you install the practice files and sample lists from the companion CD, the files are stored on your hard disk in chapter-specific subfolders under *Documents\Microsoft Press\ BuildingWebAppsSBS*. Each exercise is preceded by a Housekeeping segment that lists the sample content needed for that exercise and any extra tasks you need to complete before you start working through the exercise, as shown here:

USE the *newDefault.master* file. This practice file is located in the *Documents\Microsoft Press\ BuildingWebAppsSBS\MasterPages* folder.

BE SURE TO display the *newDefault.master* page in SharePoint Designer before beginning this exercise.

Wherever possible, we made the exercises independent of each other. However, if you choose to do exercises in a sequence other than that presented in the book, be aware that there are exercises in some chapters that depend on other exercises performed earlier in the book. If this is the case, we will tell you where in the book the prerequisite exercises are located.

After the practice files have been installed on your computer, you can import them into your SharePoint site to use during an exercise by performing the following steps:

1. Display a SharePoint site in SharePoint Designer.

2. On the **File** menu, point to **Import**, and then click **File**.

   The Import dialog box opens.

3. Click **Add File**.

   The Add File To Import List dialog box opens.

4. Navigate to *Documents\Microsoft Press\BuildingWebAppsSBS\<foldername>* (where *<foldername>* is the name of the folder that corresponds to the chapter in which you are working).

5. Select the file you want to import, and click **Open**.

   The Import dialog box shows that the selected file will be imported to the root of the open site.

6. Click **OK**.

   The file is imported into the site.

In addition, you can browse to the practice files in Windows Explorer by following these steps:

1. Click the **Start** button, and then click **Documents**.

2. In your Documents folder, double-click Microsoft Press, double-click BuildingWebAppsSBS, and then double-click a specific chapter folder.

To create the practice lists for a chapter in which you need to use a list .stp file provided on the CD, perform the following steps:

1. Log on with sufficient rights to upload a list template to the list gallery at the top level of a site collection.

2. Open the top-level SharePoint site to which you need to upload the list template in the browser.

3. Click **Site Actions**, and then click **Site Settings**.

   The Site Settings page loads in the browser.

> **Important** On Microsoft Office SharePoint Server, you will need to point to Site Settings, and then click Modify All Site Settings.

4. In the **Galleries** section, click **List Templates**.

5. Click **Upload** to display the **Upload Template: List Template Gallery** page.

6. Click the **Browse** button to open the **Choose File** dialog box.

7. Navigate to *Documents\Microsoft Press\BuildingWebAppsSBS\<foldername>*, where *<foldername>* is the name of the folder associated with the chapter.

8. Click the .stp file that you want to use to create the new list, and then click the **Open** button.

9. Click **OK.**

   The List Template Gallery: *<foldername>* page is displayed.

10. Click **OK** to redisplay the **List Template Gallery** page.

    You can now create a new list based on the template you just uploaded to the site. For chapters that require the list, there will also be a couple of list items created when the list is created, so you will have some sample data to use in the exercise.

11. Click **View All Site Content**.

12. Click **Create**.

13. Click the name of the list you uploaded in step 8.

14. Give the list the same name as the list you uploaded in step 8, and click **Create**.

    The list is created and ready to use.

Removing the Practice Files

You can free up hard disk space by uninstalling the practice files that were installed from the companion CD. The uninstall process deletes any files that you created in the *Documents\Microsoft Press\BuildingWebAppsSBS* folder while working through the exercises.

Follow these steps:

1. Click the **Start** button, and then click **Control Panel**.

2. In **Control Panel**, under **Programs and features** (Vista) or **Add or Remove Programs** (Windows XP), click the **Uninstall a program** task.

3. Select **Building Web Apps with SharePoint Designer SBS**, and click **Uninstall**.

4. Follow the prompts asking you to confirm the uninstall.

Removing the .Stp Files

After creating a list from a sample .stp file, you can remove that template from the List Gallery by performing the following steps:

1. Log on with sufficient rights to delete a list template from the top-level **List Template** gallery.

2. Open the top-level SharePoint site where you uploaded the list template .stp files.

3. Click **Site Actions**, and then click **Site Settings** to display the **Site Settings** page.

4. In the **Galleries** category, click **List templates** to display the **List Template Gallery** page.

> **Important** On Microsoft Office SharePoint Server, you will need to point to Site Settings, and then click Modify All Site Settings.

5. Click the **Edit** icon to display the details of the list template.

6. Click **Delete Item** to remove the list template from the **List Template Gallery**.

7. Click **OK** to confirm the request.

> **Tip** Even though the list template has now been deleted, any lists that were created based on that template will continue to function normally.

See Also If you need additional help installing or uninstalling the practice files, see the "Getting Help" section later in this book.

> **Important** Microsoft Product Support Services does not provide support for this book or its companion CD.

Getting Help

Every effort has been made to ensure the accuracy of this book and the contents of its CD. If you run into problems, please contact the appropriate source, listed in the following sections, for help and assistance.

Getting Help with This Book and Its CD

Microsoft Press provides support for books and companion CDs at the following Web site:

www.microsoft.com/learning/support/books/

Getting Help with Microsoft Office SharePoint Designer 2007

If your question is about Microsoft Office SharePoint Designer 2007, and not about the content of this Microsoft Press book, please search the Microsoft Help and Support Center or the Microsoft Knowledge Base at:

support.microsoft.com

You can also visit the following Web site, where you can ask John Jansen, the author of this book, any specific questions you might have about SharePoint Designer, and find other SharePoint Designer–related resources:

www.SPDAssist.com

In the United States, Microsoft software product support issues not covered by the Microsoft Knowledge Base are addressed by Microsoft Product Support Services. Location-specific software support options are available from:

support.microsoft.com/gp/selfoverview

Outside the United States, for support information specific to your location, please refer to the Worldwide Support menu on the Microsoft Help and Support Web site for the site specific to your country:

support.microsoft.com/common/international.aspx

Another source of help is the SharePoint Designer newsgroup:

social.msdn.microsoft.com/Forums/en-US/sharepointcustomization/threads/

Finally, you can read the SharePoint Designer team blog to get helpful tips as well as ideas about where the product is heading:

blogs.msdn.com/sharepointdesigner/

Questions and Comments

If you have comments, questions, or ideas regarding the book or the companion CD, or questions that are not answered by visiting the sites previously mentioned, please send them to Microsoft Press via e-mail to

mspinput@microsoft.com

Or via postal mail to

Microsoft Press
Attn: *Building Web Applications with Microsoft Office SharePoint Designer 2007 Step by Step* Editor
One Microsoft Way
Redmond, WA 98052-6399

Please note that Microsoft software product support is not offered through these addresses.

Chapter at a Glance

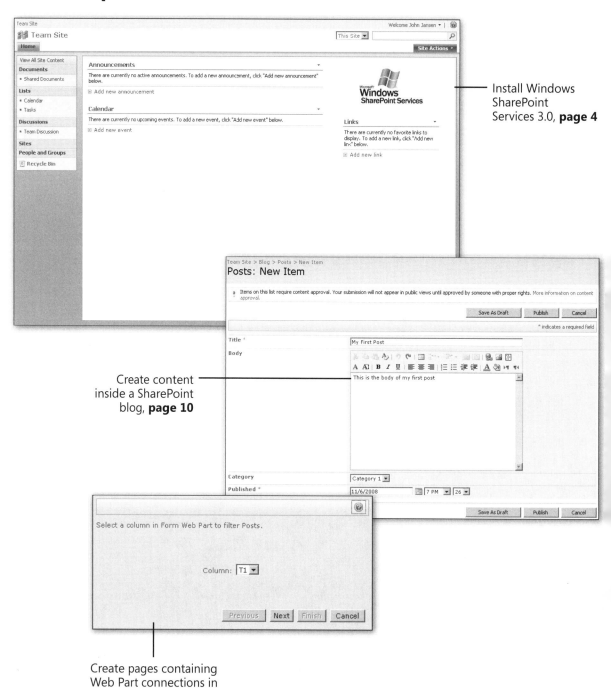

Install Windows
SharePoint
Services 3.0, **page 4**

Create content
inside a SharePoint
blog, **page 10**

Create pages containing
Web Part connections in
SharePoint, **page 12**

1 Working with Web Applications

In this chapter, you will learn to

- ✔ Recognize a Web application.
- ✔ Install Windows SharePoint Services 3.0.
- ✔ Use SharePoint site templates.
- ✔ Create a SharePoint blog.
- ✔ Create content inside a SharePoint blog.
- ✔ Create pages containing Web Part connections in SharePoint.

Web applications are everywhere. The Internet started off as a way for people to communicate in the event of an emergency, grew into a place where people could build small informational Web sites, and then grew into a place where people could sell items online. It has evolved into a place where people can interact directly with Web page content and have a rich user experience in which they gain and share information and knowledge. Almost every time you click a button, type in a search term, or post a comment to a news article on a Web site, you are interacting with a Web application. And there are many tools available now to help you create this rich user experience. Using Microsoft Office SharePoint Designer 2007, you have access to a rich platform upon which you can quickly and easily build your own applications.

In this chapter, you will learn how to recognize Web applications as they function in the real world, based on a narrow definition of what Web applications actually are. You will then install Microsoft Windows SharePoint Services 3.0 and browse the templates that ship with that platform. Next, you'll take a look at how to create sites on this platform, what the sites' structures look like, how they work out of the box, and what additional problems they might solve for you. After that, we'll take a look at the specific ways pages are created in SharePoint so you can better understand how to customize and build your own applications.

See Also For more information about the site templates that install with Windows SharePoint Services, see *Inside Microsoft Windows SharePoint Services 3.0*, by Ted Pattison and Daniel Larson (Microsoft Press, 2007).

Important There are no practice files for this chapter.

Recognizing a Web Application

As I explained in the introduction to this book, an application requires three components: objects, input, and server code.

In this exercise, you will take a brief look at the core components that make up an application on the Internet.

BE SURE TO start your Internet browser before beginning this exercise.

1. In your browser, go to *www.msn.com*.

2. Scroll down to the **Quotes** section, and type **MSFT** into the **Get quote** text box.

3. Click **Go**.

A new page loads from MSN Money with details about Microsoft stock and the company as a whole.

4. Look around this page and notice all of the rich content that loaded based on the text you typed into the text box on MSN.

Data details   Intraday chart   Stock health

According to the definition of *application* used here, this page loaded with a number of applications. For example, there are *objects* (data details, an intraday chart, and a company stock health object) on the page that reacted to *input* from a user (typing MSFT and clicking Go) to run *server code*. (Server code is invisible to the end user. On this page, this is the code that MSN Money developers wrote that queries the stock exchange and returns this content.) In addition, there is an application that returns recent news, another that returns videos, and so on. The point here is that we all experience applications on the Web all the time as we browse around, and we typically don't realize it or think about it. Another key point is that by some definitions of what an application is, this entire page is one application, or the entire moneycentral domain is considered an application. Those definitions are not relevant here: for our purposes, applications are small. Applications work well together in the container of a Web page or site, but they can also be moved around and modified to fit different specific circumstances. In later chapters, you'll build generic applications on SharePoint that will demonstrate this portability. For now, though, you need to install the platform and begin to explore it as a platform.

Installing Windows SharePoint Services 3.0

In order to create applications on top of Windows SharePoint Services or Microsoft Office SharePoint Server, you first need to install SharePoint on your server. The applications we will be building will leverage Windows SharePoint Services (WSS) but will also work on Microsoft Office SharePoint Server (MOSS). WSS and MOSS are built on the same essential platform, but MOSS has a number of additional features. When using SharePoint Designer 2007 to author applications on the SharePoint platform, these differences manifest themselves in the following ways:

- When you create a new site on MOSS, there are more site templates available to you than there are on WSS.
- When you view the toolbox in SharePoint Designer and have a MOSS site open, there will be more controls available.
- MOSS uses a concept called *layout pages*, which is outside the scope of this book.

Before installing Windows SharePoint Services, verify that your server meets the requirements given in the "Minimum System Requirements" section of "Using the Companion CD" at the beginning of this book.

For computers running Windows Server 2003, the ASP.NET v2.0.50727 status must be set to "Allowed" in the Web Service Extension section of Internet Information Services Manager.

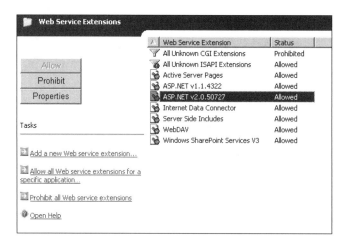

> **Important** If you cannot meet the minimum requirements for any reason, I recommend you use a hosting company for your SharePoint server. I use one myself for my wife's business site as well as for the site captured in all of the screen shots for this book, and it works great. You can find a host by searching online for terms such as "Hosted SharePoint Environment."

After you verify that your server meets these requirements, you should be ready to run the setup program. If your computer does not meet one or more of the requirements, the SharePoint installer will notify you before the installation begins. This way, you don't end up having to go through the entire process only to get a warning at the very end (as is the case with many setup programs).

In this exercise, you will download, install, and configure Windows SharePoint Services 3.0 using the default configuration settings.

> **Important** If you have already installed WSS and did not use the default settings, that should not impact your ability to follow along with the exercises in this book. I recommend that you leave your installation as it is and not try to reinstall using these steps.

 **BE SURE TO** start your Internet browser before beginning this exercise.

1. Browse to *www.microsoft.com/downloads/*.

2. Search for **WSS 3.0**.

3. In the list of results, click the **WSS 3.0 SP1** link.

> **Tip** At the time of this writing that link points to this address:
>
> *www.microsoft.com/downloads/details.aspx?familyid=4191A531-A2E9-45E4-B71E-5B0B17108BD2&displaylang=en*

4. Scroll down the page and click **Download** for the version of the server you are running (x64 or x86).

5. Click **Run**.

> **Important** If you are missing any of the prerequisites, you will be prompted to install them at this point.

6. If you agree with the Software License Terms, select the **Accept the Microsoft Software License Terms** check box and click **Continue**.

7. Click **Basic** to begin the installation.

> **Important**   There are a lot of possible choices when installing SharePoint on your server. For example, you can choose to install a *farm*, use external SQL databases, or use individual search servers. For the purposes of building applications on SharePoint, however, none of these choices directly impacts what we are going to create in this book. For more information about working with these choices in SharePoint, I recommend that you read *Microsoft SharePoint Products and Technologies Administrator's Pocket Consultant,* by Ben Curry (Microsoft Press, 2007).

After the installation completes, the SharePoint Products And Technologies Configuration Wizard launches automatically.

8. On the wizard's first page, click **Next**.

9. In the warning box that appears, click **Yes** to acknowledge that some services will need to be stopped during configuration.

10. Wait for the wizard to complete the necessary configuration steps, and then click **Finish**.

> **Troubleshooting**   Depending on how your server is configured, you may be prompted to log in to the site. If you are, be sure to use the administrator's username and password provided to you by your server administrator.

Your browser launches, displaying your new team site.

Using SharePoint Site Templates

When you created a new site by using the configuration wizard in the previous section, the WSS team site template was used as the basis for all content. In looking at the *default.aspx* page, you can get a good sense of what specific problem the site template is trying to solve.

This site is a *team site*, which was developed by the SharePoint platform team as a solution for ad hoc teams that need to keep track of upcoming events, documents, announcements, and links. Partly because this is the default template, the team site is probably the most popular site template used on SharePoint; that is not the only reason, however. This site is a fantastic use of the core requirements of any team.

Navigation system   User login   Search

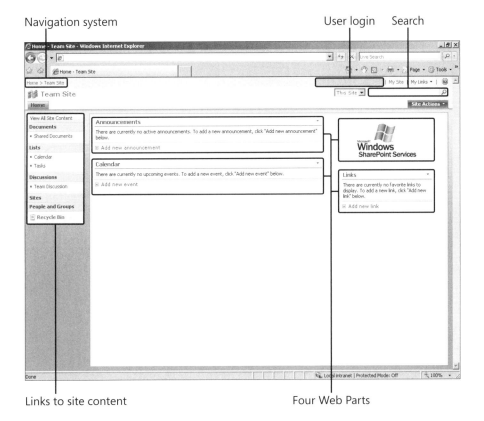

Links to site content   Four Web Parts

These core requirements are listed here:

- **A navigation system.** Across the top of each page in a SharePoint site is a *bread crumb* trail that shows you where you are and how to get back to the home page.
- **Search capabilities.** The Search box allows you to search either the entire site collection, the subsite you are navigating, or a specific list or document library.

● **A user login.** This allows a user to log in with his or her credentials or as another user with permissions to the site.

● **Four Web Parts.** The Announcements, Calendar, and Links Web Parts on this page show the default views for each of these lists, allowing the site designer to push the most important information into the home page for the site. The Image Web Part allows the site administrator to set a custom image representative of the team to show the other people who browse to this site.

● **A list of links to site content.** The list of links on the left (also called the Quick Launch bar) shows a link to each list on an opt-in basis, as well as links to other sites and the recycle bin for the site.

I typically use this site template for my work and then simply customize it to fit my needs. However, in some cases it would be a lot easier and make more sense to just select a different site template and customize that. In fact, the more familiar you become with each of the different site templates, the less you will need to customize later to get the core functionality you need.

Creating a SharePoint Blog

Out of the box in SharePoint there are a number of helpful site templates. In the previous sections, we created a team site and took a brief look at the default page for that site, which provided rich content to solve a specific need. However, there are times when you will need a more specific solution. For example, you might be in the position of needing to create a living document of text and definitions, in which case you would use the Wiki Site template. Or you might be in the position of needing to create a daily log of your thoughts and plans and allow others to comment on those posts, in which case you would use a blog.

In this exercise, you will create a blog site by using the Blog site template.

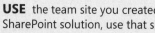

> **USE** the team site you created in the previous exercise, or if you will be using a hosted SharePoint solution, use that site.
>
> **BE SURE TO** display the site home page in your browser before beginning this exercise.

1. On the **Site Actions** menu, click **Create**.

The Create page displays a list of choices.

2. In the **Web Pages** category, click **Sites and Workspaces**.

3. On the **New SharePoint Site** page, give the new site a title of **Blog**.

4. For the description, type **My Blog Site**.

5. For the URL name, type **Blog**.

6. On the **Collaboration** tab of the **Select a Template** list, click **Blog**.

The image and the summary description for this site template change. The description lets you know this is "a site for a person or team to post ideas, observations, and expertise that site visitors can comment on."

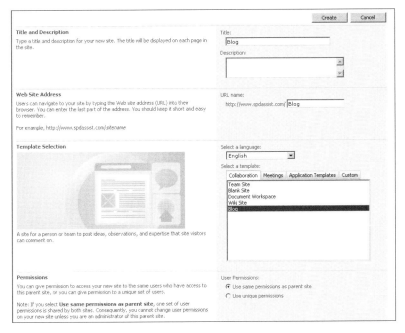

7. Leave the permissions at their default setting so that this site will inherit permissions, will be displayed on the Quick Launch bar of the parent site, will display on the top link bar of the parent site, and will use the link bar from the parent site.

8. Click **Create** to create this new site.

SharePoint creates an instance of the selected site template and puts the required content into your subsite. You now have a blog.

Creating Content Inside a SharePoint Blog

One of the reasons I chose to use a blog here is because of the relative popularity of these types of sites, but also because blog sites come with functionality you will not find in any other site template. We will leverage this functionality in a later chapter; in particular, the SharePoint blog sites have a *one-to-many* relationship of lists by default (for every one post, there can be zero or more comments).

In this exercise, you will create a blog post and comment on that post in order to leverage complex application logic.

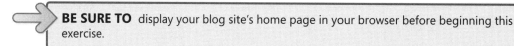

BE SURE TO   display your blog site's home page in your browser before beginning this exercise.

1. In the **Admin Links** section of the home page, click **Create a Post**.

2. Type **My First Post** as the title and **This is the body of my first post** as the body. In the **Category** list, click **Category 1**.

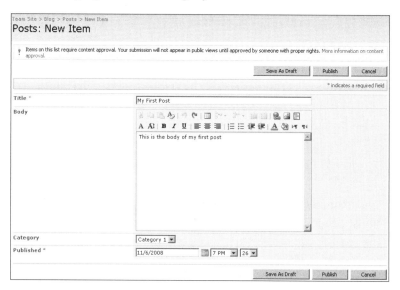

3. Click **Publish**.

SharePoint creates a blog post, which is now visible on the home page of the blog site.

4. Click **Comments (0)** at the bottom of this post.

5. Type **Great Post!** for the title of this comment, and add the body text **Great Post!**.

6. Click **Submit Comment** to save your comment, which associates it with this specific blog post.

In practical terms, you just took advantage of the out-of-the-box application that ties comments to posts by leveraging a one-to-many relationship. The application keeps track of the number of posts and allows you to browse to a page that will show you the original post as well as all the comments. Building this kind of application from scratch would be difficult, but because it is essential for a blog, it was created by the platform team for inclusion in SharePoint. What I like best about something like this is that not only is this functionality necessary for a blog, it solves a common problem necessary for a number of applications, and we can leverage it later in a site that is nothing like a blog. For example, we can use the Blog template to create a page for ratings, say for a reference to a book or training video; others could comment on the value of that material, giving it a rating of stars, and you can then create a summary of how many stars that material has received, and so on. I'm getting ahead of myself, because we will create an application that does this later in this book, but you can imagine something similar to what popular book or music Web sites have to show what their users think of the items that they are selling. All of this is to say that the more you know about the underlying functionality of any site template, the more you can take advantage of that functionality.

Creating Pages Containing Web Part Connections in SharePoint

All the functionality in the world wouldn't be worth much if there weren't Web pages on which to show the results of those applications. When creating pages in your browser, you must save them to a *document library* (in SharePoint Designer, pages can be saved to any location inside the Web site). Document libraries are special folders in SharePoint that have a lot of special logic within them. For example, document libraries come with several pages that allow you to upload items, edit items, display the details of specific items, and see a list of all the items stored in them. They also have pages for setting properties such as permissions and views.

See Also For more detailed information about document libraries, refer to *Inside Microsoft Office SharePoint Server 2007*, by Patrick Tisseghem (Microsoft Press, 2007).

SharePoint Pages (also called Web Part pages) also contain special content. They can be edited by clicking a few simple controls in the browser, dragging and dropping Web Parts from one Web Part zone on the page to another, or by changing Web Part properties (such as Extensible Stylesheet Language for Transformations, or XSLT), which will be covered in detail in Chapter 8, "Creating Views of Data."

These pages are based on the default master page for the SharePoint site. Basing these pages on master pages means that the general look and feel of SharePoint pages are consistent: all pages have the same color scheme and typically have the same header and navigation as well as search controls.

In this exercise, you will create a Web Part page in the browser and then add two Web Parts to that page to create a simple SharePoint application.

 BE SURE TO display your blog site's home page in your browser before beginning this exercise.

1. On the **Site Actions** menu, click **Create**.

   The Create page opens.

2. In the **Libraries** section of this page, click **Document Library**.

   The New page opens. On this page, you can name the document library.

3. Type **Documents** into the **Name** text box.

> **Tip** Leave the rest of the default settings alone; this will allow the Documents link to show up in the Quick Launch bar of the site and will not create a version each time a document is edited.

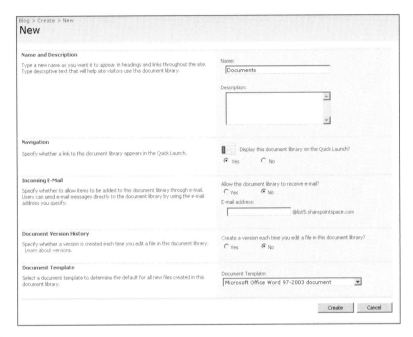

4. Click **Create** to create the document library.

5. On the *default.aspx* page of your blog site, click **Create** on the **Site Actions** menu.

6. In the **Web Pages** section, click **Web Part Page**.

The New Web Part page opens.

7. Give the page the name **testpage**.

8. Click through each of the different page templates to see the preview of each of the different pages; then click **Full Page, Vertical** for the layout of this page.

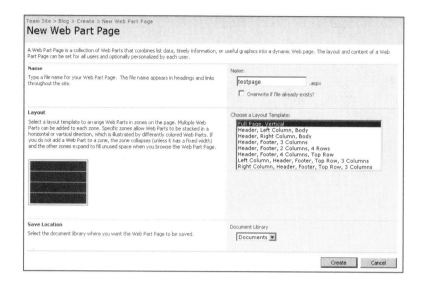

> **Important** Notice that the Save Location option is set to Documents. If you had not created a document library first, the Save Location option would be grayed out and there would be a link to create a new document library.

9. Click **Create** to create the Web Part page.

This creates a new page inside the Documents document library you just created. The page is also in Edit mode, which means that by default you are able to add new Web Parts to this page.

10. In the middle of the page, click **Add a Web Part**.

The Add Web Parts To Full Page dialog box opens.

11. Select the **Posts** check box and then under **All Web Parts**, select the **Form Web Part** check box.

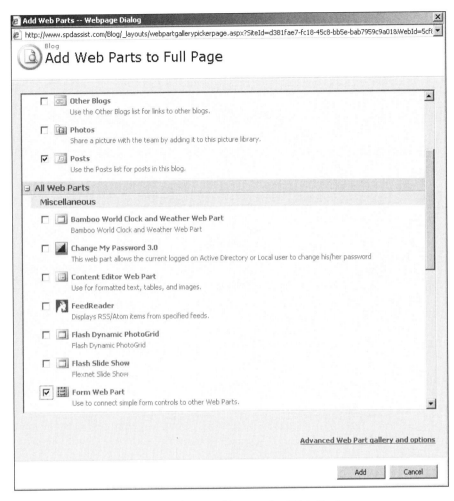

12. Click **Add** to close the dialog box and insert the Web Parts.

13. Scroll down to see the Form Web Part. On the toolbar for the Web Part, click **Edit**, point to **Connections**, point to **Provide Form Values To**, and then click **Posts**.

The Web Part Connections Wizard starts.

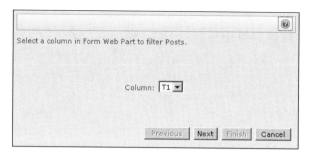

14. With **T1** selected in the **Column** list, click **Next**.

15. Leave the **Column** set to **Title** and click **Next** to finish the wizard and return to the page in Edit mode.

16. Click **Exit Edit Mode** to complete your edits and save the page.

17. Scroll down to the form and type **My First Post** into the text box.

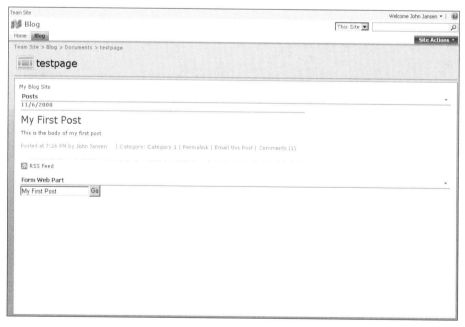

18. Click **Go**.

Congratulations! You have just created your first application in SharePoint. You'll notice that after you clicked Go, the default blog post disappeared and you were left with the post that you created earlier in this chapter. When you type text into the text box and click Go, a *postback* occurs to the page and the Posts Web Part (which is really a List View Web Part showing any posts made to your blog) is filtered so that the title of the post equals the text typed into the text box. Although this is certainly interesting, it exposes some very core functionality of SharePoint and probably has you thinking about a few things you could accomplish using Web Part connections in SharePoint. However, you might also have noticed that the Web Part connection filters correctly only when your entire text is found in the title of the Posts Web Part. In later chapters we will create more complex Web Part connections that leverage the *contains* verb to build more robust solutions.

Key Points

- Applications are ubiquitous on the Internet, and understanding how they work is paramount to understanding how to build them.

- Building applications in SharePoint means building sections of a page that interact with each other.

- SharePoint has a built-in infrastructure for building applications, and in fact ships with some very functional applications out of the box.

- Blog sites have code built into them that allows automatic one-to-many relationships to exist in SharePoint.

- Building a simple application can be as easy as dragging and dropping items inside your favorite Web browser.

Chapter at a Glance

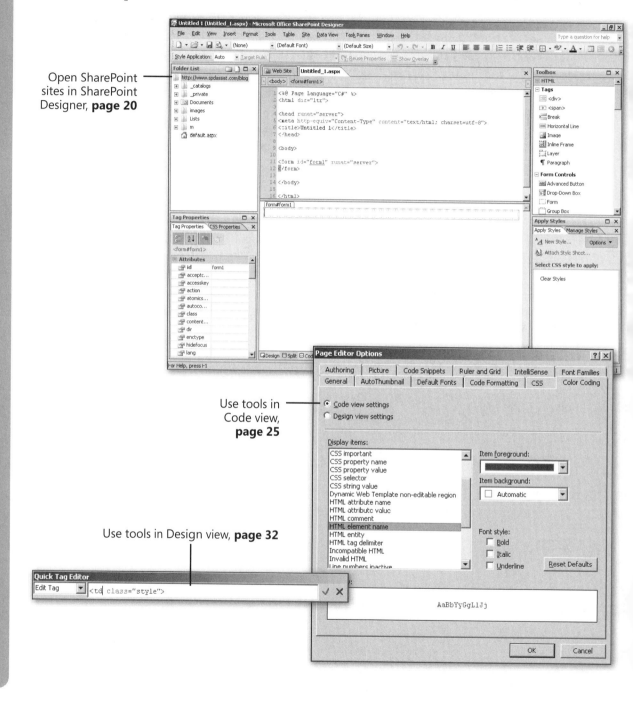

Open SharePoint sites in SharePoint Designer, **page 20**

Use tools in Code view, **page 25**

Use tools in Design view, **page 32**

2 Working with SharePoint Sites in SharePoint Designer

In this chapter, you will learn to

- ✔ Open SharePoint sites in SharePoint Designer.
- ✔ Use tools in Code view.
- ✔ Use tools in Design view.

After you install Microsoft Windows SharePoint Services 3.0 and have the root site for the server open in Microsoft Office SharePoint Designer 2007, you can create rich content on top of that provided by the default site template to design your Web application interface.

Every Web application you create should have an interface that enhances the application not only by making it nice to look at, but also by making it easier to use. SharePoint Designer has a rich set of tools targeted at making this design as straightforward as possible, while at the same time exposing you to constructs and syntax specific to the SharePoint platform. Now that you have created a blog site and seen some of the SharePoint platform exposed to you, you have already leveraged some of the rich functionality exposed when you create new sites, pages, and Web Parts. However, the more robust activities of customization and branding require using SharePoint Designer 2007. As I mentioned in the introduction to this book, I expect that you already know your way around SharePoint Designer to some degree, so this chapter is going to focus on some of the lesser-known tools in SharePoint Designer that will help you create applications faster.

In this chapter, you will work within the blog site you created in Chapter 1, "Working with Web Applications," to become familiar with how the tools in SharePoint Designer bring certain aspects of the the SharePoint platform to the surface. You will be using this same blog site throughout this book so that the lists and content on the pages are consistent with the screen shots; however, all of the constructs and tools demonstrated here are also applicable to other Windows SharePoint Services sites. After you open the site in SharePoint Designer, you will learn to create new pages that will enable you to see the specifics of the user interface for working with SharePoint. Finally, you'll be introduced to and practice using some of the Design view and Code view tools written specifically to help you rapidly create applications on SharePoint.

> **Important** The exercises in this chapter require only the blog site you created and modified in the previous chapter. No practice files are supplied on the companion CD. For more information about practice files, see "Using the Companion CD" at the beginning of this book.

Opening SharePoint Sites in SharePoint Designer

In this chapter, you will see the SharePoint platform as it is exposed in the SharePoint Designer user interface (UI). Because the SharePoint platform is built on top of Microsoft ASP.NET 2.0 as well as the Microsoft Office FrontPage Server Extensions, you will see some UI elements that are not needed for building SharePoint applications. These elements are there primarily for backward compatibility with FrontPage and also because you can use SharePoint Designer for non-SharePoint platform application development. I'll spend only cursory time in this book addressing those elements, and spend the majority of the time focused on the UI elements necessary for the task at hand. If you have read Penelope Coventry's book *Microsoft Office SharePoint Designer 2007 Step by Step* (Microsoft Press, 2008), the interface is described very effectively, so I don't want to take time here being redundant with that book. However, there are certain key elements to the UI that help us build applications in SharePoint Designer, and I do want to call attention to those.

The most important elements on this design surface are the toolbars, the page, and the task panes, all of which are described in the following list:

- **Toolbars.** Across the top are the fairly standard Microsoft Office toolbars. We'll use them throughout the book, but they don't require explanation.

- **Folder List.** The upper-left task pane is the Folder List, which shows the subsites in the current site as well as all the folders and pages in the site. I use this task pane a lot in order to create data views, open master pages, and import files.

- **Tag Properties.** The lower-left task pane loads Tag Properties by default; I usually change this one to show the cascading style sheet (CSS) properties because I am more likely to modify tag properties in Code view than in the task pane, but I modify CSS by using the task pane. You will use the CSS Properties task pane extensively throughout this book.

- **Toolbox.** In the upper-right corner you can see the Toolbox, which loads all the controls that can be inserted on a page. The Toolbox loads based on the current context of the design surface, so if you have a SharePoint page open, the Toolbox will load with SharePoint controls in addition to HTML and ASP.NET controls.

- **Apply Styles.** Below the Toolbox is the Apply Styles task pane, which is empty now because we don't yet have any style sheets applied, but which we will use extensively as well.

- **Code panel.** The Code panel displays the HTML code that is generated when you insert HTML or controls onto the design surface.

- **Design panel.** The Design panel is a near-WYSIWYG ("What You See Is What You Get") display of the HTML and controls you insert from the Toolbox or via the other pieces of the UI.

Designers usually work using multiple monitors and then drag the task panes off the application surface and drop them onto a separate monitor. I do this when I do any design work (using graphics programs, Microsoft Silverlight designers, or SharePoint Designer) in order to maximize the design surface and move the tools out of the way. Other designers I work with take this to the extreme and remove their toolbars, timelines, status bars, and task panes onto other monitors as well, so that the only thing left is the design surface.

In this exercise, you will open the blog site you created in Chapter 1 and then explore the SharePoint Designer user interface.

> **BE SURE TO** start SharePoint Designer before beginning this exercise.

1. On the **File** menu, click **Open Site**.

   The Open Site dialog box opens.

> **Important** You must click Open *Site* here and not Open *File*. SharePoint Designer provides a much different user experience depending on whether you have a page open or a site open. For example, when you have only a page open, the Site command on the Standard toolbar is disabled, the ability to insert SharePoint controls is disabled, and the tools for creating and working with master pages are disabled, as are commands for publishing and working with SharePoint pages.

2. In the **Site Name** text box, type **http://<*computername*>** if you installed SharePoint locally, or the URL of your SharePoint site if you are using a host. If prompted, provide the appropriate user name and password to load the site.

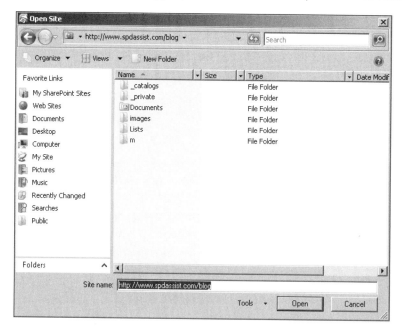

For example, I typed in *http://www.spdassist.com/blog/*, but I could just as well have typed in *http://johnjansen* (which is the name of my computer where I also have SharePoint installed).

> **Important** Remember to use the HTTP address of your site. If you are familiar with the way that servers work, you might be tempted to open the site via a network share or from the file system, but SharePoint Designer has functionality specific to running over the HTTP protocol by using remote procedure calls. If you open the site by using any other method, some features will not work, such as inserting Web Parts and Web Part zones, or inserting Web components from the Web Components dialog box.

3. Click the **Open** button to open your site.

   The Open Site dialog box might load your site in the Folder View list box and might throw an error that says "Folder name is invalid." If so, simply clear the site name in the URL and click Open again. Your site loads up in the SharePoint Designer application.

4. Click **Task Panes**, and then click **Reset Workspace Layout**.

5. Create a new page by pressing [Ctrl]+[N].

   By default, this creates a simple ASPX page.

6. Display the page in Split view by pointing to **Page** on the **View** menu and then clicking **Split**.

> **Tip** No matter what you've done to your task panes before reading this book, the above action will display them in the default designer settings. I do this not because I think this layout is the best—in fact, I do not—but because this way I can take a screen shot and describe how each of the panes helps with SharePoint application development.

Folder List　　Code panel　　Page in Split view　　Design panel　　Toolbox

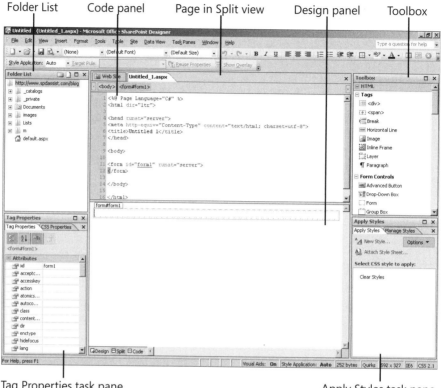

Tag Properties task pane　　　　　　　　　　　　Apply Styles task pane

As you can see, this default task pane configuration leaves the task panes inside the application, which shrinks the design surface down. In fact, at certain monitor resolutions, the design surface might shrink down to almost nothing and you will have to close the task panes to do your work. If that is the case for you, I recommend dragging the important task panes over from the right and dropping them onto task panes on the left, then closing the ones on the right completely. It is more difficult to work this way because you will need to switch between task panes a lot, but at least you will get a usable design surface.

In addition to resetting the task pane layout, I also had you put your page in Split view. I use Split view exclusively because it enables me to see both the design panel, which should render in a way that is almost WYSIWYG with Windows Internet Explorer 7, and the code panel, which allows you to see how what you do in Design view generates the necessary HTML to render as you want it to. Code view also allows you to type HTML, control properties, or other code in order to make your pages render exactly as you want them to.

In the next section, you are going to use some of the tools in Code view that make this process easier.

Using Tools in Code View

A lot of times, the only way to get something done is to use Code view. For example, if you want to build a complicated Extensible Stylesheet Language (XSL) section involving *choose/when/otherwise* logic inside a DataViewWebPart object (Data view), you would need to hand-code that. Other times, you might feel more comfortable typing in the code rather than trying to remember where the UI is to insert the necessary HTML.

To make using Code view as easy as possible, SharePoint Designer includes a number of tools at your disposal. One of the least discoverable and yet universally useful tools is the keyboard shortcut for code selection, which enables you to press three keys on the keyboard to select entire HTML blocks—thereby rapidly identifying the opening or closing tags.

In addition to allowing you to select elements for editing, Code view provides tools that link to connected stylesheets or JavaScript. For example, when there is a style attribute on a tag, that attribute becomes a "code hyperlink," which means you can click that hyperlink and open the page that has the style definition on it. Code hyperlinks come in particularly handy when you are making changes to the SharePoint style code or custom JScript files. To practice this, you'll create a style block on the page and then link to that style in the exercise at the end of this section. By doing so, you'll also see two other tools that come in handy when writing code: AutoComplete and IntelliSense.

The final Code view tools you'll work with in this section are code formatting and snippets. Code snippets allow you to create and then save HTML code that you might reuse frequently, and code formatting tools allow you to set the color and indenting defaults for different tags. For example, you might find yourself always inserting the same basic table structure, so you can save that table as a snippet and insert it later through a simple keyboard shortcut. At the same time, you might want every table to always be preceded and followed by an extra line of white space.

In this exercise, you will set some code formatting preferences and create a code snippet, insert that code snippet, create a style block on the page, click a code hyperlink, and select a block of HTML.

> **USE** the blog site you created and modified in the previous chapter. If you did not create the blog site, you can still perform these exercises by creating a new blog site, following the steps in Chapter 1; however, the screen shots in some examples will not match the ones shown here.
>
> **BE SURE TO** display the blog site in SharePoint Designer before beginning this exercise.

1. On the **Tools** menu, click **Page Editor Options**.

The Page Editor Options dialog box opens.

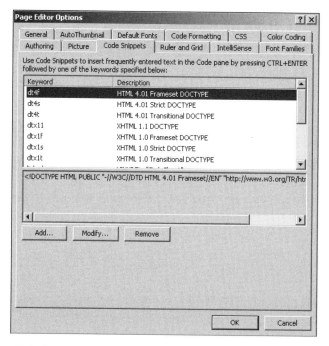

2. Click the **Code Formatting** tab.

You can use this tab to customize the Code view of your pages:

- ○ The top section allows you to control the case and spacing of the tags as they are added to Code view.

- ○ The middle section allows for specific control based on tag name. This section allows you to offset tables or Web Parts or any other tags by putting space before and after their opening and closing tags.

- ○ The bottom section applies to cascading style sheets (CSS). In the coming chapters, you'll be editing CSS directly and might find that some of these settings should change based on how you like your curly braces to appear, as well as whether to indent new properties or to use shorthand.

3. In the **Tags** list, click the **Table** tag.

4. Change the **Before Start** and **After End** values to **3**.

> **Tip** I am choosing 3 here because it is a value that will be immediately noticeable in Code view but isn't so large as to cause the page to look incomprehensible.

5. In the **Page Editor Options** dialog box, click the **Color Coding** tab, and ensure that **Code View Settings** is selected.

On this tab, you can set the default values for Code view or for Design view.

6. In the **Display items** list, click **HTML element name**.

7. Change the item foreground color to maroon.

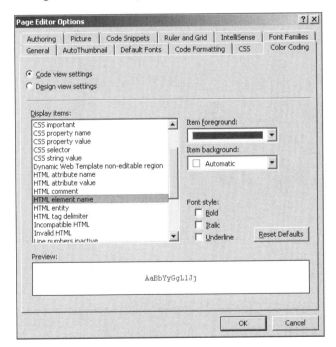

8. Click the **Code Snippets** tab.

9. Click **Add**.

The Add Code Snippet dialog box opens.

10. For the keyword, type **Table Snippet**; for the description, type **One-Cell Table**; and in the **Text** field, type the following code:

```
<table width=100%>
    <tr>
            <td>|</td>
    </tr>
</table>
```

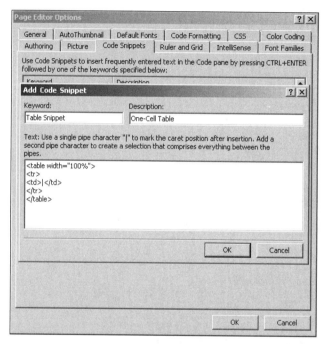

11. Click **OK**, and then click **OK** again to close the **Page Editor Options** dialog box.

12. Place your cursor into the code panel of the page you have open, inside the *<form>* tag that is there by default.

13. Press Ctrl + Enter to open the **Insert Code Snippet** window.

14. Navigate down to the snippet called **Table Snippet** and press Enter to insert the table you added to the Add Code Snippet dialog box.

> **Tip** Your cursor is flashing inside the one table cell in this table because the code snippet contains a | (pipe character), which tells the code snippet where you want your next insertion point to be.

15. Press `Ctrl`+`Shift`+`;` (semicolon) to activate the Code view tool to select the entire tag containing your current insertion point.

16. Right-click in the code panel, and then click **Reformat HTML**.

This action moves your table three line breaks below the form and three line breaks above the closing form tag based on the settings chosen above, and the tags all change to maroon.

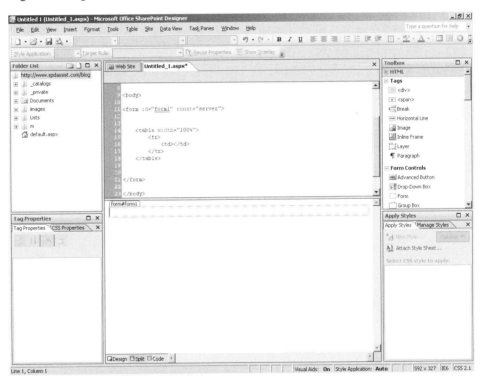

17. Place your cursor in the code panel immediately after the closing *</title>* tag and press Enter to create a blank line below the title of the page.

18. Type <.

The IntelliSense window displays a list of choices that you could type.

> **Tip** These choices are constrained by your current context. For example, you are inside the <head> of the page, so the items offered are valid inside the <head> of a page, and nothing that is invalid shows up in the list.

19. Type **S** to select the **Script** tag. Press the ↓ key to select **Style**, and then press the Tab key.

The word *style* is written onto your page.

20. Press Space to open the IntelliSense window again.

Again, this list is context-aware, so it offers you only the valid attributes on the Style tag.

21. Click **Type** to insert the type attribute.

SharePoint automatically inserts the = and symbols.

22. Select **text/css** from the new IntelliSense window that opens between the quote characters.

Your cursor automatically jumps outside the closing quote character.

23. Type > to close the script block.

Doing so writes the closing script tag for you. These two tools (IntelliSense and AutoComplete) combine to make typing HTML much less tedious than doing so in a program such as Microsoft Notepad.

24. Place your cursor inside the *<script>* tag you just generated, and press Enter.

25. Type **.style** to create a style inside the style block.

26. Type {.

SharePoint adds the closing } for you, and the IntelliSense window displays the valid values in this context. In this case, you are going to simply assign a color.

27. Click **Color** in the IntelliSense window and type : (colon).

28. Navigate down to **blue** and type ; (semicolon).

After you have followed the above steps, the following code appears in your page:

```
<style type=text/css>
.style{
    color:blue;
}</style>
```

Now you will attach this style to one of the table cells we inserted earlier, which will create a code hyperlink.

29. Place your cursor inside the opening *<td>* tag in your table, and then press `Space`.

30. Click **Class** in the IntelliSense window, and then press `Tab`.

Inside the auto-generated quotes, the word *style* appears. This is the style block you created above.

31. Click **style**, and then press `Enter`.

The word *style* here is underlined, which signifies that it is a code hyperlink.

32. Press and hold the `Ctrl` key and use the mouse to click the word **style** to jump back up to the *style* selector in the *<style>* block of code.

The benefit of this final code tool can be seen in a number of different places in SharePoint Designer. When you have external style sheets (which we will explore in the next chapter), clicking a code hyperlink opens the external file and highlights the class. When you are dealing with a large style sheet or script block (as the CSS file in SharePoint is), this highlight can be extremely helpful. In addition, XSLT has code hyperlinks to enable users to jump from one XSL template to another and track the XSLT processing, which will also be leveraged in a later chapter.

This exercise should be a good introduction to the Code view tools in SharePoint Designer. As I mentioned previously, I always work in Split view, jumping from Code to Design and back. With practice, you'll find that Code view can be an extremely powerful way of building applications on SharePoint; and by creating code snippets and formatting the code in a way that's easy for you to read and follow, your experience will be easy to master. Now we're going to move on to some of the Design view tools and look at how Design view interacts with the task panes.

Using Tools in Design View

With the Design view in SharePoint Designer, you can insert HTML content, ASP.NET controls, and SharePoint controls, as well as text and images, into a page as the building blocks for an application. In order to make the design surface meaningful, SharePoint Designer attempts to render all of these objects in a way that is WYSIWYG with Internet Explorer. That said, there are some objects that only work in Design view when they are *not* WYSIWYG. In this section, we'll take a quick look at some tools you can use while designing your pages. We'll look at tools that account for the complex HTML generated on some SharePoint pages by default, and controls and objects that render in a non-WYSIWYG format, and we'll explore leveraging other elements in the user interface.

You might be familiar with the Microsoft Visual Studio design surface from the past, which would render controls stacked on the surface as gray boxes, requiring you to constantly refresh your browser as you designed your page. Instead of forcing you into this difficult position, SharePoint Designer implemented a design-time control rendering feature so that controls could tell the design surface how they should render. For the most part, this preview works great; however, there are times when the preview doesn't match the runtime behavior, or worse, when the control itself did not implement a design-time preview for SharePoint Designer to render. In those cases, the experience will not be WYSIWYG; however, SharePoint Designer still attempts to render the controls as gray boxes, so you have the opportunity to select the control and set properties or interact with it in some other meaningful way.

In this exercise, you will begin looking at these controls by saving the page you've been working on and then switching it into Design view.

> **BE SURE TO** display the page you created in the previous exercise, in SharePoint Designer.

1. On the **File** menu, click **Save**.

The Save As dialog box opens.

2. In the **File Name** text box, type **firstPage.aspx**, and then click **Save**.

The page is saved to the root of your blog site, as you can see in the Folder List task pane.

3. On the **View** menu, point to **Page**, and then click **Design**.

The page is not completely WYSIWYG. You can see the borders that show the table cells inside the table you created. Believe it or not, this is a complicated thing to show. Because the table cells in the table we inserted via the Code Snippets window did not contain anything, it's difficult to know exactly how to render the table. To make it possible to put your cursor into the table cell, however, SharePoint Designer renders the cell at full height and shows a border around the table cell. If you want to toggle that setting, you can do so from the View menu.

4. On the **View** menu, click **Visual Aids**.

The menu that opens contains all the individual visual aids enabled in SharePoint Designer to help make designing pages easier.

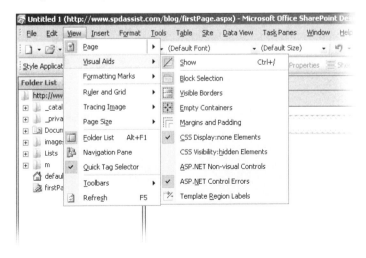

5. Click **Empty Containers**.

The table collapses, because the table cell does not contain any content. Clicking Empty Containers collapses any container that is empty.

> **Tip** The menu does not close after you click different selections. The visual aids can be tricky, so SharePoint Designer leaves the menu visible to make it easier for you to toggle between selections.

6. Click **Visible Borders**, and then click the design surface to close the **View** menu.

This time, the table disappears completely. Obviously, this makes the page very difficult to design, so SharePoint Designer does not enable these settings by default; however, because it is important to see a WYSIWYG rendering of your content at times, you can toggle these settings.

7. Toggle these two settings back by clicking **Visual Aids** on the **View** menu, clicking **Visible Borders** and **Empty Containers**, and then clicking the page to force the **View** menu to close.

> **Tip** To quickly toggle between these settings as you design your pages, double-click the Visual Aids section of the status bar at the bottom of the SharePoint Designer user interface.

8. Click to place the cursor inside the table cell of the table you inserted.

9. Press Esc to select the entire table cell.

10. Press Esc again to select the entire table.

11. Press Esc one more time to select the form on the page.

> **Tip** In addition to using the Esc key, you can use the Quick Tag Selector just above Design view to move up the HTML tree.

12. Click on the design surface again to place the cursor inside the table cell of the table you inserted.

The Quick Tag Selector above Design view shows the entire HTML tree to that point.

13. Point to the **td.style** button.

An arrow appears.

14. Click the arrow, and then click **Edit Tag**.

A small dialog box called the Quick Tag Editor opens, showing the specific HTML tag with its attributes and values.

15. Place the cursor to the right of the *<td* and press Space .

The same IntelliSense tools available in Code view are also available here. You can add attributes and values here for any tags from Code view available for selection.

16. Select the green check box to dismiss the **Quick Tag Editor** dialog box.

There are a number of other tools available in Design view, but the code and design tools discussed in this chapter are the primary tools I use during SharePoint application design. Other tools will be mentioned in later chapters, but if you have completed the exercises in this chapter, you should have a very good idea of how to be productive in both Code view and Design view.

Key Points

- With SharePoint Designer, you can create and customize SharePoint applications.
- Code view in SharePoint Designer has a lot of tools to help make designers who are comfortable with writing code more productive.
- Design view in SharePoint Designer is usually close to WYSIWYG, but not completely WYSIWYG.
- Using tools in both Code view and Design view make creating pages very fast and simple.

Chapter at a Glance

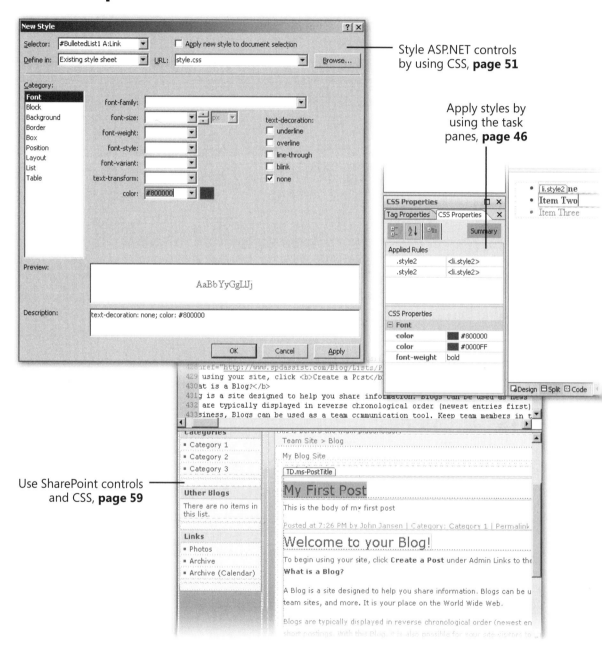

Style ASP.NET controls by using CSS, **page 51**

Apply styles by using the task panes, **page 46**

Use SharePoint controls and CSS, **page 59**

3 Accessing the Styles Behind SharePoint Pages

In this chapter, you will learn to

- ✔ Create content rendered with CSS.
- ✔ Apply styles by using the task panes.
- ✔ Style ASP.NET controls by using CSS.
- ✔ Understand CSS rules and HTML.
- ✔ Use SharePoint controls and CSS.

When writing about cascading style sheets (CSS), it is important to begin with a discussion about what it means to use "good design" when building a Web application. As you browse around on the Internet, you undoubtedly see a lot of very similar applications working in very similar ways. Yet, for sometimes inexplicable reasons, you prefer to use one over the other. Sometimes this is because one allows for more rapid checkout or has a better search mechanism, but other times you prefer one site because it looks better than another site: It "feels" more professional.

To build a professional-looking Web site and make it so that you can modify that look as easily as possible, you should use CSS. With CSS, you can create a color palette as well as a layout, store that "look and feel" separately from the actual content on the page, and modify it without breaking your applications.

In this chapter, you will create pages that render by using custom CSS. One of the challenges you will face when authoring CSS is understanding exactly how the controls and other objects on the page render when the page is accessed in a browser, so in addition to applying CSS to HTML as you will do in the first exercise, you will also apply CSS to ASP.NET and Microsoft Windows SharePoint Services controls to style SharePoint pages that render those controls.

> **Important**   The exercises in this chapter require only the blog site created and modified in earlier chapters. No practice files are supplied on the companion CD. For more information about practice files, see "Using the Companion CD" at the beginning of this book.

Creating Content Rendered with CSS

The most straightforward way to see CSS working is to create a small example HTML file that renders by using a small CSS file. Because CSS cascades into the page, the location of the CSS selectors matters for the final rendering of the output HTML. For example, if you have CSS that is applied directly inline on the HTML tags themselves, that will be applied after any CSS that is in a code block in the head of the page, which will in turn be applied after any CSS that is on a different page and that is referenced through a link in your HTML page.

In order to fully understand what that means, you need to see it in practice. When you generate any HTML on a page without any styles being applied to that HTML, the HTML will render based on your browser's default settings. To make the page look more interesting, you need to modify the CSS used to tell the browser what to render.

In this exercise, you will create the HTML to render some content, create a CSS file with styles on it to control the rendering of that HTML, and then create additional levels of CSS to see how it cascades into the page.

USE the blog site you created and modified in earlier chapters. If you did not create the blog site, you can still perform these exercises by creating a new blog site, following the steps in Chapter 1; however, the screen shots in some examples will not match the ones shown here.

BE SURE TO display the blog site in SharePoint Designer before beginning this exercise.

1. On the Common toolbar, click the **New Document** arrow and then, in the list, click **Page**.

The New dialog box opens.

2. On the **Page** tab, click **General**, select **ASPX**, and then click **OK**.

Verify that the page just created is in Split view.

3. Place the cursor in the design panel.

4. On the **Insert** menu, point to **HTML**, and then click **<div>**.

Your cursor should be between the opening and closing *div* tags, so that in code view it looks like the first < character of the *</div>* tag is selected.

5. On the **Format** menu, click **Bullets and Numbering**.

The Bullets And Numbering dialog box opens.

6. In the **Bullets and Numbering** dialog box, click the **Plain Bullets** tab, and then select the upper-right bullet style (the plain black circle).

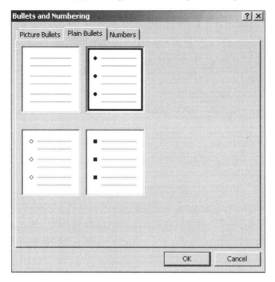

7. Click **OK** to close the dialog box.

8. Type **Item One** and press ⌨Enter, type **Item Two** and press ⌨Enter, and then type **Item Three**.

9. On the **File** menu, click **Save**. In the **Save** dialog box, type **styleDemo.aspx** in the **File name** text box, and then click **Save**.

10. Right-click the Common toolbar, and then click **Style Application**.

The Style Application floating toolbar appears.

11. Drag the Style Application toolbar and dock it under the Formatting toolbar.

12. Change the value for **Style Application** from **Auto** to **Manual** and verify that the **Target Rule** setting is (**New Inline Style**).

> **Tip** SharePoint Designer is set to automatically apply styles to your objects based on options you can set in the Page Editor Options dialog box. If you haven't made any changes, the default is to create a style block at the top of the page. When you change this setting to Manual, you have more control about where styles are saved.

13. Select the first *<li>* tag by selecting the **Item One** text and clicking the **Quick Tag Selector**.

> **Important** You must have not only the text selected, but also the tag itself.

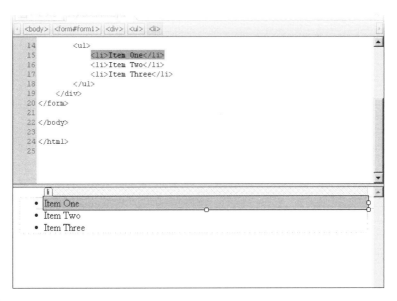

14. On the Style Application toolbar, click the **(New Inline Style)** arrow, and then click **Apply New Style**.

The New Style dialog box opens.

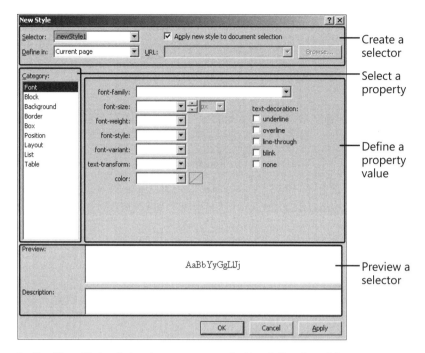

In the New Style dialog box, you can do the following things:

○ **Create a selector.** In the top area of this dialog box, you can name the selector and choose where that selector will be created.

○ **Select a property.** In the area on the side, you can pick the property of the selector you are going to modify by using the definitions in the middle of the dialog box.

○ **Define a property value.** This area shows the available choices for the property selected. In this area, you can set the value for the property in the selector.

○ **Preview a selector.** This area shows a WYSIWYG rendering of the selector as defined by your choices in the other areas of the dialog box.

15. In the **Selector** combo box, type **.style1**.

16. In the **Define in** list, click **New Style Sheet**.

17. Verify that **Font** is selected in the **Category** list, and change the **color** selection to #800000 by clicking the maroon color from the color picker for that text box.

18. Change the **font-weight** value to **bold**.

19. Click **OK**, and then click **Yes** to indicate that you want to attach the style sheet for the new style.

Doing so will cause the first *<li>* in your code to get a new class attribute with a value of *style1*, attach the new style sheet by creating a tag in the *<head>* of your document, and cause the Item One text to be maroon and bold.

20. Save your page again by clicking **Save** on the **File** menu.

> **Important** You will be prompted to save the CSS file as well, so give it the name style.css by typing *style.css* into the File Name text box and clicking Save. Because many of the modifications you will make will only affect the CSS file, SharePoint Designer keeps track of those changes and prompts you to save that page every time you save the ASPX page linked to it.

21. Select **Item Two** in the list and make sure the whole *<li>* tag is selected, as you did for **Item One** above.

22. On the **Style Application** toolbar, change **(New Inline Style)** to **(New Auto Class)**.

23. On the **Format** menu, click **Font**.

The Font dialog box opens.

24. Change the **Color** setting to blue, and then click **OK**.

Doing so will create a new class attribute on Item Two as well as a style block in the *<head>* of your page. Item Two will render blue.

25. Select **Item Three** in the same way you selected **Item One** and **Item Two**.

26. Change the Style Application toolbar setting from **(New Auto Class)** to **(New Inline Style)**.

27. On the **Format** menu, click **Font**.

28. In the **Font** dialog box, change the **Color** setting to red, and click **OK**.

Doing so will create a new style attribute on Item Three, and Item Three will render red.

BE SURE TO save your work.

After completing the above steps, you will have a page with a bulleted list of items, each of which renders in a different color and has styles applied in different ways. In the exercise in the next section, you will make subtle modifications via the task panes to change the colors being rendered, which will show how CSS cascades.

Applying Styles by Using the Task Panes

Now that you have a working set of styles, take a look at the Apply Styles task pane. You can see that "Apply Styles" is not a perfect name for the amount of functionality it contains. By using this task pane, you have the ability to perform the following actions:

● Create styles.

● Attach a style sheet to the current page.

● Change the way the styles are grouped and displayed.

● Change the background color for the style previews.

In addition to the high-level functions available in the task pane, you can also set where each style is applied. Notice in the task pane as it displays the content from the previous exercise that you can see there is one group for the attached style sheet, one group for the current page, and if you click Item Three, one group for inline styles (which shows up only when you have actually selected an item with an inline style applied). Inside each group, you can click individual styles and see a list of actions. Although you might expect that the menu that appears when you click would contain only things you can do to the item you clicked, in fact the list allows you to do page-level operations as well.

From the Apply Styles task pane you can do the following:

- **Apply Style.** Applies the style to the current selection.
- **Go to Code.** Moves the cursor to the place where the selector is defined. If the selector is defined in an unopened style sheet, that style sheet will open.
- **Select All Instances.** Selects any tags that reference the selector.
- **New Style.** Opens the New Style dialog box that you used earlier to create new styles.
- **New Style Copy.** Opens the New Style dialog box with the default values for the selector properties loaded to match the style you are clicking. This comes in handy when you have a complex selector defined and want to add properties to it without starting completely from scratch.
- **Modify Style.** Opens the New Style dialog box loaded with the values for the currently selected style so you can modify it.
- **Rename Class.** Allows you to rename the class as well as all references to that class in the page.
- **Delete.** Deletes the class but does not delete references to the class.
- **Remove Link.** Removes the link to the CSS file that contains the selector.
- **Attach Style Sheet.** Opens the Attach Style Sheet dialog box, in which you can browse to attach additional CSS files either to the current page or to all pages in the site.
- **Manage Style Sheet Links.** Opens the Link Style Sheet dialog box, in which you can see all style sheets in the site and arrange them accordingly.
- **Remove Class.** Removes the class attribute from the current selection.
- **Remove ID.** Removes the ID attribute from the current selection.
- **Remove Inline Style.** Removes the inline style from the current selection.

In this exercise, you will rename one of the selectors and see how the styles cascade into the page. You can then leverage that understanding to better control your page styles.

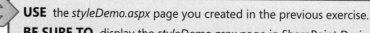

USE the *styleDemo.aspx* page you created in the previous exercise.

BE SURE TO display the *styleDemo.aspx* page in SharePoint Designer before beginning this exercise.

1. In the **Apply Styles** task pane, in the **style.css** group, click the **.style1** arrow.

   A context menu appears.

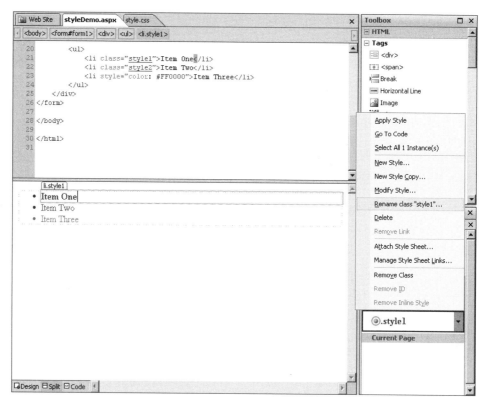

2. Click **Rename class "style1"**.

   The Rename Class dialog box opens.

3. Type **style2** for the new name and click **OK**.

4. In the message box informing you that the two pages have been updated, click **Close**.

5. Click **Item Three**. Then in the **Quick Tag Selector**, click the associated **li** tag.

6. In the **Tag Properties** task pane, scroll down to the **class** property, type **style2** as the value for this property, and then press [Enter] to commit that change.

> **Tip** Due to an issue with the way that the task panes interact with the pages, you need to save your work, close the pages, and then reopen them in SharePoint Designer in order to see the changes applied to the current selection.

7. Press [Ctrl]+[S] to save your work, and again click **OK** in the **Save Embedded Files** dialog box to save the CSS file.

8. On the **Window** menu, click **Close All Pages**.

9. Open *styleDemo.aspx* by double-clicking it in the **Folder List** task pane.

```
 9  <link rel="stylesheet" type="text/css" href="untitled_1.css" >
10  <style type="text/css">
11  .style2 {
12      color: #0000FF;
13  }
14  </style>
15  </head>
16
17  <body>
18
19  <form id="form1" runat="server">
20      <div>
21          <ul>
22              <li class="style2">Item One</li>
23              <li class="style2">Item Two</li>
24              <li style="color: #FF0000" class="style2">Item Three</li>
25          </ul>
26      </div>
27  </form>
28
29  </body>
30
31  </html>
32
```

- Item One
- Item Two
- Item Three

The text for both Item One and Item Two is blue, while the text for Item Three is still red. Before you renamed *style1* to *style2*, Item One was maroon and bold and Item Two was blue and not bold. This is a simple example of how the cascading nature of CSS works.

10. Click to select **Item Two** on the design surface.

11. Click the **CSS Properties** task pane tab.

12. Click the **Summary** button in the task pane.

This summary of the CSS actions you took above is invaluable in determining which CSS property is applied to each HTML element on the page.

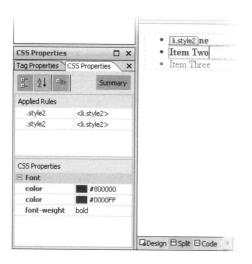

 BE SURE TO save your work.

The maroon *color* and the bold *font-weight* properties were both set in the external style sheet. The blue color was defined in the style block on the ASPX page itself, and the red color was defined inline for the tag itself. So as the page was parsed for rendering, the first thing that got loaded into memory was the external CSS file; that CSS file was then merged with the style block at the top of the page, and that CSS was then merged with the HTML markup of the page. For Item One, that means that the maroon and bold property values were merged with the color blue property value. The maroon property was overwritten by the cascade into the page-level style block and was replaced by the color blue. This is evidenced in the task pane because the *color* maroon property is crossed out, indicating that it has been overwritten. The bold property, however, was not overwritten because there was no *font-weight* defined in the page-level style block. So when applied to these two list items, maroon was overwritten, bold was not: they are both then blue and bold. As for Item Three, the inline style sets its color to red and overwrites the color property in the page-level style block, but there is again no font-weight designation, so that does not get overwritten and the item is still bold.

When you are building SharePoint applications, there will be times when you will need to troubleshoot some style application. At those times, the CSS Properties task pane will be invaluable, so understanding how the cascade works, and understanding how the task panes represent that cascade, will be very important to your application-building success.

Styling ASP.NET Controls by Using CSS

To complicate the customization of SharePoint pages further, most of the content on these pages is rendered via controls. These controls will be explored in more depth in Chapter 6, "Creating Custom Navigation Controls," but in order to understand how the styles work in SharePoint, it is necessary that you have at least a general understanding of how controls work. A *control* is an object that can be inserted into a page and that contains all of the code necessary to make it look and act the way a designer or developer wants it to.

When a control is inserted on a page, there is different markup (design-time markup) than that which renders when the page is browsed (run-time markup). What this distinction means is that you cannot simply add a class to a tag in a control and expect that style to render at run time. You need to understand the run-time HTML that is generated by the control and create CSS that will cause *that* HTML to render the way you want. In order to write the correct CSS, you need to understand exactly what HTML is generated at run time.

In this exercise, you will insert a control from the Toolbox task pane, observe the design-time code for the control, and then capture the run-time HTML for the control and add a selector that will modify that control's run-time rendering.

> **USE** the blog site you modified in the previous exercise.
> **BE SURE TO** display the *styleDemo.aspx* page in SharePoint Designer before beginning this exercise.

1. Click on the page's design surface below the current unordered list.
2. On the **Insert** menu, point to **HTML**, and then click **<div>**.

3. Click to expand the **Toolbox** task pane to its full size by clicking the **Maximize Window** button in the upper-right corner of the task pane.

4. In the **Toolbox**, scroll down to the **ASP.NET Controls** section.

5. Expand the **Standard** group, right-click **Bulleted List**, and then click **Insert**.

6. Click the On Object User Interface (OOUI), which is represented by a small arrow floating just outside the control, and click **Edit Items**.

> **Important** If the panel is not showing, you can right-click the control and then click Show Common Control Tasks.

The ListItem Collection Editor dialog box opens.

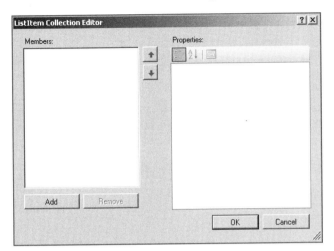

7. In the **ListItem Collection Editor** dialog box, click **Add** to create a new *ListItem*.

8. In the **Properties** box in this dialog box, add the following text to the **Text** value: **Item One**.

9. Click **Add** again and modify the **Text** value to **Item Two**.

10. Click **Add** again and modify the **Text** value to **Item Three**.

11. Click **OK**.

The following code is added to the page:

```
<asp:BulletedList runat=server id=BulletedList1>
    <asp:ListItem>Item One</asp:ListItem>
    <asp:ListItem>Item Two</asp:ListItem>
    <asp:ListItem>Item Three</asp:ListItem>
</asp:BulletedList>
```

> **Tip** The above code is what is called design-time code. It is the code that you can modify by using SharePoint Designer while designing the page. Changes to this code will then effect how the control renders at run time, when the page is accessed from a server through a browser. Take note that the *id* attribute on this control is *BulletedList1*; you will use the value in step 23 of this exercise.

12. Save the page by clicking **Save** on the **File** menu.

13. On the **File** menu, point to **Preview in Browser**, and then click a browser and resolution.

14. View the HTML source of the page. (In Windows Internet Explorer 7, right-click the page and then click **View Source**.)

15. Select all of the code and copy it. (In Microsoft Notepad, for example, click **Select All** and then click **Copy** on the **Edit** menu.)

16. Switch back to SharePoint Designer.

17. Create a new ASPX page by pressing ⌷Ctrl⌷+⌷N⌷ on your keyboard.

18. Navigate to the code panel for this page.

19. On the **Edit** menu, click **Select All**. Then on the **Edit** menu, click **Paste**.

20. Click on the design surface to cause all of the run-time code to now render on the design surface of SharePoint Designer.

> **Tip**   The *asp:BulletedList* control renders at run time in a very similar way to the unordered list you inserted above it.

21. Save the page as *temp.aspx* by pressing ⌷Ctrl⌷+⌷S⌷ on your keyboard, typing **temp** into the **File Name** text box, and clicking **Save**.

22. Expand the **Apply Styles** task pane, and then click **New Style**.

The New Style dialog box opens.

23. For the selector name, type **#BulletedList1 li**. In the **Define in** list, click **Existing style sheet**. In the **URL** box, browse to *style.css*. Then change the font **color** to **red**.

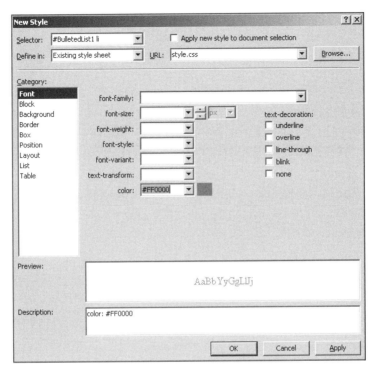

24. Click **OK**.

25. On the **File** menu, click **Save all** to save all the pages in this site.

26. Click the tab for **styleDemo.aspx** to view that page's rendering.

BE SURE TO save your work.

Because you wrote that last style to the *style.css* file and *style.css* is applied to *styleDemo.aspx*, the ASP.NET control you inserted earlier now renders each *li* tag that is inside of a tag with an ID of *BulletedList1* with red text. In other words, by browsing to the file and capturing the run-time HTML that the ASP.NET control generated, you were able to modify the CSS file in such a way that the control itself was affected—without having to modify any properties on the control, or even the page on which the control was inserted. The rules for this kind of CSS application will be explored in depth in the next section.

Understanding CSS Rules and HTML

In this exercise, you will look more closely at how modifying CSS selectors will enable you to create more robust design for controls in ASP.NET and SharePoint. Notice that in the previous exercise the selector you created began with a # (number sign). This symbol indicates to CSS that it should look for an ID rather than a style attribute. In addition, the selector ended with an *li* tag. This indicated that the selector should be applied to any *li* tag that is inside any other tag with an ID of *BulletedList1*.

There are a few CSS rules that SharePoint leverages, so understanding them from the outset is important for building applications and customizing those applications to meet your needs. Those rules are summarized in the following table:

CSS rule	Meaning
.selectorName	Apply the style to any tag with a class attribute that has a value of *selectorName*. (Notice the dot at the beginning of the string.)
tagName	Apply the style to any tag that is named *tagName*. (Notice there is no dot at the beginning of the string.)
#selectorName	Apply the style to any tag with an ID of *selectorName*. (Notice there is a # symbol at the beginning of the string.)
#selectorName, tagName	Apply the style to any tag that is named *tagName* OR any tag with an ID of *selectorName*. (Notice there is a comma between the two strings.)
#selectorName tagName	Apply the style to any tag that is named *tagName* that is inside any tag with an ID of *selectorName*. (Notice there is no comma between the two strings.)
tagName:Hover	Apply the style when the mouse "hovers" over (points to) the *tagName* element. (Notice there is a colon in the string.)

When you understand the above rules, you can take that understanding one level deeper and apply that knowledge to how hyperlinks work when it comes to CSS. When you create an *<A>* tag by inserting a hyperlink, it means you are working with an anchor tag. Anchor tags are special because most browsers have built-in styles to show them in a specific color (typically blue) and with a specific text decoration (typically underlined). In other words, most browsers on the market have default styles defined for how to render anchor tags. If you put an *A* tag inside your *li*, that *A* tag's default style will overwrite the style applied to the *li*, so you need to add a new set of styles to account for this case and overwrite the default rendering from the browser.

In this exercise, you will create hyperlinks inside the *asp:BulletedList* control inserted in the previous exercise and then add three new selectors to style.css in order to render those hyperlinks the way you want them to render by overriding the default browser settings.

> **USE** the blog site you modified in the previous exercise.
>
> **BE SURE TO** display the *styleDemo.aspx* page in SharePoint Designer before beginning this exercise.

1. In the design panel, click to select **asp:BulletedList**.

The Tag Properties task pane displays the default control properties.

2. In the **Tag Properties** task pane, scroll down to the **DisplayMode** property.

It will be set to Text by default.

3. Change the value of the **DisplayMode** property to **Hyperlink**.

After you do so, the text in the *asp:BulletedList* control will change to show the default browser setting for hyperlinks blue and underlined.

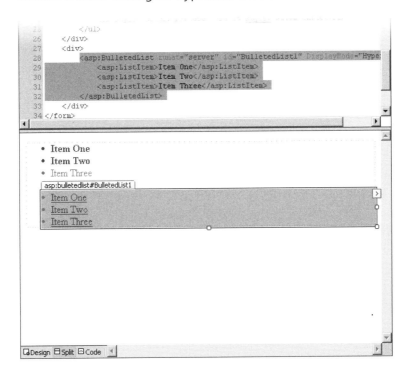

4. In the **Apply Styles** task pane, click **New Style**.

   The New Style dialog box opens

5. Change the **Selector** value to **#BulletedList1 A:Link**.

6. Change the **Define in** value to **Existing style sheet,** and then browse to select *style.css* as the **URL.**

7. In the **text-decoration** list, select the **none** check box.

8. Change the color to maroon.

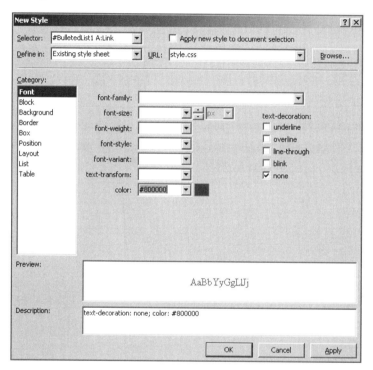

9. Click **OK**.

10. In the **Apply Styles** task pane, click **New Style**.

11. In the **New Style** dialog box, change the **Selector** value to **#BulletedList1 A: Visited.**

12. Repeat steps 6 through 9 to define this style in the *style.css* file, change the color to maroon, and change the **text-decoration** value to **none**.

> **Tip** The *A:Visited* designation checks your browser history and will render the link in a different default color if you have been to the page before. I always explicitly set *A:Visited* to match *A:Link*, to ensure that regardless of whether a user has previously been to my page, the links will display the same way.

13. In the **Apply Styles** task pane, click **New Style**. Then in the **New Style** dialog box, change the **Selector** value to **#BulletedList1 A:Hover**.

14. Repeat steps 6 through 9 to define this style in the *style.css* file, change the **font-weight** property to **bold**, the **color** property to maroon, and the **text-decoration** property to **underline**.

15. On the **File** menu, click **Save all** to save all of the pages. Then click **OK** to overwrite the previous *style.css* file, and preview your work in the browser by pressing F11 on your keyboard.

16. Point to the three links in the *asp:BulletedList* control and notice they turn bold and become underlined.

The links will not actually function at this point in your design, because you didn't yet add value attributes to the list items, but you will get to that in the next chapter.

There are clearly a lot of considerations that go into that design process, and by now you are familiar with why it is difficult to apply styles to ASP.NET controls as well as tags that might have default styles applied by the browser itself. To add yet another layer of complexity on top of this model, in addition to HTML tags and ASP.NET controls, you will also be applying styles to SharePoint controls, which render their own run-time HTML.

Using SharePoint Controls and CSS

The most common control in SharePoint is the Web Part. Web Parts have styles applied to them that allow the Web Part title to render one way, the column headers or textual content another, and the toolbar content yet another. The run-time HTML for these controls can be very complex and difficult to decipher.

In this exercise, you will capture the run-time HTML for a *ListView Web Part*, and then use the SharePoint Designer tools to modify the style of the blog heading inside this ListView Web Part by employing some of the tricks you learned in the earlier exercises in this chapter.

BE SURE TO display the blog site in SharePoint Designer before beginning this exercise.

1. In the **Folder List** task pane, double-click **default.aspx** to open the page, and then press ⌐F12⌐ to launch your browser and view the page as it will appear at run time.

2. Capture the source of the page the same way you did earlier by viewing the source on the page and then copying that source into memory.

3. Switch back to SharePoint Designer and create a new page by pressing ⌐Ctrl⌐+⌐N⌐ on your keyboard.

4. Paste the run-time code from *default.aspx* into the code panel of the page just created.

5. Click on the design surface to force the page to render that run-time code.

6. Scroll up in the design surface until you can see **My First Post**, and then select that text.

7. In the **Apply Styles** task pane, on the **Options** menu, click **Show Styles Used on Selection**. By doing so, you can see that the selector you want to modify is **.ms-PostTitle A**. Write down that selector name so you don't forget it.

Due to the way that SharePoint Designer interacts with the SharePoint platform, we do not want to modify the selector yet.

> **Important** The styles used on SharePoint pages are usually located in a style sheet called *core.css*, and this is no exception. *Core.css* is stored on the server, not inside your Web site like the *style.css* file that you created earlier is. What this means is that you need to tell SharePoint Designer that you want to pull *core.css* off the server and start storing it in the Web site itself.

8. Open *default.aspx* in SharePoint Designer by double-clicking it in the **Folder List** task pane.

9. Click the text for **My First Post**, which will select the entire ListView Web Part on the page.

10. Display the **CSS Properties** task pane.

11. In the **Applied Rules** section at the top of the task pane, click **body, form**.

Notice that the task pane indicates it is defined in *core.css*.

12. Double-click this link to open *core.css* for editing.

13. Display the **Manage Styles** task pane and scroll down in the **CSS Styles** list until you can see **.ms-PostTitle A**.

As you scroll through this list of selectors, you might begin to realize how complex the SharePoint CSS rules are. There are hundreds of selectors in here, which is why it is paramount that you capture the run-time HTML first to identify the exact selector you need to modify. In this case, the selector is very close to the bottom of the list.

14. Right-click **.ms-PostTitle A**, and then click **Modify Style**.

The Modify Style dialog box opens.

15. Change the color to maroon and click **OK**.

16. Click **New Style** to add a new style to this page.

17. For the **Selector** value, type **.ms-PostTitle A:Hover**.

18. In the **text-decoration** list, select the **underline** check box, and then click **OK**.

19. Save your work by pressing [Ctrl]+[S], and click **Yes** to acknowledge the warning that you are about to customize a SharePoint style sheet.

20. Browse to *Default.aspx* again and refresh the page.

The post title is now maroon, and when you point to the title, it becomes black and underlined.

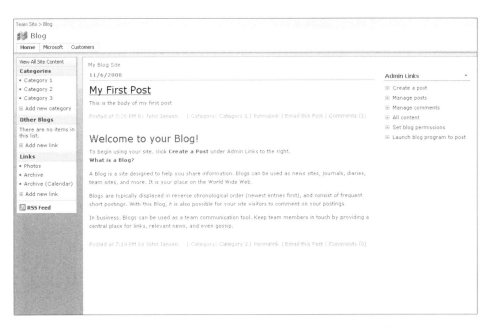

At this point, you should note that the *default.aspx* file did not get modified at all during that customization exercise. Because SharePoint uses external style sheets, there was no need to edit the page itself to get the formatting necessary, so the only modifications were made to the CSS file itself. You were able to determine which selector to modify in *default.aspx* by capturing the run-time HTML of the page and viewing that HTML in the SharePoint Designer design surface. Next, you were able to modify the correct CSS by leveraging a series of task panes at your disposal.

Key Points

- Modifying the look and feel of a SharePoint site means you have to modify the CSS behind that SharePoint site.
- SharePoint pages consist primarily of controls that make it difficult to know what needs to be modified in the CSS.
- Making changes to *core.css* in SharePoint would affect every site in the site collection if not for the SharePoint Designer feature that pulls down a copy of *core.css* and fixes the link in the CSS link control.
- Figuring out how an object is styled and then figuring out why a change you made is not showing up can be a complex process.

Chapter at a Glance

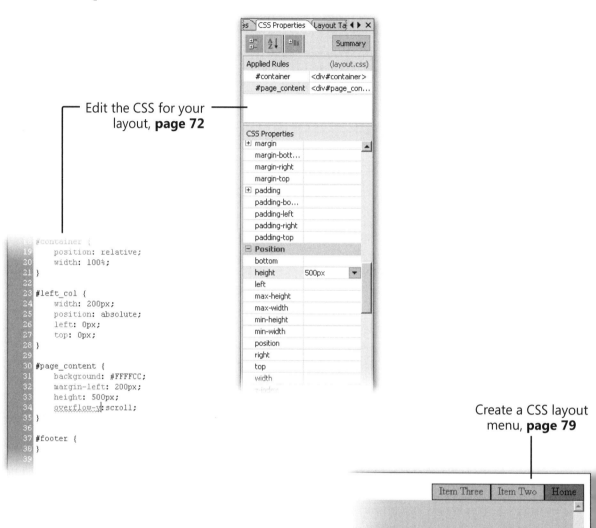

Edit the CSS for your
layout, **page 72**

```
18  #container {
19      position: relative;
20      width: 100%;
21  }
22
23  #left_col {
24      width: 200px;
25      position: absolute;
26      left: 0px;
27      top: 0px;
28  }
29
30  #page_content {
31      background: #FFFFCC;
32      margin-left: 200px;
33      height: 500px;
34      overflow-y:scroll;
35  }
36
37  #footer {
38  }
39
```

Create a CSS layout
menu, **page 79**

Item Three Item Two Home

4 Creating Layout with Cascading Style Sheets

In this chapter, you will learn to

✔ Understand table layout.

✔ Understand CSS layout.

✔ Edit the CSS for your layout.

✔ Create a CSS layout menu.

Creating pages that look good is essential to creating an application that people not only can use, but want to use. In the past, pages were typically created by using tables to control their layout. The use of tables was quite ingenious, actually: by leveraging the rectangles created in the rows and columns of a table, designers were suddenly able to place content next to other content instead of always directly below it.

Using tables for layout is really a hack. There was so little support for the *div* tag that the ease of use of tables took over, and even though using tables for layout was not recommended, everyone did it anyway. Now, however, that is changing. Windows Internet Explorer has evolved into having really good support for *divs*, as do Mozilla Firefox, Safari, and most of the rest of the browsers you might have to code for. If you do a quick Internet search for *CSS layout and tables*, you'll find a lot of debate about which is truly better and which is truly more accessible and usable. Ultimately, though, I use cascading style sheet (CSS) layout because of the purity of the model: my content is located in one place and my design is located in another.

Microsoft Windows SharePoint Services still uses tables for its master page layout and control rendering. In order to switch to using CSS layout, you will look at master pages in the next chapter and create a new master page in Microsoft Office SharePoint Designer 2007 based solely on CSS, which will allow you to replace most of the table rendering in SharePoint with CSS layout by using *div*s.

In this chapter, you will experiment with CSS layout to get a feel for how to begin to build pages. You will also learn how to design a complex layout by using the design surface in SharePoint Designer (and how to work around some of the limitations). Finally, you will build a navigation menu by using CSS layout.

> **Important**   The exercises in this chapter require only the blog site created and modified in earlier chapters. No practice files are supplied on the companion CD. For more information about practice files, see "Using the Companion CD" at the beginning of this book.

Understanding Table Layout

As I mentioned previously, during the nascent days of Internet page design, there was very little consideration given to the way a page looked. In fact, most content was simply text that might or might not have some formatting applied to it. When you look at HTML, you see the same kinds of markup that you would have seen in a print document in the 1960s: text surrounded by *<b>* tags, indicating that the printer should make that text bold; lists of items surrounded by tags indicating that they are un-ordered or ordered; and so on. In fact, HTML is a subset of Standard Generalized Markup Language (SGML), which is itself a subset of Generalized Markup Language (GML). At its core, GML tries to separate content from markup. *Content* is the stuff on the page you want people to see, and *markup* is the instruction to the computer for *how* that content should be displayed. This design was meant to allow users to write a document and then send that document to different devices and have it render in the same way on each device; you could send it to a laser printer, the computer screen, or a copy editor, and all would understand the layout in the same way.

To make pages look interesting and place content side by side on the page, users were forced to use tables. In theory, tables should only be used when rendering a repeating set of data (such as a list of customers or products), but they became the de facto way of rendering all content on a page.

In this exercise, you will create a typical table-based layout for a page.

 USE the blog site you created and modified in earlier chapters. If you did not create the blog site, you can still perform these exercises by creating a new blog site, following the directions in Chapter 1; however, the screen shots in some examples will not match the ones shown here.

BE SURE TO display the blog site in SharePoint Designer before beginning this exercise.

1. Create a new page by pressing [Ctrl]+[N].

> **Tip** As before, when you create a page with a SharePoint Site open, SharePoint Designer defaults to creating an ASPX page because that is the most likely page type you will want to use.

2. On the **View** menu, point to **Page**, and then click **Design** to place the page in Design view.

3. Click to place the cursor in the design surface of the page.

4. On the **Table** menu, click **Layout Tables**.

The Layout Tables task pane opens.

5. In the **Layout Tables** task pane, click the third layout in the layout gallery. (When you point to the template, the description text will say **Corner, Header, Left, and Body**.)

The page now has a table layout, as indicated by green and blue borders surrounding a table that takes up the full page in Design view.

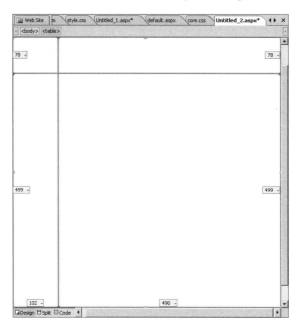

6. Save the file as **newDefault.aspx**.

 BE SURE TO leave the *newDefault.aspx* file open in SharePoint Designer.

You can see how easy that was to create, and you now have a page that is relatively easy to understand. In this layout, you can imagine putting your company logo in the upper-left table cell, your navigation controls across the top next to your logo, perhaps a menu down the left side of the page, and then the content of the page in the main body area. Unfortunately, this technique also creates a page in which the content and markup are inextricably linked; when you want to later modify the content on the page, you also end up in the unenviable position of modifying the layout of the page as well. This means that maintenance can be very difficult—and maintaining consistent branding even more so.

Understanding CSS Layout

Unlike table layout, CSS layout allows the content to remain completely separate from the layout. At its most basic level, a page that renders by using CSS looks like a text file with *div* tags and lists. Each tag contains an attribute value that references a style, and that style is contained in a CSS block or CSS page that holds the information for how that tag should be formatted. What this means in practice is that you can cause the same content to lay out in myriad different ways simply by changing the CSS file that is attached to it.

See Also Search for *CSS Demonstration* in your favorite search engine and you will find several Web sites that demonstrate the power of using CSS layout.

In this exercise, you will create a page based on one of the CSS templates that ships with SharePoint Designer. The layout will look similar to the table layout you created in the previous section, but rather than using tables, it will use *div*s and CSS.

BE SURE TO display the blog site in SharePoint Designer before beginning this exercise.

1. On the **File** menu, point to **New**, and then click **Page**.

The New dialog box opens.

2. On the **Page** tab, in the left column, click **CSS Layouts**.

3. In the center column, click **Header, logo, 2 columns, footer**.

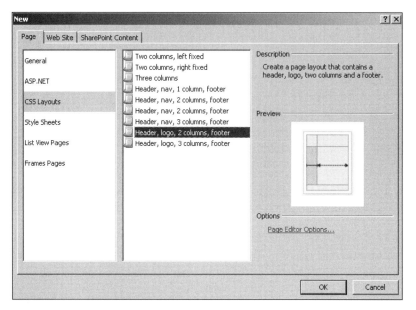

4. In the **New** dialog box, click **OK**.

5. On the **View** menu, point to **Page**, and then click **Split** to display the page in Split view.

6. Scroll the code pane to see the kind of code that was just generated.

7. Save the file as *newDefault.aspx*, and when prompted, save the CSS file as *layout.css*.

When you look at the code portion of this page, you will see two interesting constructs:

● There is a link to an external CSS file called *layout.css*.

● There are three main *div* tags and four nested *div* tags, all containing ID attributes (respectively: *masthead, container, footer, top_left, header, left_col,* and *page_content*).

In addition, the design portion of the page shows the *div*s as being collapsed.

This rendering is because there is currently no instruction in the CSS file telling the *divs* what height and width to use. By default, all *div* tags render only as large as the content inside them needs them to render, and because there is no content in these *divs*, they are collapsed.

> **Tip** SharePoint Designer makes one subtle modification to the rule of rendering here: if the tags truly rendered as collapsed, there would not be any way for you to put your cursor inside them, so SharePoint Designer renders empty *divs* just large enough for you to place your cursor inside of them to add content.

If you want to change the layout for *this* page at a later time, all you would have to do is change the CSS file. If you wanted to change the layout of the page with the *table* on it, you would have to either create a whole new page from scratch or very carefully modify the markup in the page itself. Granted, CSS has a higher introductory learning curve, but when it comes to maintaining pages long term, CSS layout really is the preferred way to design.

Editing the CSS for Your Layout

After you create a page, you will want to make additional edits in order to make it lay out exactly as you expect. You will always want to work in Split view when doing CSS layout, because there are some tricky concepts at play. SharePoint Designer is the first application to provide a WYSIWYG design surface for CSS layout editing; as such, there are some areas that need improvement and will require you to jump into the code to make some tweaks.

In the exercise later in this section, you will modify the CSS behind the page layout that you created in the previous exercise, to create areas in which you can insert SharePoint content later. In order to be truly effective at modifying CSS layout, you need to be comfortable jumping back and forth from Code view to Design view, as well as from the ASPX page to the CSS page, so the exercise is meant to give you some practice with that working style. But first, you should spend a bit of time to understand the CSS that was generated to make the page render as it does. You can switch to the *layout.css* page and look at the code line by line. The first style affects the *div* that has an ID of *masthead*:

```
/* CSS layout */
#masthead {
     position: relative;
     width: 100%;
}
```

The masthead is set to be relatively positioned at 100 percent of the browser window.

The *div* with an ID of *top_left* is next:

```
#top_left {
     width: 200px;
     position: absolute;
     left: 0px;
     top: 0px;
}
```

The *top_left div* has a width of 200 pixels. Typically, monitors render content close to 72 pixels per inch, though some are now reaching 85 or even 92, and there are newer high-DPI monitors coming out every year, so this *div* should render on most monitors between 2 and 3 inches wide. Its position is absolute and is locked into being 0 pixels in from the left and 0 pixels down from the top of its container. (In this case, because it is inside the *div* with an ID of *masthead*, that *div* is its container.)

The *div* with an ID of *header* follows:

```
#header {
     margin-left:200px;
}
```

This style has a left margin of 200 pixels, which accounts for the width of the *div* with an ID of *top_left*. If you ever want to make the *top_left div* wider, you have to also change the *margin-left* setting here to account for that change. Notice as well that there is no width coded in here, which means this *div* will stretch to be 100 percent of its container, minus the 200-pixel left margin.

Next is the *div* with an ID of *container*:

```
#container {
     position: relative;
     width: 100%;
}
```

This style has the same settings as the *div* with the ID of *masthead*, so it will be positioned at 100 percent of the browser window as well.

The *div* with an ID of *left_col* looks the same as the *div* with an ID of *top_left*:

```
#left_col {
     width: 200px;
     position: absolute;
     left: 0px;
     top: 0px;
}
```

This setting can be confusing for people, because it looks like it should be absolutely positioned so that its upper-left corner would be 0 pixels from the left and 0 pixels from the upper edge of the page, but that is not accurate. Absolute positioning always refers to the current container, not the page itself. So this *div* will render 0 pixels from the left and 0 pixels from the top of the *div* with an ID of *container*.

The *div* with an ID of *page_content* is next:

```
#page_content {
     margin-left: 200px;
}
```

It behaves in the same way as the header *div*. If you want to widen the left column, you have to remember to increase the *margin-left* setting for the *div* with an ID of *page_content*.

The footer is here purely as a placeholder:

```
#footer {
}
```

We will add some styles to it later in this chapter. Now you should better understand the CSS that was generated by default to make the page render the way that it does.

In this exercise, you will change the CSS discussed in this section to create appropriate containers for SharePoint content.

> **BE SURE TO** display the blog site in SharePoint Designer before beginning this exercise.

1. Display the *newDefault.aspx* page you created in the previous exercise in this chapter in Split view, and place the cursor on the design surface inside the *page_content div*.

2. If the **CSS Properties** task pane isn't visible, click **CSS Properties** on the **Task Panes** menu.

3. In the **CSS Properties** task pane, scroll down to the **Background** category and expand it.

4. Click the first **background-color** value field.

   An arrow appears.

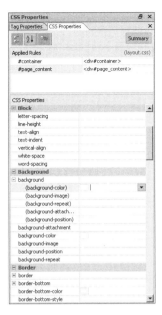

5. Click the arrow and then click **More Colors**.

The More Colors dialog box opens.

6. In the **Value** text box, delete the word **Automatic**, and then type **Hex={FF,FF,CC}**.

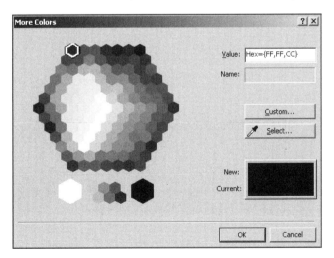

7. In the **More Colors** dialog box, click **OK**.

The background color for the *page_content div* is now off-white.

8. In the **CSS Properties** task pane, scroll down to the **Position** group.

9. In the **height** box, type **500px**.

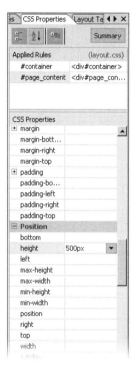

10. Press [Enter] to commit the change.

11. Save the pages, clicking **OK** in the **Save Embedded Files** dialog box to save the changes in the CSS file.

12. Switch to the *layout.css* page you created in the second exercise in this chapter.

The *page_content* class has new code added to it to account for the color and height you just set. It now looks like this:

```
#page_content {
    background: #FFFFCC;
    margin-left: 200px;
    height: 500px;
}
```

13. Place your cursor to the right of the final semicolon in this class and press [Enter].

The IntelliSense menu opens and shows you a list of allowable choices given your current context.

14. Type **overflow**, and then press [Enter].

15. On the IntelliSense menu, click **scroll**, and type ; (semicolon) to close that command. Then press the [Esc] key to dismiss the IntelliSense menu that subsequently appears.

16. For the property you just added, change **overflow:scroll;** to **overflow-y:scroll;**.

```
18  #container {
19      position: relative;
20      width: 100%;
21  }
22
23  #left_col {
24      width: 200px;
25      position: absolute;
26      left: 0px;
27      top: 0px;
28  }
29
30  #page_content {
31      background: #FFFFCC;
32      margin-left: 200px;
33      height: 500px;
34      overflow-y: scroll;
35  }
36
37  #footer {
38  }
39
```

17. Add an additional property, **overflow-x:hidden;**.

> **Important** *overflow-y* and *overflow-x* are unsupported properties in the current schema, so SharePoint Designer underlines them with a red squiggle, but you will use them anyway because if you don't, you will see scroll bars along the bottom of your *div* as well as along the side. The goal here is that when the content in the div grows beyond a height of 500 pixels, a scrollbar will appear for the overflow along the y-axis, but not along the x-axis.

18. Click in the *footer* class and press [Enter].

19. Select **text-align** from the IntelliSense window, click **Center**, and then type ; (semicolon).

20. Click inside the *left_col* class and add **height:500px;** to that selector so that its height will match the height of the *page_content div* you set earlier.

 BE SURE TO save your work.

Tip Even though the *newDefault.aspx* page now renders in a way that is different from before, it does so due only to the modifications of the CSS file. No change has been made to the content of the *newDefault.aspx* page.

You'll be able to see these changes the next time you view the *newDefault.aspx* page in Design view. The *page_content div* should be off-white and 500 pixels high, and the *left_col div* should also be 500 pixels high.

Of course, the page still has no meaningful content. You will begin adding content in the next section, and continue to add content and modify this page throughout the book. As you do so, you will also see some slightly unexpected behavior, so I will call that out as best as I can and try to explain why it is happening. For now, you are going to add a menu control to the top of the page that will be used to navigate through the main pages of the applications you will build.

Creating a CSS Layout Menu

One typical use of tables in HTML is to create a menu across the top of the page that contains links to other parts of the Web site. Using tables for this kind of menu made sense in the past because tables maintain horizontal layout and make horizontal layout very simple to create. However, using tables is also restrictive; when adding a new link to the menu, you need to edit the table, add a new table cell, add the new text, and then style the text appropriately.

With CSS layout, adding a new link is as simple as adding a new item to a list of items. For example, in the previous chapter you created an ASP.NET control that renders an unordered list of items. By default, the browser renders this unordered list with bullets, stacking one item on top of the other. By using CSS, however, you can change that rendering to make the list items render side by side and look like a navigation menu.

In this exercise, you will use the ASP.NET control you created in Chapter 3 to build a simple menu application by using CSS layout.

> **USE** the blog site you modified in the previous exercise.
>
> **BE SURE TO** display the *styleDemo.aspx* page in SharePoint Designer before beginning this exercise.

1. Select the ASP.NET *BulletedList* control, and then press Ctrl + C to copy it.

2. Switch to the *newDefault.aspx* page you created in the first exercise in this chapter and, in the design panel of your page, place the cursor inside the *div* with an ID of *header*.

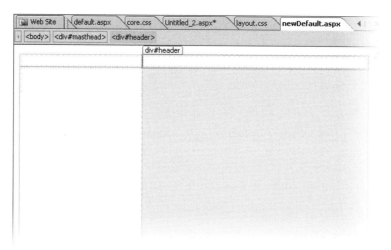

3. Click ⌨Ctrl⌨ + ⌨V⌨ to paste the *BulletedList* control into this location.

4. Select the *BulletedList* control, click the On Object User Interface (OOUI) control, and then click **Edit Items** on the **Common BulletedList Tasks** menu.

The ListItem Collection Editor dialog box opens.

5. In the **ListItem Collection Editor** dialog box, verify that **Item One** is selected. Then change the **Text** property to **Home** and the **Value** property to **newDefault.aspx**.

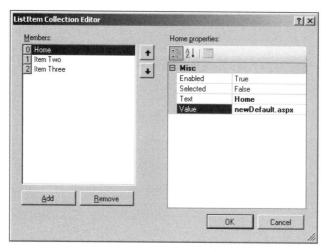

6. Click **OK**.

> **Tip** You changed only one link here to point to something meaningful, but you will be changing the rest of the links in later chapters.

7. Switch to the *layout.css* page you created in the second exercise in this chapter.

8. Under the *#header* selector, add a **#header ul** selector that sets the left padding and left margin of any *ul* inside a *div* with an ID of *header* to be 0, by hand-coding the following:

```
#header ul{
      padding-left: 0;
      margin-left: 0;
}
```

```
#top_left {
     width: 200px;
     position: absolute;
     left: 0px;
     top: 0px;
}

#header {
     margin-left:200px;
}

#header ul {
     padding-left: 0;
     margin-left: 0;
}

#container {
     position: relative;
     width: 100%;
}

#left_col {
     width: 200px;
```

9. Under the *#header ul* selector, add a **#header ul li** selector that removes any style from any *li* tag that is inside any *ul* tag that is inside any *div* with an ID of *header*, so that the bullets themselves stop rendering. In addition, set the display property so that the list items render inline rather than on top of each other by adding the following code:

```
#header ul li{
      list-style: none;
      display: inline;
}
```

10. Under the *#header ul li* selector, add a new **#header ul li a** selector that sets the layout on any *a* tag that is inside any *li* tag that is inside any *ul* tag that is inside any *div* with an ID of *header* so that the following characteristics are set: 10-pixel padding on the left and right, 3-pixel padding on the bottom, no text decorations, list items float from the right, list items have a font color that is black and a background of light gray, and list items are surrounded by a 1-pixel solid black border. You do this by adding the following code:

```
#header ul li a{
        padding-left: 10px;
        padding-right: 10px;
        padding-bottom: 3px;
        text-decoration: none;
        float: right;
        color: black;
        background-color: #C0C0C0;
        border: 1px solid #000;
}
```

11. Under the *#header ul li a* selector, add a new **#header ul li a:hover** selector that sets the background color for the hyperlink to darker gray when the hyperlink is active:

```
#header ul li a:hover{
        background-color: #808080;
}
```

12. Save your work, then switch to the *newDefault.aspx* page.

The bulleted list that you pasted into this page is now rendering in a way that looks like a navigation menu.

13. Preview your new menu in the browser by selecting the *newDefault.aspx* page in the Folder List task pane and pressing the [F12] key.

 BE SURE TO switch back to SharePoint Designer and save your work.

Key Points

- When designing pages, you can use either primarily table layout or primarily CSS layout.
- CSS layout is easy to maintain and easy to create, though initially there is a learning curve to using CSS.
- With CSS, you can modify the default rendering of different HTML constructs and ASP.NET controls so that they match your design expectations.
- SharePoint Designer has a rich set of tools that you can use to modify CSS in Code view, in the CSS property grid, and in the CSS files themselves.

Chapter at a Glance

Read a master page
at design time,
page 89

Create an ASPX page based
on a master page, **page 93**

Create a master page,
page 97

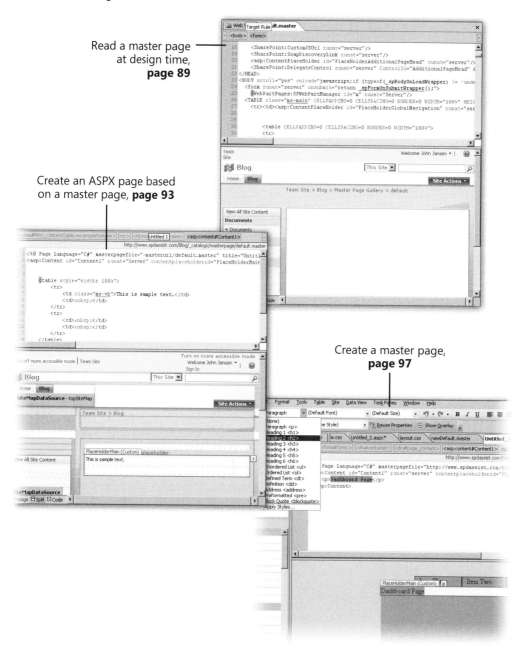

5 Working with Master Pages

In this chapter, you will learn to

✔ Explore the Master Page Gallery.

✔ Read a master page at design time.

✔ Create an ASPX page based on a master page.

✔ Create a master page.

✔ Create the minimal SharePoint master page.

Master pages are an important part of any good application. They allow you to create a consistent look and feel for all of your pages without needing to repeat the same code over and over again as you would typically need to do when building a Web application. However, master pages are also very complex, which is why I am going to spend an entire chapter looking at them.

The most important thing that you need to understand about master pages is that they contain tags called *ASP:ContentPlaceHolder* tags (also referred to as *content regions* in the Microsoft Office SharePoint Designer 2007 user interface) that are used as place-holders for content in the pages that derive from them. These content regions are placed within the content on the master page—a page that you will share between all the pages in your application—and then "unlocked" so they can contain custom content that is unique to that page. The simplest master pages contain only one content region (typically given an ID of *PlaceHolderMain*), which is then unlocked on each page that derives from the master page.

After completing the exercises in this chapter, you will have a master page that contains the shared content of your application (a navigation system, links to CSS pages for styling and layout, and the minimum number of content regions necessary for use with SharePoint pages). Because all ASPX pages that derive from a master page *must not* contain any content *tags* that do not match the content *regions* in the master page, you need to ensure that you have a content region for every content tag in the default SharePoint pages.

In this chapter, you will begin by looking at the Master Page Gallery itself to see where it is located in the file structure of the Web site and to view the functions available in the gallery. After becoming familiar with the gallery, you will open a master page in SharePoint Designer to learn how to read the content as it is rendered at design time. Then you will create new pages based on the master pages in the site, and create custom master pages. Finally, you will add the necessary content onto your custom master page so that it will work with every SharePoint page in the Web site.

> **Important** Before you can use the practice files in this chapter, you need to install them from the book's companion CD to their default location. For more information, see "Using the Companion CD" at the beginning of this book.

Exploring the Master Page Gallery

By default, all of the master pages created when a site is created are placed in the Master Page Gallery in the SharePoint site. You can access this gallery via the browser to see the list of master pages, but you can also open it in SharePoint Designer. I prefer to view it in SharePoint Designer because I can then more easily edit the pages (which cannot be browsed themselves) as well as rename, check out, and delete those pages if necessary.

In this exercise, you will open the Master Page Gallery in SharePoint Designer and explore the options discussed in the previous paragraph.

> **USE** the blog site you created and modified in earlier chapters. If you did not create the blog site, you can still perform these exercises by creating a new blog site, following the steps in Chapter 1; however, the screen shots in some examples will not match the ones shown here.
> **BE SURE TO** display the blog site in SharePoint Designer before beginning this exercise.

1. Click the **Web Site** tab located just below the toolbars.

The Web Site tab displays a full list of the folders and files in the site.

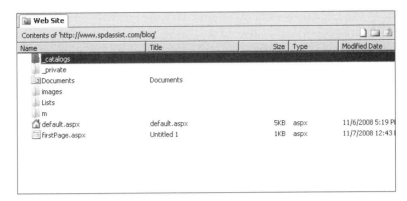

2. Double-click the *_catalogs* folder, and then double-click the *masterpage* folder.

> **Tip** Because you are working with a "blog" site, there is only one master page: *default.master*. Most templates have only one master page in them, but some (such as the Publishing Portal site template in Microsoft Office SharePoint Server 2007) have many master pages.

3. Right-click *default.master* to see the list of available commands you can perform on the master page. These commands are described here:

- ○ **Check Out.** With this command, you can check out the file so that no one else can edit it while you make your changes.

- ○ **Version History.** This command opens a dialog box showing you the major and minor check-ins that have occurred to this file. From this dialog box, you can also restore the current version back to an earlier version.

- ○ **Open.** This command opens the file for editing in SharePoint Designer.

- ○ **Open With.** This command offers a menu with a list of alternative applications to use to open the file, and allows you to choose a program from a list of those installed on your computer.

- ○ **Open In New Window.** This command opens the file in a new instance of SharePoint Designer. This can be helpful if you want to have Code view open and full size in one instance of SharePoint Designer and Design view open and full size in another instance of SharePoint Designer.

- ○ **Set As Default Master Page.** This command is unavailable in this example because the *default.master* page already is the default master, but if it weren't the default, you could click this command to set it as such.

○ **Set As Custom Master Page.** This command is unavailable in this example because the *default.master* page already is the custom master, but if it weren't the custom master, you could click this command to set it as such.

○ **New From Master Page.** You'll use this command quite a bit. This command creates a new ASPX page that is linked to the current master page and opens that page for editing.

○ **Preview In Browser.** This command is always unavailable for master pages because they cannot be browsed.

○ **Cut.** This command removes the page from the Master Page Gallery and places it into memory.

○ **Copy.** This command copies the page into memory. You could then use the Paste command to create a new master page. You could do this when you want to make only subtle changes to the current master page for your application's look and feel.

○ **Paste.** This command pastes a new page into the gallery.

○ **Rename.** This command renames the file and then forces a link fixup to occur so that any pages that are referencing the old name are fixed to then reference the new name.

○ **Delete.** This command removes the page from the Master Page Gallery.

○ **Publish Selected Files.** This command opens the Remote Web Site Properties dialog box, which is primarily used for ASP.NET development and to move pages from one server to another. In the SharePoint context, it will cause a warning to appear explaining that SharePoint-specific content will not work after being published.

○ **Don't Publish.** This command prevents the specified page from being published when a full Publish command is used. Again, this functionality does not make a lot of sense in the SharePoint context.

○ **Properties.** This command opens the Properties dialog box, in which you can view the file name and title, as well as other file properties.

Reading a Master Page at Design Time

Master pages contain a lot of content and are therefore difficult to read and understand when opened for design in SharePoint Designer. Like standard HTML or ASPX pages, master pages contain HTML markup that controls how their content is rendered (for example, a master page contains a body, and within that body a form, and within that form a table, and so on). However, a master page also contains all of the ASP.NET content region controls necessary to allow other pages to be derived from it and create custom content themselves. A master page might also contain a series of ASP.NET controls, SharePoint controls, Web Parts, and links to CSS (.css) or Javascript (.js) files. The most important SharePoint elements that a master page cannot contain are Web Part zones.

> **Tip** Web Part zones are containers on a page that allow Web Parts to be stored exclusively in the backend database. If there are no zones on the page, all Web Parts become part of the actual page markup, which might affect performance of the page at run time.

In this exercise, you will open the *default.master* page in the SharePoint Designer design surface, change some rendering commands, select a content region, and add some custom content to the page to see how it affects the rendering of other pages in the site.

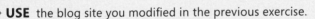

> **USE** the blog site you modified in the previous exercise.
> **BE SURE TO** display the Web Site tab of the blog site in SharePoint Desiger before beginning this exercise.

1. In the **Master Page Gallery**, right-click **default.master**, and then click **Open**.

   The *default.master* page opens in SharePoint Designer.

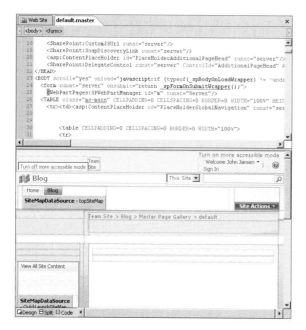

Some controls render as gray boxes on some SharePoint pages, and the *default.master* page here is no exception. This rendering is because the control does not have any design-time HTML because it doesn't render as anything at run time; however, SharePoint Designer shows it as a box so that you can select it and then set properties, move it, or in some other way interact with the control.

2. On the **View** menu, point to **Visual Aids**, and then click **Show**.

> **Tip** As demonstrated in Chapter 2, "Working with SharePoint Sites in SharePoint Designer," SharePoint Designer turns on some visual aids by default to allow designers to see all of the elements on the page. This creates a situation in which the page is no longer WYSIWYG, but these aids are necessary for you to be able to actually design the page effectively.

All of the boundaries in each content region control stop rendering, making it impossible to find any content regions on the page. In addition, the gray box for SiteMapDataSource disappears.

3. Repeat step 2 to redisplay the visual aids.

> **Tip** Each content region's border renders as a light purple rectangle. As you point to one of the rectangles, you can see its name appear in a tooltip.

4. Click in the middle of the page to place the cursor inside the **PlaceHolderMain** content region.

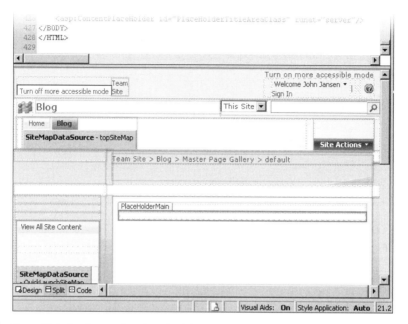

5. Type **This is the main placeholder.**

6. Use the ⬅ key to move the cursor back to the beginning of the text you just typed, and then use the ⬅ key again to move one more character over so the cursor is flashing just outside the **PlaceHolderMain** content region.

7. Type **This is before the main placeholder.**

8. Save the page.

   SharePoint warns you that you are saving changes to a page from the site definition.

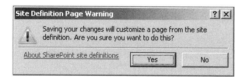

9. In the **Site Definition Page Warning** message box, click **Yes**.

See Also For more information about site definitions, see *Inside Microsoft Windows SharePoint Services 3.0*, by Ted Pattison and Daniel Larson (Microsoft Press, 2007).

> **Troubleshooting** Occasionally, editing master pages does not update the design surface. If you find yourself in this state, simply press F5 to force a refresh for the page.

10. On the **File** menu, click **Open**, browse to *default.aspx,* and then click **Open**.

The *default.aspx* page opens in SharePoint Designer.

11. Scroll through the design surface and observe the text you added to the master page.

 BE SURE TO save your work.

You can see that the text added above the content region is visible, but the text inside the content region is not visible. This is an important feature of master pages: any content that is outside a content region will be seen on all pages that are derived from that master page, but any content inside a content region can be overwritten by the individual pages that are derived from it.

Creating an ASPX Page Based on a Master Page

There are essentially two ways to create pages that are derived from a master page. You can either begin from the master page and create a page that displays all of the master page content, or you can create all of your custom content first and then attach a master page to your custom page, which prompts you to map your custom content to a content region on the master page.

In this exercise, you will create a page with some styled content on it and then attach that page to the *default.master* page for this site.

BE SURE TO display the blog site you modified in the previous exercise, in SharePoint Designer, before beginning this exercise.

1. On the **File** menu, point to **New**, and then click **ASPX** to create an ASPX page.

2. Make sure the cursor is inside the page's design surface, and then click **Insert Table** on the **Table** menu.

The Insert Table dialog box opens.

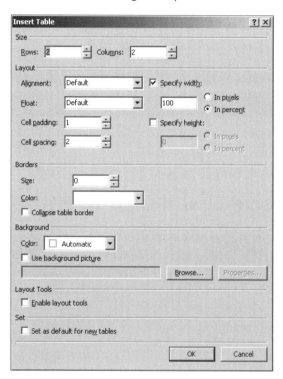

3. Accept the default settings, and click **OK**.

This inserts the table on your page with the cursor in the upper-left table cell.

4. Display the **Tag Properties** task pane and scroll down to the **class** property.

5. Type **ms-vb** as the property value for this class.

6. Click to ensure that the cursor is in the table cell that now has the class attribute added, and type **This is sample text.**

7. On the **Format** menu, click **Master page**, and then click **Attach master page**.

The Select A Master Page dialog box opens.

With this dialog box, you can select the default master page for the site, the custom master page, or a unique master page.

8. Click **OK** to select the default master page.

The Match Content Regions dialog box opens. With this dialog box, you can map content on the current page to render inside content regions on the master page.

9. In the **Match Content Regions** dialog box, click **OK**.

This maps the contents of the entire body of the current page and places it inside the PlaceHolderMain content region.

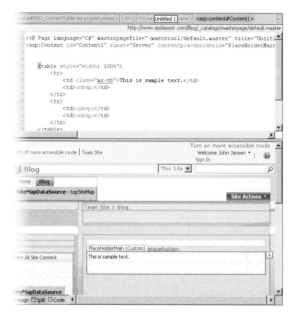

 BE SURE TO save your work.

You can see that not only is the table you inserted above now rendering inside the main placeholder, but also it is surrounded by all the *default.master* page content. Another key thing to note here is that the text you added to the table cell has a style applied to it. This important rendering is because you added the *ms-vb* class to the table cell and then applied a master page that has a reference to a CSS file that contains a definition for this class.

Creating a Master Page

As demonstrated in the previous exercise, you can have many master pages in a site. There can only be one default master page, and only one custom master page, but you can create any number of additional master pages. For the most part, you'll be creating one master page and setting it as the default, as you will be doing in this chapter. However, there are times when you might want to brand one group of pages differently from another group of pages; in that case, you can create new master pages and then create pages from those master pages without setting the master pages as the default.

In this exercise, you will modify the page created in Chapter 4, "Creating Layout with Cascading Style Sheets," to contain the necessary content so that it can be a master page, add some content to that master page, and save it to the Master Page Gallery.

 BE SURE TO display the blog site in SharePoint Designer before beginning this exercise.

1. On the **File** menu, click **Open**, and then double-click *newDefault.aspx*.
2. On the **File** menu, click **Save As**.

The Save As dialog box opens.

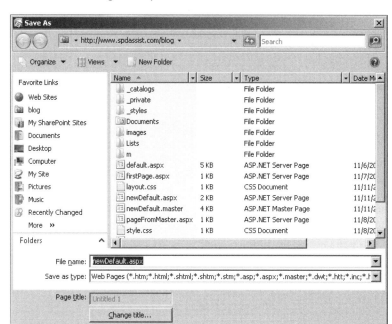

3. Type **newDefault.master** in the **File name** box, and then click **Save**.

Because you have not yet added any master page content regions, you are prompted with a message box indicating that you do not have any content regions defined.

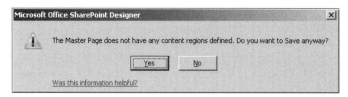

4. Click **Yes** to save the page anyway.

Because you have not added a SharePoint Robots Meta Tag control, you are prompted to add one. This tag is very important for security considerations when you are leveraging fine-grained permissions on list data.

5. Click **Yes** to add this meta tag.

6. Right-click the design surface directly above the off-white **page_content** area, and then click **Manage Microsoft ASP.NET Content Regions**.

The Manage Content Regions dialog box opens.

> **Tip** There is already one content region in the page, as represented by this dialog box. SharePoint Designer puts a content region in the head of the page in order to allow you to overwrite the title of the page.

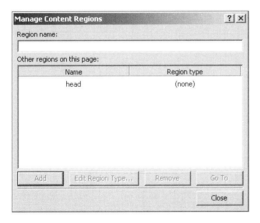

7. In the **Region name** text box, type **PlaceHolderMain**.

8. Click the **Add** button.

9. In the **Manage Content Regions** dialog box, click **(none)**.

The Region Type column displays a menu from which you can specify the type of content that is allowed to be inserted into the content region. This setting alters the design-time markup of the control so that the SharePoint Designer user interface changes based on this setting by leveraging the SharePoint Designer Contributor mode.

See Also For more information about Contributor mode in SharePoint Designer, see *Microsoft Office SharePoint Designer 2007 Step by Step*, by Penelope Coventry (Microsoft Press, 2008).

The following settings are available for this column:

○ **(none).** This is the default setting for region content. You will probably never need to change away from this unless you want to specifically lock down the regions on your pages.

○ **Text And Image.** This setting allows users to insert only text or images into the region. It prevents users from inserting HTML tags, for example.

○ **Text Only.** More restrictive than the Text And Images setting, this setting allows users to insert only text into the region.

○ **Text, Layout, And Images.** This setting allows users to insert text, images, and layout content such as *div* tags and tables.

10. Accept the **(none)** setting, and then click **Close** to close the **Manage Content Regions** dialog box.

A new content region is added to your master page. This region can now be overwritten by other pages that will be based on this master page.

11. Press ⌈Ctrl⌉+⌈S⌉ to save this page.

12. On the **File** menu, click **New**, and then click **Page**.

13. In the **New** dialog box, click **Create from Master Page**.

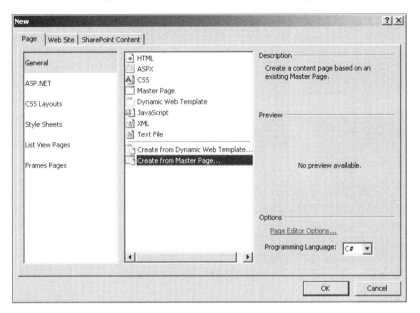

14. Click **OK**.

The Select A Master Page dialog box opens.

15. Click **Select a Master Page**.

16. In the **Select a Master Page** dialog box, browse to the blog Web site and double-click *newDefault.master*.

17. Click **OK**.

18. Point to **PlaceHolderMain(Master)**, and click the arrow that appears.

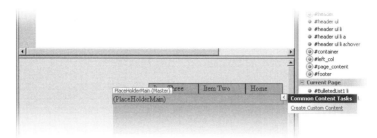

19. Click **Create Custom Content** to unlock this content region.

20. Replace the **(PlaceHolderMain)** default text with **Dashboard Page**.

21. Select **Dashboard Page**.

22. In the **Style** list on the Common toolbar, click **Heading 2 <h2>**.

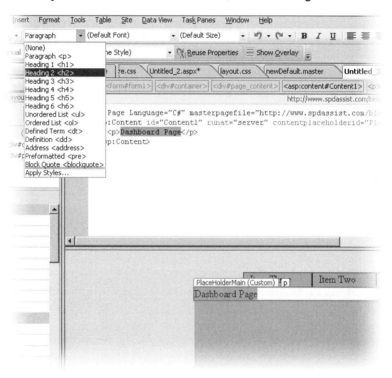

23. Save the page as *tempDefault.aspx,* and then preview it in the browser to see your changes.

Creating the Minimal SharePoint Master Page

As mentioned at the beginning of this chapter, when you are using master pages it is important that pages that are derived from that master page not have *asp:Content* tags that do not map directly to an *asp:ContentPlaceHolder* on the master page. If a page does contain extra *asp:Content* tags, the page will render with an error when you try to browse to it.

What this means to an application developer is that if you want to set your custom master page to be the default master page for the site, you will need to include *asp:ContentPlaceHolders* to account for all the *asp:Content* tags that exist on SharePoint pages that are not in your control. When you create SharePoint content in the browser, that content might include ASPX pages that are designed to render by using the *default.master* page. To protect yourself against the possible errors the rendering of these pages might generate, you need to create a minimum master page.

In this exercise, you will modify your current master page so that it includes this minimum number of content regions.

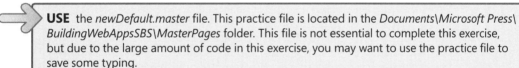

USE the *newDefault.master* file. This practice file is located in the *Documents\Microsoft Press\ BuildingWebAppsSBS\MasterPages* folder. This file is not essential to complete this exercise, but due to the large amount of code in this exercise, you may want to use the practice file to save some typing.

BE SURE TO display the *newDefault.master* page in SharePoint Designer before beginning this exercise.

1. On the **View** menu, point to **Page**, and then click **Code** to display *newDefault.master* in Code view.

2. Place the cursor immediately before the opening *<html>* tag and paste in the following code:

```
<%@ Register
    Tagprefix="SharePoint"
    Namespace="Microsoft.SharePoint.WebControls"
    Assembly="Microsoft.SharePoint,
        Version=12.0.0.0,
        Culture=neutral,
        PublicKeyToken=71e9bce111e9429c" %>
<%@ Register
    Tagprefix="WebPartPages"
    Namespace="Microsoft.SharePoint.WebPartPages"
    Assembly="Microsoft.SharePoint,
        Version=12.0.0.0,
        Culture=neutral,
        PublicKeyToken=71e9bce111e9429c" %>
```

3. Select *<SharePoint:RobotsMetaTag runat="Server"></SharePoint:RobotsMetaTag>* and replace it with the following code:

```
<WebPartPages:SPWebPartManager runat="server"/>
<SharePoint:RobotsMetaTag runat="server"/>
  <Sharepoint:CssLink runat="server"/>
  <asp:ContentPlaceHolder
        id="PlaceHolderAdditionalPageHead"
        runat="server" />
```

4. Change the opening *<body>* tag so that it includes an onload event:

```
<body onload="javascript:_spBodyOnLoadWrapper();">
```

5. Change the opening *<form>* tag so that it includes an onsubmit event:

```
<form id="form1" runat="server" onsubmit="return _
spFormOnSubmitWrapper();">
```

6. Just before the closing *</form>* tag in the page, add an *asp:Panel* control that contains the remaining necessary content regions:

```
<asp:Panel visible="false" runat="server">
<asp:ContentPlaceHolder
      id="PlaceHolderSearchArea"
      runat="server"/>
<asp:ContentPlaceHolder
      id="PlaceHolderTitleBreadcrumb"
      runat="server"/>
<asp:ContentPlaceHolder
      id="PlaceHolderPageTitleInTitleArea"
      runat="server"/>
<asp:ContentPlaceHolder
      id="PlaceHolderLeftNavBar"
      runat="server"/>
<asp:ContentPlaceHolder
      ID="PlaceHolderPageImage"
      runat="server"/>
<asp:ContentPlaceHolder
      ID="PlaceHolderBodyLeftBorder"
      runat="server"/>
<asp:ContentPlaceHolder
      ID="PlaceHolderNavSpacer"
      runat="server"/>
<asp:ContentPlaceHolder
      ID="PlaceHolderTitleLeftBorder"
```

```
      runat="server"/>
<asp:ContentPlaceHolder
      ID="PlaceHolderTitleAreaSeparator"
      runat="server"/>
<asp:ContentPlaceHolder
      ID="PlaceHolderMiniConsole"
      runat="server"/>
<asp:ContentPlaceHolder
      id="PlaceHolderCalendarNavigator"
      runat ="server"/>
<asp:ContentPlaceHolder
      id="PlaceHolderLeftActions"
      runat ="server"/>
<asp:ContentPlaceHolder
      id="PlaceHolderPageDescription"
      runat ="server"/>
<asp:ContentPlaceHolder
      id="PlaceHolderBodyAreaClass"
      runat ="server"/>
<asp:ContentPlaceHolder
      id="PlaceHolderTitleAreaClass"
      runat ="server"/>
<asp:ContentPlaceHolder
      id="PlaceHolderBodyRightMargin"
      runat="server"/>
</asp:Panel>
```

You need to clean up the *<head>* section of your master to include a link to the core JavaScript file from SharePoint, and include one additional content region so that the titles of pages can be overwritten.

7. Select the *<title>Untitled 1</title>* tag and replace it with the following:

```
<SharePoint:ScriptLink
      language="javascript"
      name="core.js"
      Defer="true"
      runat="server"/>
<title ID=onetidTitle><asp:ContentPlaceHolder
      id=PlaceHolderPageTitle
      runat="server"/></title>
```

8. Add a link to the *style.css* file you created earlier in this book by adding the following immediately above the *<link ...>* tag that is currently in the head of your page:

```
<link rel="stylesheet" type="text/css" href="/blog/style.css" />
```

9. Delete the *<style ...>* block that contains definitions for *#BulletedList1 li* and *#BulletedList1 A:Link*.

The code now looks like this:

```
<!DOCTYPE html
    PUBLIC "-//W3C//DTD XHTML 1.0 Transitional//EN"
    "http://www.w3.org/TR/xhtml1/DTD/xhtml1-transitional.dtd">
<%@ Master language="C#" %>
<%@ Register
    Tagprefix="SharePoint"
    Namespace="Microsoft.SharePoint.WebControls"
    Assembly="Microsoft.SharePoint,
        Version=12.0.0.0,
        Culture=neutral,
        PublicKeyToken=71e9bce111e9429c" %>
<%@ Register
    Tagprefix="WebPartPages"
    Namespace="Microsoft.SharePoint.WebPartPages"
    Assembly="Microsoft.SharePoint,
        Version=12.0.0.0,
        Culture=neutral,
        PublicKeyToken=71e9bce111e9429c" %>
<html dir="ltr"
    xmlns="http://www.w3.org/1999/xhtml">
<head runat="server">
<META name="WebPartPageExpansion"
    content="full">
<title ID=onetidTitle>
    <asp:ContentPlaceHolder
        id=PlaceHolderPageTitle
        runat="server"/>
</title>
<SharePoint:RobotsMetaTag runat="server"/>
<Sharepoint:CssLink runat="server"/>
<asp:ContentPlaceHolder
    id="PlaceHolderAdditionalPageHead"
    runat="server"/>
<link rel="stylesheet"
    type="text/css"
    href="/blog/style.css" />
<link rel="stylesheet"
    type="text/css"
    href="/blog/layout.css" />
<asp:ContentPlaceHolder
    runat="server"
    id="head">
</asp:ContentPlaceHolder>
</head>
<body onload="javascript:_spBodyOnLoadWrapper();">
<form id="form1"
    runat="server"
    onsubmit="return _spFormOnSubmitWrapper();">
```

```
<WebPartPages:SPWebPartManager runat="server"/>
<div id="masthead">
    <div id="top_left">
    </div>
    <div id="header">
    <asp:BulletedList runat="server"
        id="BulletedList1"
        DisplayMode="HyperLink">
        <asp:ListItem
            Value="newDefault.aspx">
            Home
        </asp:ListItem>
        <asp:ListItem>
            Item Two
        </asp:ListItem>
        <asp:ListItem>
            Item Three
        </asp:ListItem>
    </asp:BulletedList>
    </div>
</div>
<div id="container">
    <div id="left_col">
    </div>
    <div id="page_content">
    <asp:ContentPlaceHolder
        runat="Server"
        id="PlaceHolderMain">
        <p>(PlaceHolderMain)</p>
    </asp:ContentPlaceHolder>
    </div>
</div>
<div id="footer">
</div>
<asp:Panel visible="false" runat="server">
<asp:ContentPlaceHolder
    id="PlaceHolderSearchArea"
    runat="server"/>
<asp:ContentPlaceHolder
    id="PlaceHolderTitleBreadcrumb"
    runat="server"/>
<asp:ContentPlaceHolder
    id="PlaceHolderPageTitleInTitleArea"
    runat="server"/>
<asp:ContentPlaceHolder
    id="PlaceHolderLeftNavBar"
    runat="server"/>
<asp:ContentPlaceHolder
    ID="PlaceHolderPageImage"
    runat="server"/>
<asp:ContentPlaceHolder
    ID="PlaceHolderBodyLeftBorder"
    runat="server"/>
```

```
                    <asp:ContentPlaceHolder
                        ID="PlaceHolderNavSpacer"
                        runat="server"/>
                    <asp:ContentPlaceHolder
                        ID="PlaceHolderTitleLeftBorder"
                        runat="server"/>
                    <asp:ContentPlaceHolder
                        ID="PlaceHolderTitleAreaSeparator"
                        runat="server"/>
                    <asp:ContentPlaceHolder
                        ID="PlaceHolderMiniConsole"
                        runat="server"/>
                    <asp:ContentPlaceHolder
                        id="PlaceHolderCalendarNavigator"
                        runat ="server"/>
                    <asp:ContentPlaceHolder
                        id="PlaceHolderLeftActions"
                        runat ="server"/>
                    <asp:ContentPlaceHolder
                        id="PlaceHolderPageDescription"
                        runat ="server"/>
                    <asp:ContentPlaceHolder
                        id="PlaceHolderBodyAreaClass"
                        runat ="server"/>
                    <asp:ContentPlaceHolder
                        id="PlaceHolderTitleAreaClass"
                        runat ="server"/>
                    <asp:ContentPlaceHolder
                        id="PlaceHolderBodyRightMargin"
                        runat="server"/>
                </asp:Panel>
            </form>
        </body>
    </html>
```

> **Troubleshooting** If there are any errors in your master page at this point, you should repeat these steps very carefully. The most common reason for an error is that one of the tags did not get closed properly. In addition, you should browse to *tempDefault.aspx* and verify that it also does not render with any errors.

10. Save the page, and then switch to Design view.

11. In the **Folder List** task pane, right-click the page, and then click **Set as Default Master Page** to set this page as the default master page for the blog site template.

SharePoint warns you that attached pages that do not have a matching set of named content regions will break.

12. In the warning box, click **Yes**.

The steps above will prevent any pages in the SharePoint site from breaking.

> **Tip** All the pages in the blog site will now start by using *newDefault.master* as their master page. Because you have not placed the navigation bar on this master page yet, the content in the blog site is only moderately usable.

Key Points

- Master pages are created in the Master Page Gallery at site creation time.
- The content in master pages is complex, but SharePoint Designer has design tools that help you make sense of it.
- By creating a page from a master page, you can share content easily from page to page.
- SharePoint pages contain a large number of content regions, so it is important that any master pages you create account for these regions.
- Setting the default master page for a SharePoint site is as easy as making a selection from the master page context menu.

Chapter at a Glance

Insert an ASP.NET menu control, **page 112**

Set menu control properties, **page 114**

Modify style properties of an *asp:menu* control, **page 116**

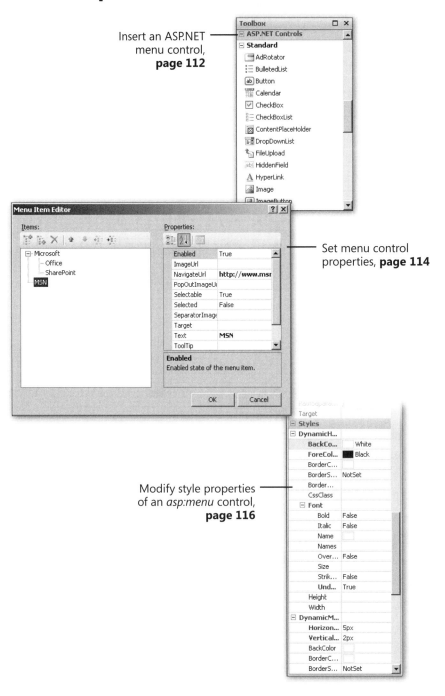

6 Creating Custom Navigation Controls

In this chapter, you will learn to

- ✔ Insert an ASP.NET menu control.
- ✔ Set menu control properties.
- ✔ Modify style properties of an *asp:menu* control.
- ✔ Add a link to a SharePoint navigation control.
- ✔ Add style to SharePoint navigation controls.

Navigation in Microsoft Windows SharePoint Services 3.0 is strongly tied to the site structure and to the lists and document libraries in the site. You have probably noticed that when you create a list in a SharePoint site, you are given the opportunity to add that list to the Quick Launch menu. However, what is not apparent is how to subsequently remove items from the Quick Launch menu or how to add items that are not lists to the Quick Launch menu. To do that, you need to understand how the *asp:menu* control works in general, as well as how to customize that control in order to then add links to the SharePoint navigation control.

In most applications on the Web, JavaScript is used to create the navigation experience. By using JavaScript, you can create pages that enable dynamic user interaction (meaning that the pages change in appearance as users interact with them) without passing the code back to the server for processing. One of the most common uses of JavaScript is to create dynamic "flyout menus" that display to the right of the current mouse position (if the menu is laid out vertically on the page) or below the current mouse position (if the menu is laid out horizontally on the page).

In this chapter, you will create this effect by using two different techniques. The first technique is to create an XML file that contains your navigation structure and then render that structure via a general ASP.NET menu control. The second is to modify the out-of-the-box SharePoint navigation control by using both the browser and Microsoft Office SharePoint Designer 2007, and then modify the cascading style sheet (CSS) file behind SharePoint to alter the look of that control.

> **Important** Before completing the exercises in this chapter you must install the practice files from the companion CD, or complete the exercises in earlier chapters. For more information about practice files, see "Using the Companion CD" at the beginning of this book.

Inserting an ASP.NET Menu Control

As you learned in Chapter 4, "Creating Layout with Cascading Style Sheets," ASP.NET and SharePoint controls have their own design-time experience, which is different from their run-time HTML. So you'll only be seeing a *representation* of a control, not the control itself, when you insert it in SharePoint Designer. When you edit the look and feel of the control, you will again be modifying the cascading styles for the controls.

In this exercise, you will insert an ASP.NET menu control.

> **USE** the *newDefault.master* page of the blog site you modified in Chapter 5, "Working with Master Pages." If you did not build the blog site as instructed earlier in this book, use the *newDefault.master* practice file located in the *Documents\Microsoft Press\ BuildingWebAppsSBS\ASPControls* folder.
>
> **BE SURE TO** display the *newDefault.master* file in Split view before beginning this exercise.

1. If the **Toolbox** task pane is not showing, click **Toolbox** on the **Task Panes** menu.

2. Expand the **ASP.NET Controls** section of the Toolbox.

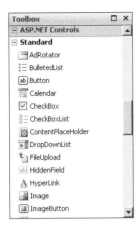

3. Expand the **Navigation** section.

4. Drag and drop the **Menu** control onto the design panel of your page inside the *div* with an ID of *left_col*.

   SharePoint Designer inserts an *asp:menu* control into the page.

5. Click the arrow in the upper-right corner of the panel to show the On Object User Interface (OOUI) menu for this control, and the commands available for customizing this control.

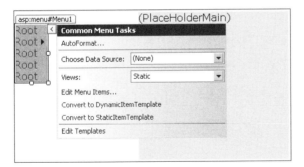

 BE SURE TO save the *newDefault.master* file.

Setting Menu Control Properties

The *asp:menu* control will not do you any good until you tell it what menu items to display. On ASP.NET sites, you can create a dynamic XML file to make the menu dynamic. In SharePoint, you can use either a list of items inside the control or the Site Map control.

In this exercise, you will launch the Menu Item Editor dialog box and add a few items inside the control to demonstrate the rich run-time experience of this control.

> **USE** the *newDefault.master* file you modified in the previous exercise.
>
> **BE SURE TO** display *newDefault.master* in Split view before beginning this exercise.

1. Press Ctrl + S to save the page.

   > **Tip** Whenever you work with ASP.NET controls in SharePoint Designer, save the page first, and often after that. If you don't, you might find that setting some properties causes the controls to start rendering as gray boxes with error text. Usually, saving the page and then refreshing it removes those errors.

2. Either click the arrow on the *asp:menu* control, or right-click the control and then click **Show Common Control Tasks** to display the OOUI menu for the control.

3. In the **Common Menu Tasks** panel, click **Edit Menu Items**.

   The Menu Item Editor dialog box opens.

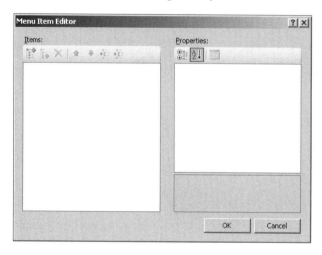

Add a Root Item

4. Click the **Add a Root Item** button.

5. Set the **NavigateUrl** property to **http://www.microsoft.com** and the **Text** property to **Microsoft**.

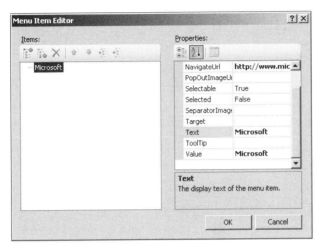

Add a Child Item

6. Click the **Add a Child Item** button, and set the **NavigateUrl** property to **http://www.microsoft.com/office** and the **Text** property to **Office**.

7. Click the **Microsoft** node, and then click the **Add a Child Item** button again. Set the **NavigateUrl** property to **http://www.microsoft.com/sharepoint** and the **Text** property to **SharePoint**.

8. Click the **Microsoft** node again and click the **Add a Root Item** button. Set the **NavigateUrl** property to **http://www.msn.com** and the **Text** property to **MSN**.

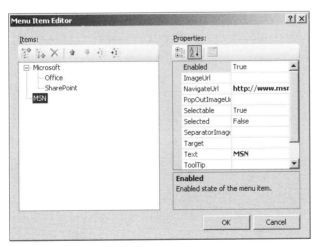

9. Click **OK**.

10. Save the page and browse to any of the pages that are derived from the master page.

> **Tip** If you have not been following along, you can simply right-click the *newdefault.master* page in the Folder List task pane, click New on Master Page, and then save this new page and preview it in the browser.

When you browse, a menu of the Microsoft and MSN items appears. If you point to the word *Microsoft*, you see the sublinks for Office and SharePoint. Clicking a link takes you to the site you specified in the *NavigateUrl* property of that menu item.

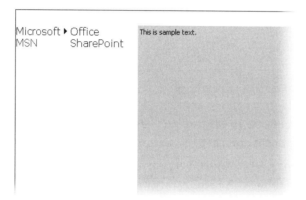

This menu is functional, but it is not branded and does not render the way we want it to, to match the look of our application. This is an ASP.NET control, so the code generated by the control at run time is not the same as the code you can modify for the control at design time. To correctly modify the look and feel of this control, you must use SharePoint Designer to modify properties of the control.

Modifying Style Properties of an *asp:menu* Control

The *asp:menu* control renders the content of the menu items by using templates. It is not within the scope of this book to look specifically at the ASP.NET design model; however, I do want to show you how modifying the formatting for a control can expose its CSS properties and affect how it renders on the SharePoint Designer design surface. I'll also explain how those properties are exposed for modification in the Tag Properties task pane. When you click the OOUI for the *asp:menu* control, you can see the robust choices available out of the box for customizing the control.

There are several commands for customizing this control, as described here:

- **AutoFormat.** This opens the AutoFormat dialog box, which contains four ASP.NET themes that generate the necessary CSS to render the control in standard ways.

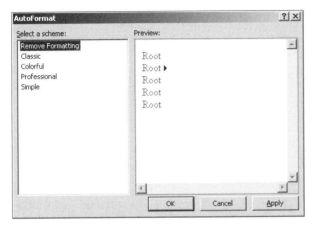

- **Choose Data Source.** Clicking the arrow displays a list of the data sources that are already on the page, along with a <New Data Source> option, which launches the Data Source Configuration Wizard. In SharePoint, this wizard only has one choice: Site Map, which causes the *asp:menu* control to render the SharePoint navigation structure.

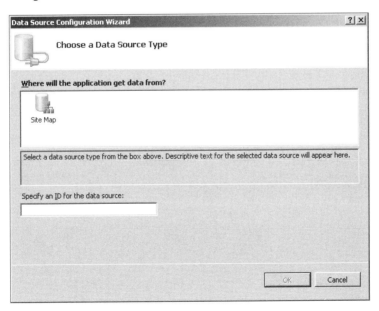

> **Tip** If you were creating an ASP.NET site instead of a SharePoint site, *xmldatasource* would also be available in this wizard. On SharePoint, however, this control is not allowed.

- **Views.** Clicking this arrow displays the Static and Dynamic options. These options allow you to modify the way that different layers of your menu render at run time.

- **Edit Menu Items.** Clicking this launches the Menu Item Editor, which allows you to add items to the *asp:menu* control. We will use this wizard in the next section.

- **Convert to DynamicItemTemplate.** Clicking this command causes *DynamicItemTemplate* to insert the *<%# Eval("Text") %>* code block. This block of code gets the Text value you will set on the menu in the next exercise. In SharePoint, code blocks are not allowed, so this template causes an error; if you were on an ASP.NET site, it would allow you to put other text next to the link text.

- **Convert to StaticItemTemplate.** As with *DynamicItemTemplate*, this template inserts a code block and so causes a SharePoint error as well.

- **Edit Templates.** This launches the ASP.NET template editor, which allows you to customize either the DynamicItem or the StaticItem template.

In this exercise, you will apply a scheme to the *asp:menu* control and then use the Tag Properties task pane to alter the look and feel of that control.

> **USE** the *newDefault.master* file you modified in the previous exercise.
> **BE SURE TO** display *newDefault.master* in Split view before beginning this exercise.

1. In the SharePoint Designer design panel, click the *asp:menu* control.

2. Click the arrow to display the OOUI menu.

3. Click **AutoFormat** to open the **AutoFormat** dialog box.

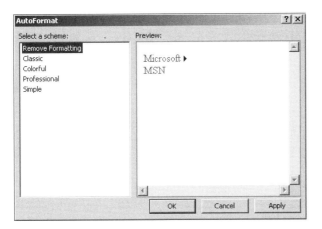

4. In the **Select a scheme** list, click **Simple** to see a preview of the simple scheme as it will apply to the *asp:menu* control.

5. Click **OK**.

6. Click the OOUI arrow to close the **Common Menu Tasks** panel.

7. Click in the code panel for this page to see the code that was just generated.

   Several attributes were added to the *asp:menu* control tag:

   ○ *StaticSubMenuIndent*

   ○ *BackColor*

   ○ *Font-Names*

   ○ *Font-Size*

   ○ *ForeColor*

   ○ *DynamicHorizontalOffset*

   In addition to these attributes, there were also a number of property nodes added inside the control:

   ○ *StaticSelectedStyle*

   ○ *StaticMenuItemStyle*

   ○ *DynamicHoverStyle*

   ○ *VerticalPadding*

   ○ *DynamicHoverStyle*

   ○ *DynamicMenuStyle*

   ○ *DynamicSelectedStyle*

   ○ *DynamicMenuItemStyle*

These are the elements you must modify in SharePoint Designer to change the look and feel of this control.

8. Select the *asp:menu* control in the design panel.

9. Verify that the **Tag Properties** task pane is showing. If it is not showing, click **Tag Properties** on the **Task Panes** menu.

10. Expand the **Tag Properties** task pane to full size.

11. In the **Appearance** group, change the **BackColor** property to **White**.

12. Expand the **Font** property and change the **Size** value to **Small**.

13. Scroll down in the **Tag Properties** task pane to the **Styles** group.

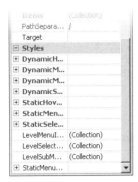

14. Expand **DynamicHoverStyle** to display its properties and change the **BackColor** property to **White** and the **ForeColor** property to **Black**.

15. Expand the **Font** property and change the **Underlined** property to **True**.

16. Expand **DynamicMenuItemStyle** and set the width to **100px**, the **BorderStyle** property to **Outset**, and the **BorderWidth** property to **1px**.

17. Expand **DynamicMenuStyle** and change the **BackColor** property to **White**.

18. Expand **StaticHoverStyle** and change the **BackColor** property to **White** and the **ForeColor** to **Black**.

19. Save the *newDefault.master* page in SharePoint Designer and refresh an ASPX page that derives from this master page in the browser to see how your changes have affected the run-time rendering of the *asp:menu* control.

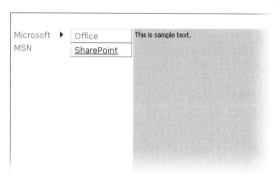

> **Troubleshooting** Sometimes saving the page when your cursor is inside the Tag Properties task pane does not work. If the control doesn't render the way you expect it to, switch to SharePoint Designer and verify that the master page was saved. Click in the design panel and press Ctrl+S, then switch to the browser and refresh the page again.

Adding a Link to a SharePoint Navigation Control

SharePoint navigation is based on the *asp:menu* control navigation you modified in the previous section. The primary difference for the SharePoint navigation control is that the menu items are controlled by the *topSiteMap* data source. This means that you don't have direct access to the menu items being displayed in the same way you did before; however, this design does not prevent you from modifying that data source via other means, nor does it prevent you from modifying the look and feel of the menu control itself.

In this exercise, you will insert a top navigation bar into your master page, use the Site Settings controls in the browser to add a link to the data source that points to an external Web site, and then add a link to an individual page in your site by using the SharePoint Designer Navigation task pane.

> **USE** the *newDefault.master* file you modified in the previous exercise and the *tempDefault.aspx* page of the blog site you modified in Chapter 5. If you did not build the blog site as instructed earlier in this book, use a new blog site created from the blog site template and the *tempDefault.aspx* practice file located in the *Documents\Microsoft Press\BuildingWebAppsSBS\ASPControls* folder.
>
> **BE SURE TO** display *newDefault.master* in Split view before beginning this exercise.

1. In the **Folder List** task pane, expand the *_catalogs\masterpage* folder, and open the *default.master* file.

2. Click the top navigation **SharePoint:AspMenu** control in the design panel.

The *SharePoint:AspMenu* control is selected in the code panel as well.

3. Switch to the code panel.

4. Select the *SharePoint:AspMenu* control and the *SharePoint:Delegate* control immediately below the *AspMenu* control.

5. Press Ctrl + C to copy these two controls into memory.

6. In the *newDefault.master* page code panel, click to place the cursor inside the *top_left div* area.

7. Paste the controls into this *div* area.

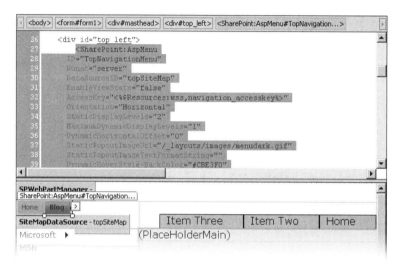

8. Save the master page and browse to the *tempDefault.aspx* file.

    The SharePoint navigation control rendering appears above the *asp:menu* control created in the previous exercise.

9. Modify the URL so that instead of pointing to the *newDefault.aspx* page it points to *_layouts/settings.aspx*.

    The site settings page for the blog site renders in the browser.

10. In the **Look and Feel** category, click **Top Link Bar**.

11. Click **Stop Inheriting Links** so that the top link bar can be customized.

    The Top Link Bar page opens.

12. Click **New Link**.

13. In the **Type the web address** text box, type **http://www.microsoft.com**.

14. In the **Type the description** text box, type **Microsoft**.

15. Click **OK** to add this link to the top navigation bar.

16. Switch back to SharePoint Designer and refresh the *newDefault.master* page. Then verify that the top navigation bar is rendering with two links: **Home** and **Microsoft**.

17. On the **Task Panes** menu, click **Navigation** to display the **Navigation** task pane.

18. Right-click **SharePoint Top Navigation Bar** and point to **New**.

19. Click **Page**.

SharePoint Designer adds a link to Untitled 1 under the current Microsoft link.

20. Right-click **Untitled 1** and click **Rename**, then rename this link **Customers**.

The link itself still points to *Untitled_1.htm* in your Web site, but you will change that in a later chapter.

21. Browse back out to *tempDefault.aspx* and verify that the top navigation bar now contains three links: one to **Home**, one to **Microsoft**, and one to **Customers**.

 BE SURE TO save your work.

Adding Style to SharePoint Navigation Controls

Now that you understand how to add pages or Web sites to the navigation control in SharePoint, you need to spend some time customizing the look and feel of the control. In much the same way that you modified styles in earlier chapters, as well as the *asp:menu* control in this chapter, you will make a modification to the *core.css* file that will affect the rendering of all of the menu controls on your pages.

In this exercise, you will modify one of the classes referenced by the *SharePoint:AspMenu* control, so that the control renders with different font and background colors than the default.

 USE the *newDefault.master* file you modified in the previous exercise.
BE SURE TO display *newDefault.master* in Split view before beginning this exercise.

1. Select the navigation control that has the **Home**, **Microsoft**, and **Customer** links in it.

2. Scroll down in the code panel to the *DynamicMenuItemStyle* tag.

Because these CSS classes are attribute values of ASP.NET controls, they do not render as you might expect in the CSS Properties Task pane. To customize the rendering of this control, use Code view.

3. Press ⎡Ctrl⎤ and click the code hyperlink for *ms-topnav* to open *core.css* with the *ms-topnav* selector selected.

4. Delete *background-image:url("/_layouts/images/topnavunselected.gif");* to prevent the navigation bar from rendering with an image in the background.

5. Delete the *background-repeat:repeat-x;* value.

6. Delete the *border-bottom:none;* value.

7. Change *background-color:#e2efff;* to **background-color:#ffffff;**.

8. Change *color:#3764a0;* to **color:#000000;**.

9. Scroll down to the *.ms-topnavselected* selector and delete the following values: *background:url("/_layouts/images/topnavselected.gif");* *background-repeat:repeat-x;*.

10. Change *background-color* to **#ffffff** and *color* to **#000000**.

```
    .ms-topnav {
644 border:solid 1px #c2dcff;
645 border-left:solid 1px #ffffff;
646 font-family:Tahoma;
647 font-size:8pt;
648 background-color:#ffffff;
649 color:#000000;
650 }
651 .ms-topnav a{
652 display:block;
653 white-space:nowrap;
654 padding:1px 8px 0px 8px;
655 height:18px;
656 }
657 .ms-topnavselected{
658 color:#000000;
659 font-weight:bold;
660 border:solid 1px #79a7e3;
661 border-bottom-width:0px;
662 border-left:solid 1px #e3efff;
663 background-color:#ffffff;
664 }
665 .ms-topnavselected a{
666 color:#003399;
667 }
668 .ms-topNavHover{
669 background-image:url("/_layouts/images/topnavhover.gif");
670 background-color:#ffe6a0;
    border:solid 1px #c2a770;
```

11. Save *core.css* to commit your changes.

12. Browse to your site's *tempDefault.aspx* page and refresh the page if necessary.

The navigation bar renders with a white background and black text.

 BE SURE TO save your work.

As you have seen, there are a number of ways to build a navigation structure in SharePoint. Ease of navigation is a core component to a successful application, so it is important to understand all of the options available. The master page that you have built in this book now contains an ASP.NET bulleted list with some items in it, an *asp:menu* control with links to external sites, and a *SharePoint:AspMenu* control that links to the navigation structure on your SharePoint site. Each of these techniques is important in its own way, so determining which one to use will depend on your specific Web application needs..

Key Points

- Modifying navigation in ASP.NET and SharePoint is relatively straightforward when you understand the different rendering methods for controls.

- ASP.NET has controls that enable rapid development of navigation in Web sites. Those controls can easily be modified in SharePoint Designer.

- The navigation of SharePoint sites can be controlled via the browser or via SharePoint Designer.

- When you understand what CSS is used for the rendering, customization of the SharePoint navigation control is as simple as modifying the default ASP.NET menu control.

Chapter at a Glance

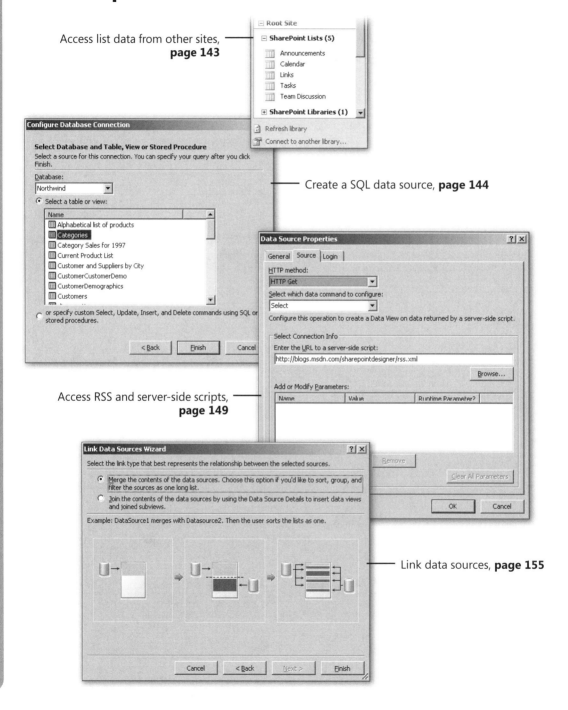

Access list data from other sites, **page 143**

Create a SQL data source, **page 144**

Access RSS and server-side scripts, **page 149**

Link data sources, **page 155**

7 Creating Data Sources in SharePoint

In this chapter, you will learn to

✔ Access list data from within the current site.

✔ Copy and modify a list data source.

✔ Access list data from other sites.

✔ Create a SQL data source.

✔ Access RSS and server-side scripts.

✔ Access XML Web services.

✔ Link data sources.

So far in this book, the exercises have focused on building a simple navigation structure, customizing and modifying ASP.NET and SharePoint controls, and building master pages. However, building the look and feel of your application is only part of the challenge. The heart and soul of your application is the data it accesses and displays.

Building the data back end for an application can be challenging, but Microsoft Office SharePoint Designer 2007 has an interface that allows you to easily see the data sources you have already created, and by extension, the data sources you still need to create. When you view the Data Source Library, SharePoint Designer performs a query across your Web site and automatically displays any lists or document libraries in your site, as well as any XML files. These sources are "auto-enumerated" and are managed in ways that are unique from the other data sources in the library.

The other sources are displayed in the Data Source Library as well, but they are stored in a special document library called *fpdatasources* (the *fp* is because this was originally written for Microsoft Office FrontPage 2003 working on Microsoft SharePoint Team Services 2.0 sites). When you create data sources, the necessary connection information (including user names and passwords) is stored in XML format inside this document library. It is important to remember that all of the query information is there—which means that anyone who has Designer (or higher) permissions on your Web site can read your data sources and see any information stored there.

Each data source type requires a different method of interaction, so refer to the following list when considering which type of source to create:

- **SharePoint lists.** Lists are usually auto-enumerated sources that appear in the library simply because they exist in the site. However, to create a unique data source based on list data, you can simply click a data source, copy it, and save it with new properties (by applying a sort or filter, for example).

- **SharePoint libraries.** Essentially, these are identical to list data sources, except that they have a different content type. SharePoint libraries are also auto-enumerated and can be copied and modified, allowing you to create rich data sources based on libraries.

- **Database connections.** This type of source is one of the most challenging to work with. SharePoint application developers consistently experience problems understanding the authentication model to access data from a Microsoft SQL Server. Connecting to a database requires that you either include the user name and password in your connection string or leverage single sign-on (SSO) or Kerberos. We discuss this in greater detail later in this chapter.

  See Also For more information on databases and authentication in ASP.NET, refer to the article on the Microsoft Developer Network (MSDN) site at *msdn.microsoft.com/ en-us/library/ms998292.aspx.*

- **XML files.** Another auto-enumerated source, XML files show up in the library simply by being included in the site. When you add an external XML file as a data source, SharePoint Designer prompts you to import the XML file into the current site.

- **Server-side scripts.** Any script that returns properly formatted XML as its response works here. There aren't a lot of these around, but in certain cases you might find a script that returns something you can use. Included in this group, however, are *really simple syndication (RSS) feeds*. RSS is very common across the Internet today. This data source allows you to include rich content from many other locations on pages inside your own site. There is a security consideration that needs to be made here, however: When you are accessing data from someone else's server, you have no control over that server. If that server is hacked or if the administrator of that server turns malicious, you might expose yourself to attacks. We'll talk more about this in Chapter 8, "Creating Data Views."

- **XML Web services.** Web services are also very popular across the Internet today. The security concerns for server-side scripts are true here as well. If you do not have a trust relationship with the provider of your data, you put yourself at risk.

- **Linked sources.** This data source type lets you combine any of the above sources with any other source to create very rich data views. An example of this is a Web service that shows books from an online retailer combined with a SharePoint list of authors.

In this chapter, you will explore the Data Source Library and add a new source to each group in the library. You will consider the pros and cons of each type of source, as well as what happens behind the scenes when you create a source. In addition, you will take a look at the properties of the different data sources in the library to better understand how to manage your data and build the best applications you can.

> **Important** The exercises in this chapter require only the blog site created and modified in earlier chapters. No practice files are supplied on the companion CD. For more information about practice files, see "Using the Companion CD" at the beginning of this book.

Accessing List Data from Within the Current Site

List data is by far the most common type of data source used in SharePoint applications. You can think of lists as similar to tables inside a SQL database—though an important difference is that they do not maintain *one-to-many* and *many-to-many* relationships well. Lists can be created either in the browser or in SharePoint Designer, but when you want to add new fields (or columns) to a list, you can do so only in the browser.

To make your data sources as robust as possible, you need to understand what can be done to lists, and where best to perform those actions. In this exercise, you will create two lists in your SharePoint site by using SharePoint Designer. Then you will modify the columns in a list to generate the schema (the underlying structure of the list) you need for your application. Finally, you will populate the lists with usable data.

USE the blog site you created and modified in earlier chapters. If you did not create the blog site, you can still perform these exercises by creating a new blog site, following the steps in Chapter 1; however, the screen shots in some examples will not match the ones shown here.

BE SURE TO display the blog site in SharePoint Designer before beginning this exercise.

1. On the **Task Panes** menu, click **Data Source Library**. Then expand the **Data Source Library** task pane to its full size.

Troubleshooting If the Data Source Library starts to show incorrect "redraw" issues where part of the library overlaps with another part of the library, save your work and exit SharePoint Designer, then relaunch SharePoint Designer and reopen your site and page.

Within the library, the seven categories of data sources described at the beginning of this chapter are displayed. The SharePoint Lists group contains the five default lists, and the SharePoint Libraries group contains the two document libraries included within the blog site template.

2. In the **SharePoint Lists** group, click **Create new SharePoint list**.

The New dialog box opens, with the SharePoint Content tab active and the Lists category selected.

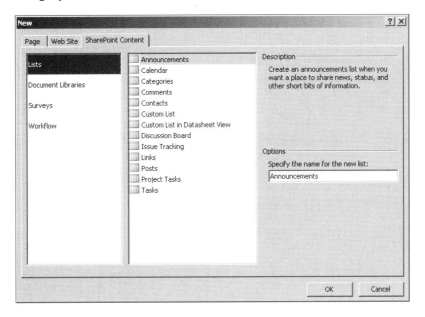

> **Tip** The available lists in this dialog box are populated automatically when SharePoint Designer queries the server itself for the available lists. If you or another server administrator has uploaded any custom list templates to the server, those lists automatically show up here.

3. Click **Contacts** and then, in the **Specify the name for the new list** box, type **Customers**. Then click **OK**.

This creates the Customers list based on the Contacts content type and automatically refreshes the Data Source Library, displaying this list as a new data source.

4. Click **Create new SharePoint list** again.

5. Select **Custom List**, give the new list a name of **CustomerType**, and click **OK** to create that list.

The new list again shows up in the Data Source Library's SharePoint Lists group. In addition to being listed in the Data Source Library, the new lists are also displayed in the Folder List task pane.

6. Click the **Customers** folder in the **Folder List** task pane to select it, and then press F12 to preview the list in the browser.

You are automatically directed to the *AllItems.aspx* page for this list, which renders based on the *newDefault.master* page you created in Chapter 4, "Creating Layout with Cascading Style Sheets."

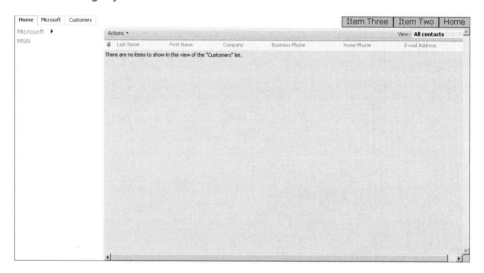

> **Troubleshooting** Depending on the way that permissions are configured for your Web site, you might see only the Actions command in the List View toolbar. If this is the case, browse to your site's authentication page (*/blog/_layouts/authenticate.aspx*) to log in as any user with the Manage Lists right.

7. On the **Settings** menu in the upper-right corner, click **List Settings**.

The *Customize Customers* page for this list appears.

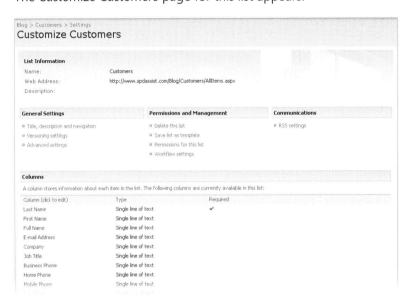

On this page you can modify several properties for the list, including its name or description, workflow settings, permissions, and other advanced settings. In addition, you can create new columns or new views of the list.

8. In the **Columns** section of the page, below the list of existing columns, click **Create column**.

The *Create Column* page appears.

9. In the **Column name** box, type **PreferredContactMethod**.

> **Tip** The column name entered above does not have any space characters in it because spaces in field names are encoded as _*x0020*_ in XPath. When you later want to modify the XPath expression for fields with spaces in them, you have to remember to add those characters every time you type a field name.

10. Click **Choice (menu to choose from)** for the type of information to be stored in this column.

11. In the **Type each choice on a separate line** box, type the following four choices (pressing the [Enter] key after each): **E-mail**, **Phone**, **Text**, and **Mail**.

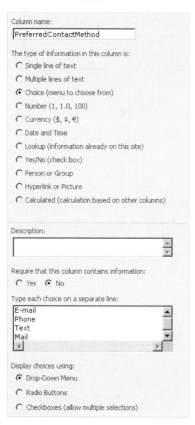

12. At the bottom of the *Create Column* page, click **OK** to create this column.

The *List Settings* page is displayed in the browser.

13. In the **Columns** section of the page, click **Create Column** again.

14. This time, give the column a name of **CustomerTypeLookup,** and click **Lookup (information already on this site)** in the list of column types.

15. Click the **Get information from** arrow, and click **CustomerType**.

16. In the **In this column** list, click **Title**.

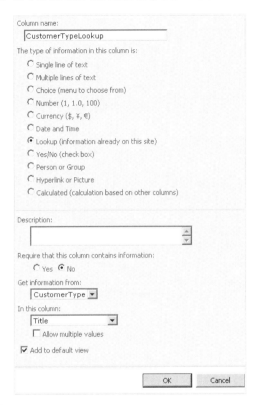

17. Click **OK** to create this column.

18. View the CustomerType list by browsing to */Blog/CustomerType/AllItems.aspx*.

19. Click **New** (and then **New Item,** if necessary).

20. Type **Cold Lead** as the title, and then click **OK**.

21. Repeat steps 19 and 20 to create five additional list items: **Warm Lead**, **Hot Lead**, **Active**, **Regular**, and **Maintenance**.

22. View the Customers list by browsing to */Customers/allitems.aspx*.

23. Click **New** (and then **New Item,** if necessary).

24. Set the following values, and then click **OK** to create this item:

Column Name	Value
Last Name	Park
First Name	Dan
Mobile Phone	206-555-1212
PreferredContactMethod	Text
CustomerTypeLookup	Warm lead

Notice that the possible values for CustomerTypeLookup were populated from the CustomerType list you created. In the future, you can modify *that* list to make changes to the customer types, which is good database design.

25. Create a second item in the Customers list with the following values:

Column Name	Value
Last Name	Haas
First Name	Jonathan
Email	jonathan@spdassist.com
PreferredContactMethod	E-mail
CustomerTypeLookup	Active

 BE SURE TO close the browser.

Copying and Modifying a List Data Source

As mentioned earlier, list data sources are auto-enumerated sources that are in the Data Source Library simply by virtue of being in the site. What this means is that you cannot delete the data source for a list from the Data Source Library without actually deleting the list from the site. In addition, you cannot modify the properties of a list data source without first copying it to create a new entry in the Data Source Library.

In this exercise, you will make a copy of the Customers list data source and modify its properties to create a new data source.

> **BE SURE TO** display the blog site in SharePoint Designer and ensure that the Data Source Library is available before beginning this exercise.

1. In the **Data Source Library**, point to **Customers**, and then click the arrow to display the **Customers** menu.

Notice that several of the commands in this list are unavailable. Those commands (such as Mail Recipient and Move To) only apply to non–auto-enumerated data sources. Those sources are stored as XML files in the *fpdatasources* document library and so can be moved around. For list data, however, the choices are more limited until you copy and modify that data source to create an XML file for it.

2. On the **Customers** menu, click **Copy and Modify**.

The Data Source Properties dialog box opens.

3. In the **Query** area, click **Fields**.

The Included Fields dialog box opens. In this dialog box, you choose the fields to include in the data source.

4. In the **Included Fields** list, click **Content Type ID.** Then click the **Remove** button.

5. Continue clicking **Remove** until you remove all of the fields except the **Last Name**, **First Name**, **CustomerTypeLookup**, and **ID** fields.

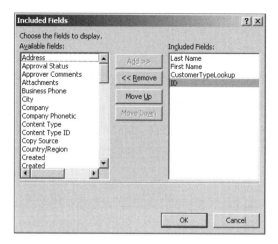

> **Tip** If you try to remove the ID field, you will see a message warning you that the ID is a primary key field for this data source. Click No to keep this field in the new data source.

6. Click **OK** to return to the **Data Source Properties** dialog box.

7. Click **Sort**.

The Sort dialog box opens.

8. In the **Available fields** list, click **Last Name**, and then click **Add** to add the field to the **Sort order** list.

9. Click **OK** to close the **Sort** dialog box.

10. Click **OK** to close the **Data Source Properties** dialog box.

The new data source is created in the Data Source Library.

11. Click this new data source to view its menu.

Notice that now you have the full list of commands available.

Accessing List Data from Other Sites

In addition to accessing data from SharePoint lists inside your current Web site, some applications must access data from other lists in other sites on the same server. The most common reason for doing so is to access data across an entire division that might be stored at the root of a site, but that you want to filter and display as part of your own team's application.

In this exercise, you will create a link to the Data Source Library at the root of the site collection so that you can access the data found there.

BE SURE TO display the blog site in SharePoint Designer before beginning this exercise.

1. If the **Data Source Library** for your site is not showing, click **Data Source Library** on the **Task Panes** menu.

2. Click to expand the library to full size.

3. At the bottom of the library, click **Connect to another library.**

The Manage Library dialog box opens.

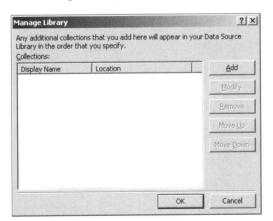

4. Click **Add**.

The Collection Properties dialog box opens.

5. For the **Display Name** property, type **Root Site**.

6. For the **Location** property, type the URL for the parent of your current site collection.

7. Click **OK** and then **OK** again to add that library to your site.

8. Click the + (plus sign) to expand the **Data Source Library** for the root site.

At this point, SharePoint Designer sends a query to the site collection, and if you have permission to view the data sources at the root site level, the data sources populate. (You must have Open Web permission, which is included in the Designer role—so you have to be at least a Designer on the root for this to work.)

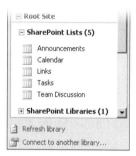

Creating a SQL Data Source

Displaying SQL data presents a unique set of challenges, not just in SharePoint, but in server technologies in general. When the SQL server is not on the same physical machine with the Internet Information Services (IIS) you are using for your Web application, the Web page that is trying to display information from that SQL server will fail to authenticate. Briefly: the ASPX page "hops" to the IIS server and is authenticated there, but cannot then "hop" again to the SQL server to authenticate there.

> **Tip** To learn more about the "double-hop" problem, search online for *double hop authentication*. You will find a rich array of information on the subject.

To get around this problem, you can use one of three techniques. The first is to implement a *Kerberos* authentication model, which is a way of securely passing credentials from one server to another (for example, from the SharePoint Web server to the SQL server). This method is very complex (though simplified in Windows Server 2008) and is therefore not very common and is not within the scope of this book. However, if you are the server administrator, you might want to investigate Kerberos and implement it on your own.

The second method is to use *single sign-on (SSO)*. SSO is available in Microsoft Office SharePoint Server, but not Microsoft Windows SharePoint Services; it allows you to create an authentication model in which the server administrator creates the necessary connections to resources for you, and then you call into those resources to get at the external data.

See Also For more information on Kerberos and single sign-on authentication, see the following two MSDN articles: *msdn.microsoft.com/en-us/library/ms580316.aspx* and *msdn.microsoft.com/en-us/library/aa378747.aspx*.

The third method for getting at SQL data is to include a user name and password directly inside the connection string to the SQL database. As mentioned earlier in this chapter, it is important to realize that doing so means that any "author" (or person granted "Designer" privileges) of your site can open the connection file and read the user name and password in clear text.

In this exercise, you will create a connection to a SQL server by using this third method and including the user name and password embedded within the SQL connection string.

Troubleshooting If you do not have access to a SQL server, you will not be able to complete this exercise. Contact your server administrator for the necessary server name and authentication information.

BE SURE TO display the blog site in SharePoint Designer before beginning this exercise.

1. On the **Task Panes** menu, click **Data Source Library**. Then maximize the **Data Source Library** task pane.

2. In the **Data Source Library**, expand the **Database Connections** group, and then click **Connect to a database**.

The Data Source Properties dialog box opens.

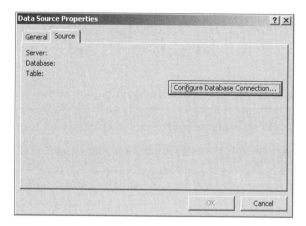

3. Click **Configure Database Connection**.

The Configure Database Connection dialog box opens.

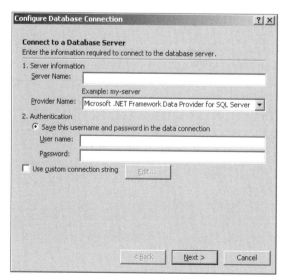

4. In the **Server Name** box, type the name for the SQL server to which you have permissions to connect.

5. In the **Provider Name** list, leave **Microsoft .NET Framework Data Provider for SQL Server**.

6. In the **Authentication** area, type the user name and password of the user who has permission to read (or write to) the SQL database.

7. Click **Next**.

A message appears, warning you that the user name and password will be stored in clear text.

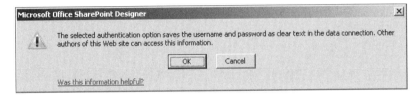

8. Click **OK** to advance to the next step in the wizard.

9. In the **Database** list, click the name of the database for which the user has permissions.

For demonstration purposes, I am connecting to the Northwind sample database.

10. In the **Select a table or view** list, select a table to display.

For demonstration purposes, I am connecting to the Categories table in the Northwind sample database.

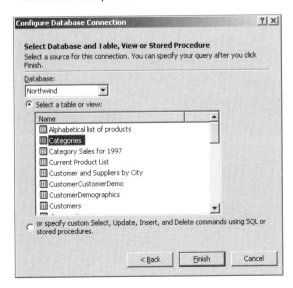

> **Tip** You can also write your own Select, Update, Insert, and Delete commands by using SQL or stored procedures. If you click that option, the next step of the wizard asks you for the SQL query to use.

11. In the **Configure Database Connection** dialog box, click **Finish**.

The Data Source Properties dialog box displays the results of your efforts.

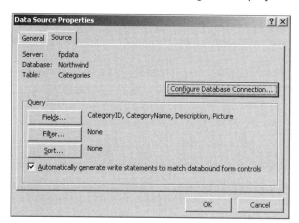

You can see the fields that are included in the SQL query, as well as any filtering and sorting that was explicitly added. In addition, there is a check box that indicates whether SharePoint Designer should automatically generate *write* statements to match databound form controls. When you use custom SQL, this is cleared by default. When this check box is selected, if you insert a view of the SQL data source and then later format one of the values in that view as an ASP.NET control, SharePoint Designer modifies the SQL query to make that new control work. With custom SQL, you would rarely want to do that. With SQL generated automatically by the wizard, it is likely that you would want to do that.

12. On the **General** tab, type a friendly name for the database connection so you can easily find it later, and then click **OK**.

SharePoint Designer adds the data source to the Data Source Library.

Accessing RSS and Server-Side Scripts

As I mentioned earlier, RSS is pervasive on the Internet today. To find interesting RSS data sources, you can simply launch your browser and conduct searches across newspaper sites, magazine sites, or other information-centric Web sites. In addition, you can access the list data on your site via the RSS link for that data.

In this exercise, you will create a data source that points to the RSS feed for the SharePoint Designer team blog.

BE SURE TO display the blog site in SharePoint Designer and ensure that the Data Source Library is available before beginning this exercise.

1. In the **Data Source Library**, click to expand the **Server-side Scripts** group.

2. Click **Connect to a script or RSS Feed**.

    The Data Source Properties dialog box opens.

3. Accept the default **HTTP method** and **Select which data command to configure** list settings of **HTTP Get** and **Select**, respectively.

4. In the **Enter the URL to a server-side script** box, type **http://blogs.msdn.com/ sharepointdesigner/rss.xml**.

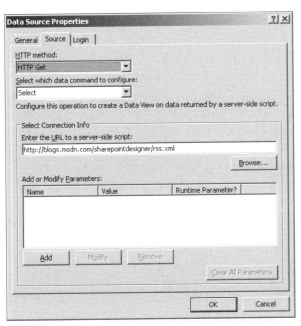

5. Leave the **Add or Modify Parameters** list empty.

This area is primarily used for scripts that take in values and act upon those values, which you will see in practice with the SOAP data source in the next exercise.

6. Click the **Login** tab and verify that **Don't attempt to authenticate** is selected.

7. On the **General** tab, give this data source the friendly name of **SharePointDesignerBlog**, and then click **OK**.

SharePoint Designer adds the new data source to the Data Source Library.

Accessing XML Web Services

XML Web services are increasing in popularity. They travel over the Simple Object Access Protocol (SOAP) via HTTP and HTTPS. This method of transport allows server administrators and Web developers to create complex code on their own end that can be leveraged by disparate Web sites. SOAP data sources can consume parameters in their methods and return complex results in XML format. Each SOAP method is described by using the Web Services Description Language (WSDL), which tells the consumer of that Web service what parameters to supply in order to get valid results.

SharePoint Designer can read the WSDL and then display the necessary parameters in the Data Source Properties dialog box. After you create a new SOAP data source, SharePoint Designer again creates the necessary XML file in the *fpdatasources* document library that contains all of the necessary information to connect to that SOAP service in the future.

In this exercise, you will create a connection to the Lists Web service available in Windows SharePoint Services. You will create a data source that will return a list of the lists on your site, and then you will create a data source that takes a list name as a parameter to enable the service to return dynamic XML data of list data based on the list name passed into the parameter. Finally, you will use the data returned from one of the SOAP methods to populate the parameter with meaningful data.

BE SURE TO display the blog site in SharePoint Designer and ensure that the Data Source Library is available before beginning this exercise.

1. In the **Data Source Library**, expand the **XML Web Services** group, and then click **Connect to a web service**.

The Data Source Properties dialog box opens. You might notice that this dialog box looks very similar to the Data Source Properties dialog box in the preceding exercise. These two sources share many of the same types of security and authentication issues, so the user interface in which you create the two sources is almost identical.

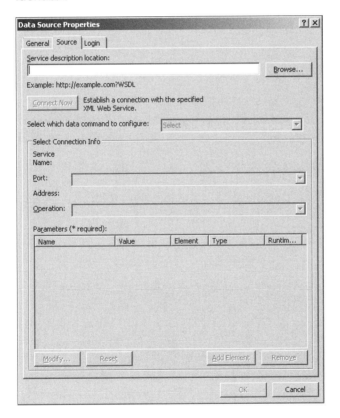

2. In the **Service description location** box, type the URL to the Lists Web service for your blog site: **http://www.<*servername*>.com/blog/_vti_bin/lists.asmx?WSDL** (where <*servername*> is the name of your SharePoint server).

3. Click **Connect Now**.

> **Tip** The URL to Web services on SharePoint is always located in the *_vti_bin* folder for the site in which you are trying to access data. Each of these Web services is documented extensively on MSDN and team blog sites on the Internet.

4. In the **Port** box, click **ListsSoap12**.

5. Click the **Operation** arrow.

Notice that the Operation list is populated with the available methods in the *lists.asmx* Web service.

6. In the **Operation** list, click **GetListCollection**.

Notice that the Parameters list box becomes unavailable. That is because GetListCollection does not take any parameters. It simply returns an XML response that contains the list of lists in your Web site.

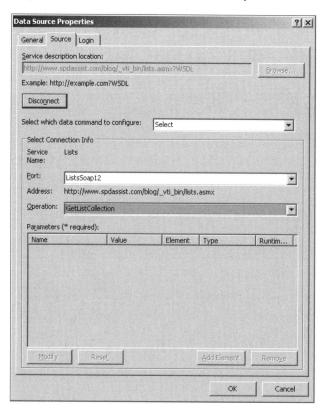

7. Click the **General** tab and name this data source **ListsOnBlog**.

8. Click **OK** to create this data source.

9. Repeat steps 1 through 4 to begin creating another SOAP data source.

10. In the **Operation** list, click **GetListItems**.

Notice that this time there are seven parameters that you can populate for this data source.

11. In the **Parameters** list, double-click **listName**.

The Parameter dialog box opens.

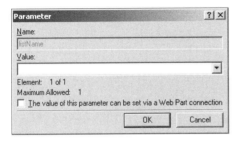

12. In the **Value** box, type **Customers**.

13. Select the **The value of this parameter can be set via a Web Part connection** check box, and then click **OK**.

14. In the **Data Source Properties** dialog box, click the **General** tab.

15. Name this data source **ListItemsOnBlog**.

16. Click **OK** to create the second SOAP data source.

> **Important** This data source will not work as expected unless you change the default value for the *listName* property. To do so, you need to find the *Globally Unique Identifier (GUID)* for the Customers list and replace the *listName* value with that. Each list in the ListItemsOnBlog data source that you just created has an XML node that contains the GUID. In these next steps, you will get the GUID value.

17. In the **Data Source Library**, click the **ListsOnBlog** data source, and then click **Show Data**.

The Data Source Details task pane opens, showing the results for the XML Web service.

18. Scroll through the result set until you see **Customers** displayed as the **Title** value.

19. Point to the **ID** value to see the GUID for the Customers list.

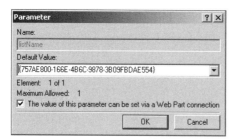

See Also In Chapter 8, "Creating Data Views," you will explore this task pane further.

20. Write down the GUID for this list.

21. Click the **Data Source Library** task pane tab.

The Data Source Library is displayed.

22. Click **ListItemsOnBlog** and, in the menu that appears, click **Properties**.

The Data Source Properties dialog box opens.

23. Click **Reconnect**, and then double-click **listName**.

24. Replace **Customers** with the GUID you wrote down in step 20.

25. Click **OK** twice to close the dialog boxes and update the value.

The data source contains a reference to the Customers list by using the GUID for that list.

Linking Data Sources

Sometimes when you are creating an application in SharePoint Designer, you want to combine the data from two different data sources into the same view. The most common method for this is creating a *join* in a SQL query to create a data source that shows items from two SQL tables. With arbitrary XML data, however, creating a join like a SQL join is a very complex task. To make this task as straightforward as possible, SharePoint Designer lets you create data sources that join other data sources from any of the groups in the Data Source Library. When it's time to insert views of these sources, you will be prompted to map the columns that match to create a meaningful relationship.

In this exercise, you will create a linked data source between two lists in the blog site.

BE SURE TO display the blog site in SharePoint Designer and ensure that the Data Source Library task pane is available before beginning this exercise.

1. Click to expand the **Linked Sources** group in the **Data Source Library**.

2. Click **Create a new Linked Source**.

   The Data Source Properties dialog box opens.

3. Click **Configure Linked Source**.

   The Link Data Sources Wizard starts, displaying the list of currently available data sources.

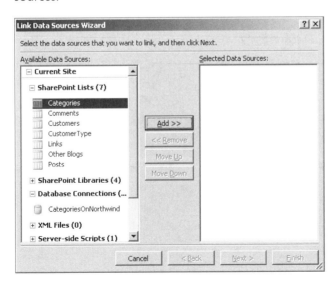

4. In the **SharePoint Lists** group, click **Categories**.

5. Click **Add** to add **Categories** to the **Selected Data Sources** list.

6. In the **SharePoint Lists** group, click **Posts** and add it to the **Selected Data Sources** list.

7. Click **Next** to move to the second page of the Link Data Sources Wizard.

This page allows you to either merge or join the two data sources.

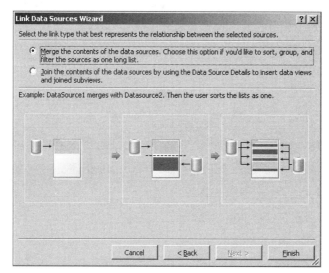

8. Click **Join the contents of the data sources by using the Data Source Details to insert data views and joined subviews**.

9. Click **Finish** to exit the wizard.

10. In the **Data Source Properties** dialog box, click **OK**.

SharePoint Designer creates the linked data source.

Key Points

- By using the Data Source Library, you can create several data sources that you can use to build your application.

- Lists, document libraries, and XML files are all auto-enumerated data sources, so they appear in the Data Source Library without your having to explicitly add them.

- When you create a list data source based on an auto-enumerated list, you can subsequently modify that list data source.

- Creating a data source that points to an RSS feed or SOAP service is as easy as typing the appropriate URL and parameters into the Data Source Properties dialog box.

- Linked data sources can be created to connect to data sources that otherwise would have to exist in separate data views on your pages.

Chapter at a Glance

Drag a data source
onto the design surface,
page 160

<form#form1>	<webpartpages:webpartzone#g_CE78031EC32...>	<WebPartPages:DataFormWebPart>

a Source Library Data Source Details

Current Data Source:
Customers...

SPWebPartManager - WebPartManager
WebPartPages:DataFormWebPart   Zone 1

Customers

Common Data View Tasks

Last Name	Modified By	Modified
Park	John Jansen	11/16/2008 11:11 PM
Haas	John Jansen	11/17/2008 10:43 PM

Filter:

Sort and Group:

Paging:

Edit Columns...

Change Layout...

Data View Preview: Default

☐ Show with sample data

Conditional Formatting...

Web Part Connections...

Parameters...

Refresh Data View

Data View Properties...

Mobile Phone

Related Data Sources ▾

☑ Show data values

Refresh data source

Advanced Grouping ? X

☐ Always hide group details

☐ Maintain groups when paging

☐ Show column names per group

☐ Show column totals per group

OK   Cancel

Set a custom sort and group
for a data view, **page 164**

Web Part Connections Wizard ? X

Create a new connection between the source and target Web Parts.

Source Web Part: **Customers**
Source action: **Send Row of Data To**
Target Web Part: **<untitled Web Part> (customerDetails.aspx)**
Target action: **Get Filter Values From**

Choose the target Web Part and action for the connection:

Target Web Part: <untitled Web Part>

Target action: Get Filter Values From

Description

Filter the selected Data View based on data values received from another Web Part.

Connect data views from
one page to another with
Web Part connections, **page 174**

< Back   Next >   Cancel

8 Creating Data Views

In this chapter, you will learn to

✔ Drag a data source onto the design surface.

✔ Set a custom sort and group for a data view.

✔ Insert specific fields from the Data Source Details task pane to enable inline editing.

✔ Connect data views from one page to another with Web Part connections.

✔ Convert a list view to a data view.

In Chapter 7, "Creating Data Sources in SharePoint," you created several different types of data sources. Of course, the creation of these sources is only the foundation for building Web applications; the real application building doesn't start until you use those data sources to get data and then create interesting views of that data.

When you use Microsoft Office SharePoint Designer 2007 to create views of data in SharePoint, you create new Web Parts called *Data Form Web Parts* (also known as *data views*). Data views render on the design surface by leveraging two interesting constructs:

- **Data source controls.** A Microsoft ASP.NET data source is markup on a page that includes all of the connection information from that data source, as well as specific properties such as the Data Source ID and the parameters that ensure the return of the correct set of data.

- **XSLT rendering.** Extensible Stylesheet Language Transformations (XSLT) is a programming language that is able to iterate over a set of XML data, by moving from node to node and attribute to attribute, and convert that XML data set into a different format (another XML document, HTML, or even programming code). The data view converts the XML data it gets from the data source control and uses XSLT to generate the HTML necessary to display that XML data in a meaningful way.

Because data views use XSLT to render the data that is returned to them, there is a rich rendering engine that you can use to create highly formatted Web applications that run server-side code.

The best Web applications provide dynamic content to keep users coming back. But in addition to the appeal that new and ever-changing data has, the real benefit of live data is measurable in the increased productivity of the people who access that Web application. For example, you might create an application that tracks current inventory so users can browse to that application and see what's in stock. Most of the time when you create data views, you want simply to display data to the user, and by leveraging conditional formatting, you can call the user's attention to something important in the data (by displaying in red a product that is running low, for example). However, the Data Form Web Part also allows you to create an interactive experience by using ASP.NET controls that bind to the data source and allow users who have permission to update the data source itself.

In this chapter, you will build data views of one of the SharePoint list data sources you created in the previous chapter. By using different techniques in SharePoint Designer, you will modify those views to show complex groupings, ASP.NET form interaction, and conditional formatting. All of these views combine to create an interactive user experience.

> **Important** Before you can use the practice files in this chapter, you need to install them from the book's companion CD to their default location. For more information, see "Using the Companion CD" at the beginning of this book.

Dragging a Data Source onto the Design Surface

Creating a view of list data by dragging and dropping is the easiest way to get a data view onto your page, but almost never does the drag-and-drop method actually insert the columns of data that you want to display. With auto-enumerated data sources (lists and XML files), you can either drag the source from the Folder List task pane and drop it onto the design surface, or you can drag the data source from the Data Source Library task pane onto the design surface. With other data sources (such as RSS feeds), you can drag only from the Data Source Library because those sources do not exist in the Folder List task pane.

In this exercise, you will drag and drop a view of the Customers list from the Folder List task pane. After you insert the view, you will modify the fields that are displayed in that view. Finally, you will save the page to link to it from the top navigation bar you created in Chapter 6, "Creating Custom Navigation Controls."

> **USE** the *Customers.stp* template file. This practice file is located in the *Documents\Microsoft Press\BuildingWebAppsSBS\DataViews* folder. Also use the blog site you created and modified in earlier chapters. If you did not create the blog site, you can still perform these exercises by creating a new blog site, following the steps in Chapter 1; however, the screen shots in some examples will not match those shown here.
>
> **BE SURE TO** display the blog site in SharePoint Designer before beginning this exercise.

1. Create a new page by pressing [Ctrl]+[N] on your keyboard.

2. On the **View** menu, point to **Page,** and then click **Design** to place the page in Design view.

3. On the **Insert** menu, point to **SharePoint Controls**.

   The SharePoint Controls menu appears.

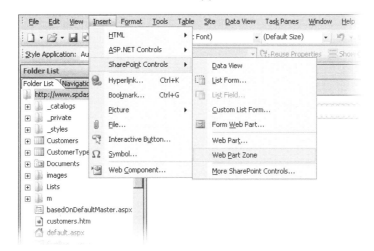

4. Click **Web Part Zone**.

   A Web Part zone is inserted in the page. Web Part zones are objects that allow the Web application's users to customize pages by using the browser. Web Part zones can contain only Web Parts (no text, images, or other HTML), which allows their content to be stored in the SharePoint *content database* (this is the database that was created on the SQL server when you created a new site collection, as you did when you installed Microsoft Windows SharePoint Services 3.0).

See Also For more information on Web Part zones, see *Microsoft Office SharePoint Designer 2007 Step By Step* by Penelope Coventry (Microsoft Press, 2008).

5. If the **Folder List** task pane for your site is not visible, click **Folder List** on the **Task Panes** menu.

6. Drag the **Customers** folder from the **Folder List** task pane into the Web Part zone on the page.

A data view of the Customers list appears inside the Web Part zone. The data from the Customers list is rendered by a Data Form Web Part, which displays the data in a table with repeating rows. The data view code queries SharePoint for the schema of the list, then queries for the data from that list, and then predicts what fields are most likely important in that list.

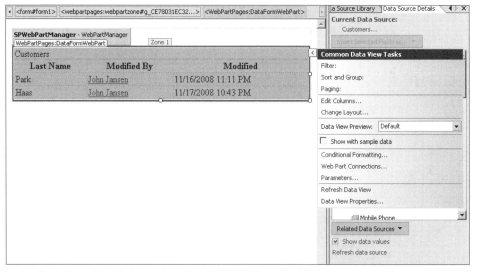

7. If the On Object User Interface (OOUI) for the data view does not display the **Common Data View Tasks** panel, click the OOUI icon to display it.

OOUI

8. In the **Common Data View Tasks** panel, click **Edit Columns**.

The Edit Columns dialog box opens. In this dialog box, you can modify the fields that are in the current data view.

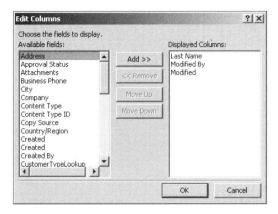

9. In the **Available fields** list, select **First Name**.

10. Click **Add** to add it to the **Displayed Columns** list.

11. In the **Displayed Columns** list, select **Modified by** and **Modified**. Hold down the
    [Ctrl] key and click the items to make multiple selections.

12. Click **Remove**.

    The two items are removed from the Displayed Columns list.

13. Click **OK**.

    The fields in the view change to Last Name and First Name.

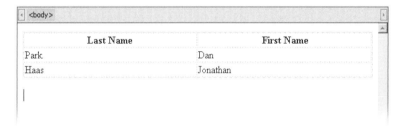

14. Save the page as *Customers.aspx* by pressing [Ctrl]+[S] on your keyboard, typing
    Customers.aspx into the **Save As** dialog box's **File Name** box, and clicking **Save**.

> **Important** If you completed the exercises in Chapter 6, you created a page called
> *Customers.aspx* there as well. If a message appears telling you that *Customers.aspx*
> already exists, click OK to overwrite the current file with this one.

Setting a Custom Sort and Group for a Data View

In the exercise in the previous section, you created a view that displays the last name and first name of the items in the Customer list in this Web site. However, a view like that one is not as compelling as it could be. To make the view more interesting, the data view has a set of tools that you can use to add columns as you did in the previous exercise, create parameters (which you will do in a later chapter), and establish filters, custom paging, conditional formatting, formulas, and custom sorts and groups. Because XSLT is used to render the data values as well as some of the customized interaction scenarios, there are times when it is necessary to modify that XSLT directly. SharePoint Designer has a tool called the XPath Expression Builder that makes the job of hand-coding XSLT easier.

In this exercise, you will sort the data view and then use the Expression Builder to modify the sort command so that it uses a simple XSLT substring method. Finally, you will enable grouping by using that XSLT expression so that the view is grouped by the first initial of each customer's last name (as in a phone book).

USE the *Customers.aspx* file from the previous exercise.

BE SURE TO display the blog site in SharePoint Designer open in Design view before beginning this exercise.

1. Click to place your cursor in the data view of the Customers list.

2. From the **Data View** menu, click **Sort and Group**.

   The Sort And Group dialog box opens.

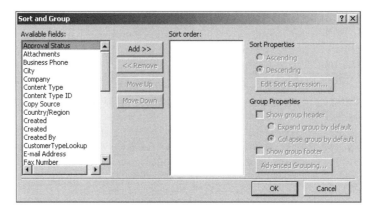

3. Scroll down in the **Available fields** list until you see **Last Name**.

4. Select **Last Name**, and then click the **Add** button.

Last Name is added to the Sort Order list.

5. Click **Edit Sort Expression**.

The Advanced Sort dialog box opens with *@Title* displayed in the Edit The XPath Expression area. In this dialog box, you can edit the current XPath selection by using built-in XPath functions; similar to SharePoint Designer's Code view, this dialog box also uses IntelliSense and AutoComplete.

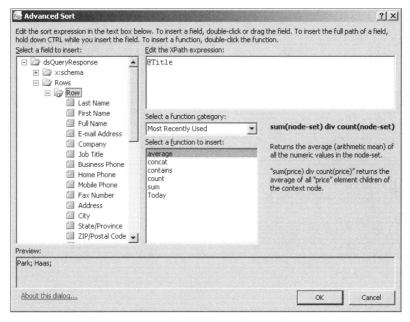

6. In the **Edit the XPath expression** box, select **@Title**.

7. In the **Select a function category** box, click **Text / String**.

The Select A Function To Insert list changes to display only those XPath choices specific to text and string manipulation.

8. Double-click **substring**.

@Title is wrapped in the substring function, and a tooltip pops up above the function indicating the expected parameters.

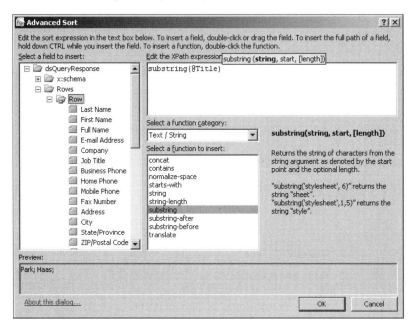

9. Type a **,** (comma) between **@Title** and the closing parenthesis.

10. After the comma, type **1** as the *start* parameter.

   This tells the method to begin selecting a substring of the *@Title* data value starting at the first character in the word.

11. Type another **,** (comma) followed by **1**, to complete the parameters.

   This tells the method to select a substring that has a length of 1. In addition, the Preview section of the dialog box shows that the letters *P* and *H* will be selected based on this XPath expression.

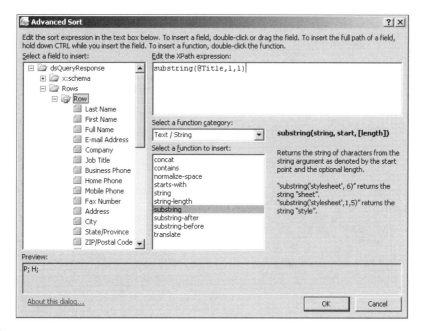

12. Click **OK**.

The Advanced Sort dialog box closes and the Sort Order list in the Sort And Group dialog box displays the XPath expression you just entered.

13. Select the **Show group header** check box.

This makes the Expand Group By Default and Collapse Group By Default choices available.

14. Select **Collapse group by default**.

15. Click **Advanced Grouping**.

The Advanced Grouping dialog box opens.

16. Select the **Show column totals per group** check box, and then click **OK** to close this dialog box.

17. In the **Sort and Group** dialog box that opens, click **OK**.

The data view is now rendered with group headers.

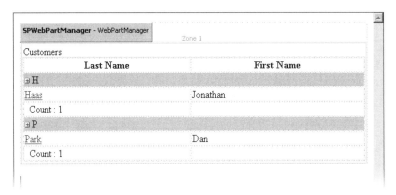

The groups are based on the last name of the customer in the Customers list. In addition, the data view shows the total number of people in each group.

BE SURE TO save your work.

Inserting Specific Fields from the Data Source Details Task Pane to Enable Inline Editing

Earlier in this chapter, you inserted a view of a list by dragging that list from the Folder List task pane directly onto the page. That technique is a very easy way to get a view on the page, but it often requires you to modify the fields that are displayed. An alternative way to get a data view onto the page is to first show the data that is in a specific data source and then select the fields that you want to insert. After doing so, you can still modify the columns displayed if you determine that a change needs to be made, but by selecting the fields first, you have greater control at the outset.

In this exercise, you will show data in the Customers list and insert a view of that list by explicitly selecting some of the fields and then clicking the type of view you want to insert. Finally, you will enable inline editing so users can easily click to edit the list data.

USE the Customers list you modified earlier in this chapter.

BE SURE TO display the blog site in SharePoint Designer before beginning this exercise.

1. Press Ctrl + N to create a new page in SharePoint Designer.

2. On the **Data View** menu, click **Manage Data Sources**.

The Data Source Library task pane is displayed.

3. In the **SharePoint Lists** group, click **Customers**.

4. Click **Show Data**.

The Data Source Details task pane is displayed, which renders a tree of the XML data returned from the Customers list data query. With this task pane, you can modify the properties of this data source query in much the same way you did in Chapter 7, except that modifying properties here does not impact the source in the Data Source Library—it creates a copy of the data source, and the changes are stored there.

5. Click the arrow next to the **[1/2]** designation near the top of the task pane.

The second item in the data source tree is displayed.

6. Hold down the [Ctrl] key and click to select the **Last Name**, **First Name**, **E-Mail Address**, **Business Phone**, **Mobile Phone**, **PreferredContactMethod**, and **CustomTypeLookup** fields.

7. Click **Insert Selected Fields as**.

A menu appears with a list of choices for the views or forms that can be inserted based on this data source.

8. Click **Single Item View**.

A view of the fields selected in step 6 is inserted. Unlike the view that was inserted in the earlier exercise, this view shows only a single item.

9. On the **Data View** menu, click **Change Layout**.

The Data View Properties dialog box opens.

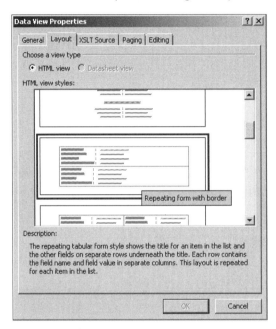

10. Click the **Editing** tab.

11. Select the **Show edit item links** check box, and then click **OK**.

A new row is inserted in the data view just below the rows displaying the list data. That row contains an Edit hyperlink.

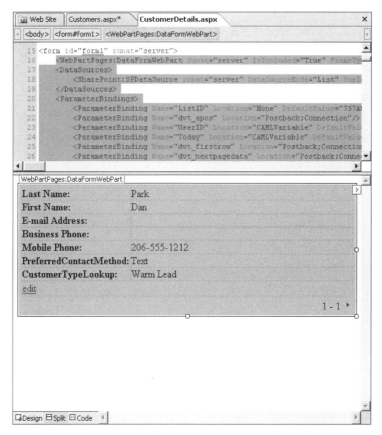

12. At the bottom of this data view is a row that contains **1 – 1** with an arrow that is used to page through data values. Place the cursor into this table row.

13. On the **Table** menu, point to **Select**, and then click **Table**.

The entire table nested inside the bottom row of the data view is selected.

14. On the **Table** menu, point to **Delete**, and then click **Table**.

The bottom table is deleted from the data view.

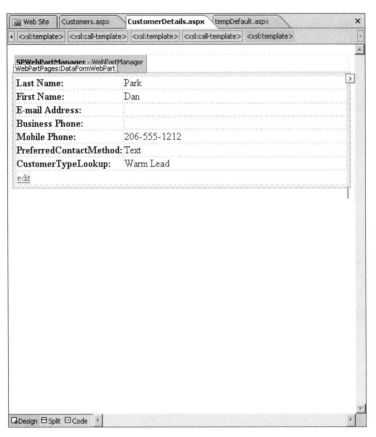

15. Save this page as *CustomerDetails.aspx*.

16. Browse to *CustomerDetails.aspx*, and then click the **Edit** link.

    The view changes to display the correct form fields necessary to update the list's data, and the Edit link has changed to Save and Cancel.

Connecting Data Views from One Page to Another with Web Part Connections

In Chapter 1, "Working with Web Applications," you used the browser to connect a form to a list view by using Web Part connections. The limitation to this approach is that Web Part connections made in the browser must be on the same page. If you want to create a Web Part connection on one page that is linked to a Web Part on a different page, you need to use SharePoint Designer. Connecting data views from one page to another is an easy way to build dynamic Web applications.

You might have noticed that the grouped data view you inserted in *Customers.aspx* in the earlier exercise is displayed on the design surface as if it were expanded by default, although you chose to collapse it by default. SharePoint Designer does this so that you can modify the list item formatting at design time, even though the items will appear grouped at run time. If that weren't the case, you would not be able to create Web Part connections from that view.

In this exercise, you will create a Web Part connection from the view you created in the *Customers.aspx* page to the view you created in the *CustomerDetails.aspx* page, so that the single item view will be filtered to show the details of only the customer you click in the grouped view.

> **USE** the Customers list you modified earlier in this chapter.
>
> **BE SURE TO** display the *Customers.aspx* file in Design view in SharePoint Designer before beginning this exercise.

1. In the **Last Name** column of the data view, select **Haas**.

2. On the **Data View** menu, click **Web Part Connections**.

   The Web Part Connections Wizard opens.

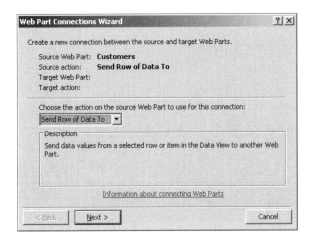

   The top part of the Web Part Connections Wizard shows the source Web Part, the action from the source Web Part, the target Web Part, and the target action. These are the values that will be populated as you proceed through this wizard.

3. In the **Choose the action on the source Web Part to use for this connection** list, accept the default selection of **Send Row of Data To**.

> **Tip** SharePoint Designer populates this wizard dynamically by parsing the page and gathering the necessary information. For example, any Web Part connection interfaces that the Web Part supports are displayed in this list. When there are no other Web Parts on the page, the wizard defaults to creating a cross-page connection, and then displays only the supported interfaces on the consumer Web Part of the other page that is selected.

See Also For more information on Web Part connections and the interfaces supported by the Data Form Web Part, see the developer documentation on MSDN at *msdn.microsoft.com/en-us/library/microsoft.sharepoint.webpartpages. communication.aspx.*

4. Click **Next**.

   The second step in the Web Part Connections Wizard is shown. Notice that this step has defaulted to creating a cross-page connection because there is only one Web Part on this page.

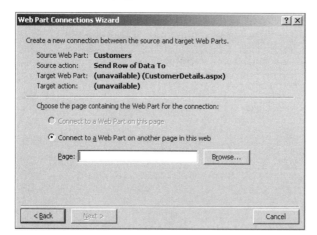

5. Click **Browse**.

   The Edit Hyperlink dialog box opens.

6. Scroll in the folder list and select **CustomerDetails.aspx**.

7. Click **OK**.

   The Edit Hyperlink dialog box is closed and the Web Part Connections Wizard is populated with *CustomerDetails.aspx.*

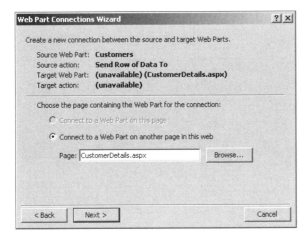

8. Click **Next**.

   The next page in the wizard appears. On this page, you specify the settings for the target Web Part and target action.

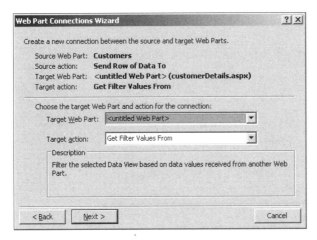

9. For **Target Web Part**, accept the default selection of **<untitled Web Part>**, and for **Target action**, accept the default selection of **Get Filter Values From**.

10. Click **Next**.

    The next page in the wizard is where you set the filter that will be passed by the Web Part connection.

11. In the **Inputs to <untitled Web Part>** column, scroll down the list until you see **ID,** and then click the arrow in the **Columns in Customers** column.

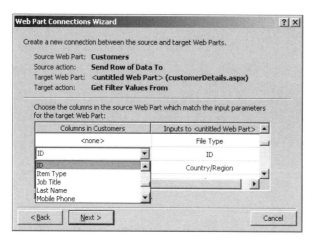

12. Click **ID,** and then click the **Next** button.

The final page in the Web Part Connections Wizard is displayed. On this page you specify where to create the hyperlink that will be used to create the connection. Because you selected the last name in step 1, that value is prepopulated; however, you do have the opportunity to change it now.

13. Accept the default selection of [**Current Selection: xsl:value-of**] and click **Next.**

The wizard displays a summary of the connection you created and warns you that both pages used in this connection must be saved in order for the connection to work.

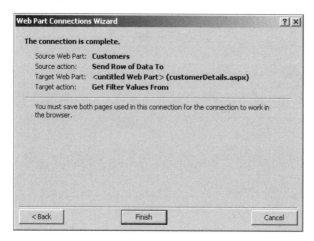

14. Click **Finish**.

15. Save your work.

> **Important** Remember to save both pages involved in the Web Part connection.

16. On the **Format** menu, point to **Master Page**, and then click **Attach Master Page**.

The Select A Master Page dialog box opens.

17. Accept the default selection of **Default Master Page**, and then click **OK**.

The Match Content Regions dialog box opens.

18. Click **OK** to leave the default matching as it is.

Customers.aspx renders with the shared content from the master page surrounding the data view.

19. Click the **CustomerDetails.aspx** tab to display *CustomerDetails.aspx* in Design view.

20. Repeat steps 16 through 18 to attach the default master page to *CustomerDetails.aspx* as well.

21. Browse to *Customers.aspx*.

22. Click the + (plus sign) next to a group to expand that group.

The list expands to show the items in that group.

23. Click one of the last name data values to create the Web Part connection.

You are taken to *CustomerDetails.aspx,* where the view is filtered to show only the customer whose name you clicked.

Converting a List View to a Data View

So far in this chapter, you have created data views by using two different techniques: one was a simple process of dragging and dropping from the Folder List task pane, and the other was the explicit selection of the fields you wanted to insert and the insertion of a type of data view based on that selection. The final way to insert a data view is by converting a List View Web Part (list view) into a data view.

List views look very similar to data views and can be inserted either in the browser (by creating a new view page of a list or by using the Insert Web Part dialog box) or in SharePoint Designer. In the same way that data views use data sources to query for data and then XSLT to render that data, list views use Collaborative Application Markup Language (CAML) queries to query for data, and then CAML markup to render that data. However, list view customization is not nearly as rich as data view customization. In fact, that simple Web Part connection created in the previous exercise is not possible with list views, because there is no way to choose where to place the Web Part connection link. (Instead of a hyperlink, a list view creates bullets.)

In this exercise, you will insert a Web Part zone, and then insert a list view into that zone. After that, you will convert that list view into a data view and perform conditional formatting on one of the data values.

USE the *tempDefault.aspx* and *newDefault.master* files. These practice files are located in the *Documents\Microsoft Press\BuildingWebAppsSBS\DataViews* folder. Although you will not access *newDefault.master* directly in this exercise, the page will render with an error if you have not imported this file.

BE SURE TO display the blog site in SharePoint Designer before beginning this exercise.

1. On the **File** menu, click **Open**, and then click *tempDefault.aspx*.

2. Click **OK**.

   The *tempDefault.aspx* page opens in SharePoint Designer.

3. Click to place the cursor immediately to the right of the words **Dashboard Page** on the design surface.

4. Press Enter.

5. On the **Insert** menu, point to **SharePoint Controls**, and then click **Web Part Zone**.

   A Web Part zone is inserted below the words *Dashboard Page*.

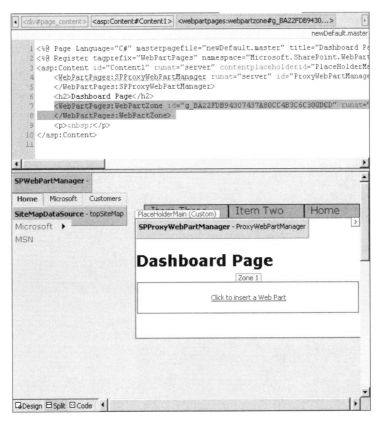

6. Click the link inside the Web Part zone.

   The Web Parts task pane opens.

7. Scroll down in the task pane until you see the Customers list.

8. Click **Customers**.

9. Click **Insert Selected Web Part.**

    A list view of the Customers list is inserted into the Web Part zone.

Smart Tag

10. Click the **Smart Tag** button at the top of the list view to see the **List View Options** menu.

11. On the **List View Options** menu, click **Filter**.

    The Filter Criteria dialog box opens.

12. Click the space immediately below **Field Name**, and then click **CustomerTypeLookup** on the menu. On the **Comparison** menu that appears, verify that **Equals** is selected.

13. On the **Value** menu, click **Cold Lead**, and then click **Hot Lead**.

14. On the **And/Or** menu, click **Or**.

15. Repeat steps 12 through 14 to create a total of three filter criteria, in which **CustomerTypeLookup** equals **Hot Lead** or **Warm Lead** or **Cold Lead**.

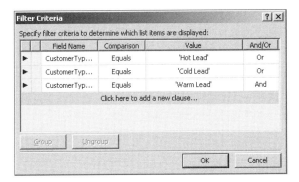

16. Click **OK**.

The list item for Haas is no longer in the view, because it was saved as an Active CustomerTypeLookup value, which was not included in the filter.

17. Right-click the list view, and then click **Convert to XSLT Data View**.

The view changes from a list view into a data view. The most noticeable difference is that now you can put your cursor inside the view.

18. Click to select the word **Park** in the data view.

19. On the **Data View** menu, click **Conditional Formatting**

The Conditional Formatting task pane opens.

20. Click **Create**, and then click **Apply Formatting**.

The Conditional Criteria dialog box opens.

21. Create a condition the same way you created a Filter condition above, but set **CustomerTypeLookup** as **Equal** to **Hot Lead**.

22. Click **OK**.

The Modify Style dialog box opens.

23. In the **Category List**, click **Font**.

24. Change the **font-size** value to **medium**.

25. Change the **color** value to **red**.

26. Click **OK**.

A new condition is added to the Conditional Formatting task pane, indicating that the color of the font will be red and the size of the font will be medium when the CustomerTypeLookup value is equal to Hot Lead. The font in the data view does not change, because Park was saved as a Warm Lead and so does not meet the condition.

27. On the **Data View** menu, click **Change Layout**.

The Data View Properties dialog box opens.

28. On the **General** tab, clear the **SharePoint List Toolbar** check box.

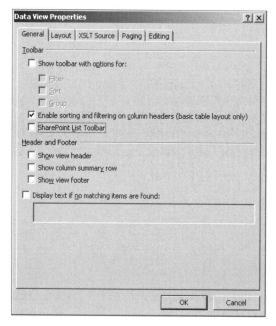

29. Click **OK**.

The view no longer has a toolbar.

30. Save this page.

31. Browse to *tempDefault.aspx*.

A view of the Customers list containing one item is displayed.

32. Click **Customers** in the top navigation bar on this page.

You are taken to the *Customers.aspx* page. Any new customers added to this list will also appear on the *tempDefault.aspx* page if they meet the filter criteria and will be shown in red text if they meet the conditional formatting criterion.

Key Points

- There are several ways to create data views in SharePoint Designer.
- No matter which technique you use to create a data view, there are many tools at your disposal to customize the view to meet your needs.
- SharePoint Designer has an XPath editor that makes generating custom XPath expressions very simple.
- With SharePoint Designer, you can create cross-page Web Part connections to build multiple-page Web applications.
- List views can be converted into data views to enable rich customization and conditional formatting.

Chapter at a Glance

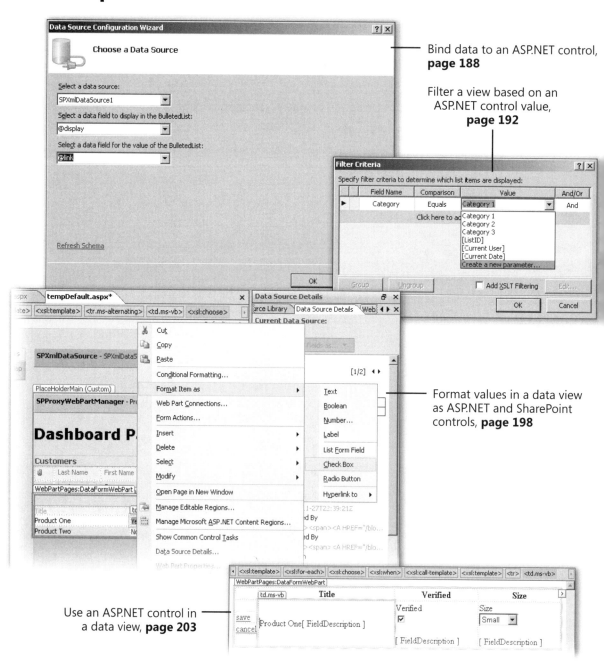

Bind data to an ASP.NET control, **page 188**

Filter a view based on an ASP.NET control value, **page 192**

Format values in a data view as ASP.NET and SharePoint controls, **page 198**

Use an ASP.NET control in a data view, **page 203**

9 Using ASP.NET and SharePoint Controls in Data Views

In this chapter, you will learn to

✔ Bind data to an ASP.NET control.

✔ Filter a view based on an ASP.NET control value.

✔ Format values in a data view as ASP.NET and SharePoint controls.

✔ Use an ASP.NET control in a data view.

Microsoft ASP.NET is an important aspect of Microsoft Office SharePoint Server and Microsoft Windows SharePoint Server 3.0. Although SharePoint provides a rich set of controls and tools that enable your Web site to realize a wide range of collaborative scenarios, SharePoint is built squarely on the shoulders of the underlying ASP.NET model. In fact, most SharePoint controls are derived from ASP.NET controls, so they have similar properties and a similar user interface.

As mentioned earlier in this book, ASP.NET is a platform that was built so that application builders (both developers and designers) would not have to write redundant code to perform common tasks. ASP.NET provides a set of controls that take care of the basic functionality, and application builders can extend those controls by using *declarative markup* in a page or by writing *code behind* the page. When authoring on the SharePoint platform, ASP.NET developers might be surprised to find that security restrictions prevent them from writing that code behind unless they are server administrators and write it directly into the server file structure. (Writing code onto the file system is beyond the scope of this book.) Despite this security limitation, application builders can accomplish quite a lot by simply editing the control markup itself and leveraging the XSLT engine in a data view.

In this chapter, you will explore the ASP.NET control model. Microsoft Office SharePoint Designer 2007 has a rich user interface that exposes the platform to you, as long as you know where to look. First, you will write a simple XML file and bind that data source to a bulleted list. Then you will insert several data views based on techniques learned in previous chapters. Finally, you will expand the functionality of these data views by inserting ASP.NET and SharePoint controls.

> **Important** Before you can use the practice files in this chapter, you need to install them from the book's companion CD to their default location. For more information, see "Using the Companion CD" at the beginning of this book.

Binding Data to an ASP.NET Control

Almost any ASP.NET control can be bound to a data source control. Without the ASP.NET model, binding data to HTML requires you to write code on your page to access data from a data source and then write code to display that data in an interesting way. Using the ASP.NET model, you can simply insert a data source control, insert an ASP.NET control, and then bind the ASP.NET control to the data source via some simple dialog boxes.

Chapter 5, "Working with Master Pages," showed several ASP.NET controls rendering on a page, and in Chapter 6, "Creating Custom Navigation Controls," you inserted a bulleted list control and hard coded some values to it, so you already have experience looking at design-time controls and modifying their properties.

In this exercise, you will create an XML file and insert a data source control based on that file. Then you'll bind that data source to an ASP.NET control to render a dynamic view of links.

USE the *menu.xml* XML file and the *newDefault.master* master page file. These practice files are located in the *Documents\Microsoft Press\BuildingWebAppsSBS\DataViewControls* folder. If you have completed the exercises in the previous chapters, the *newDefault.master* file is already in your blog site. The *menu.xml* file is included only to save you from having to type the menu items by hand. Also use the blog site you created and modified in earlier chapters. If you did not create the blog site, you can still perform these exercises by creating a new blog site, following the steps in Chapter 1; however, the screen shots in some examples will not match the ones shown here.

BE SURE TO display the blog site in SharePoint Designer before beginning this exercise.

1. On the **File** menu, point to **New**, and then click **Page**.

The New dialog box opens.

2. On the **Page** tab, click **General,** and then click **XML**.

3. Click **OK**.

A new XML file is created, with the necessary opening line to make it valid.

```
1 <?xml version="1.0" encoding="utf-8" ?>
```

4. Click to place the cursor immediately below the opening line of code.

5. Add the following code:

```
<root>
    <menu id="1" display="Sign In" link="_layouts/authenticate.aspx"/>
    <menu id="2" display="Products" link="products.aspx"/>
    <menu id="3" display="Home" link="default.aspx"/>
</root>
```

6. Save this page as **menu.xml**.

7. In the **Folder List,** click *newDefault.master* to open it.

8. On the **View** menu, point to **Page**, and then click **Design**.

This places *newDefault.master* in Design view.

9. Click **asp:BulletedList** in the header of the page to select it.

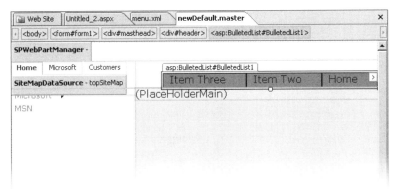

10. Press ⬅ to move the cursor to the left of the *asp:BulletedList* control.

11. On the **Task Panes** menu, click **Data Source Library**.

The Data Source Library is displayed, showing that *menu.xml* is now in the XML Files group because that data source was auto-enumerated by the Data Source Library code.

12. Click **menu.xml**, and then click **Insert Data Source Control**.

The *SPXmlDataSource* control is inserted into the page.

The *SP* here stands for *SharePoint*, which means this is a SharePoint control that derives from the ASP.NET *XmlDataSource* control. Because this control only derives from the ASP.NET control, the dialog boxes that you would have if you were working directly with the ASP.NET control are not available, so you need to add one attribute to this source by using Code view.

13. On the **View** menu, point to **Page**, and then click **Code**.

This puts *newDefault.master* in Code view with the cursor flashing immediately to the left of the *SharePoint:SPXmlDataSource* control.

14. Click in the markup for the control, immediately to the right of the *SharePoint: SPXmlDataSource* opening tag name, and to the left of the *runat* attribute.

15. Press ⎡Space⎤.

The IntelliSense menu appears, showing the valid attributes that can be inserted inside this control.

16. Scroll down to **XPath** and double-click it to insert it in the control.

17. Type **root/menu** for the attribute value.

```
64    <SharePoint:SPXmlDataSource XPath="root/menu" runat="server" id="SPXmlDataS
65        <DataFileParameters>
66            <asp:Parameter Name="FileName" DefaultValue="menu.xml"/>
67            <asp:Parameter Name="FilePath"/>
68        </DataFileParameters>
```

18. On the **View** menu, point to **Page**, and then click **Design**.

19. Click *asp:BulletedList* again in Design view to select it.

20. Click the On Object User Interface (OOUI).

The Common BulletedList Tasks panel appears.

21. Click **Choose Data Source**.

The Data Source Configuration Wizard opens.

22. In the **Select a data source** list, click **SPXmlDataSource1**.

23. In the **Select a data field to display in the BulletedList** list, click **@display**.

24. In the **Select a data field for the value of the BulletedList** list, click **@link**.

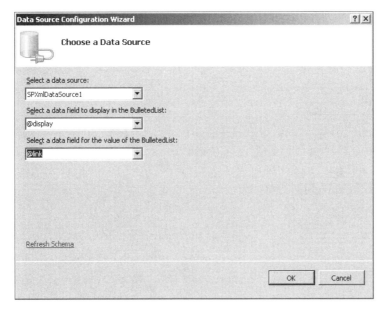

25. Click **OK** to data bind the *asp:BulletedList* control to the XML file you saved in step 6.

This ASP.NET control does not generate a What You See Is What You Get (WYSIWYG) experience. After you click OK, the only indication that this control is correctly data bound is that it is labeled as Databound in Design view. To test this change, you must create a page from this master page and preview it in a browser.

26. Save *newDefault.master.*

27. In the **Folder List** task pane, right-click **newDefault.master**, and then click **New from Master Page**.

28. Save this new page as **test.aspx**.

29. On the **File** menu, point to **Preview in Browser**, and then click your favorite browser.

The new data bound menu is rendered correctly in the browser.

Filtering a View Based on an ASP.NET Control Value

In addition to binding to data, an ASP.NET control can also perform an *AutoPostBack* operation on the page. When the control performs an *AutoPostBack* operation, the data in the value of the control is passed into the page. After that value has been passed into the page, other controls or Web Parts can access it. This enables you to create a page that has an ASP.NET control on it that posts data to a data view to perform a filter operation.

In the exercise in this section, you will use the ASP.NET Controls section of the Toolbox task pane. When you click More ASP.NET Controls, you can see all the possible ASP.NET controls and get an idea of how robust the ASP.NET framework is. This section of the task pane has six subcategories:

- **Standard.** Controls in this section emulate basic HTML constructs. Here you find form controls such as *CheckBox*, *Button*, *HiddenField*, and *RadioButton*.

- **Data.** Controls in this section perform retrieval and display of data. Some controls in this section are not available to be inserted when authoring on a SharePoint site. Two of these controls are the *AccessDataSource* and *XmlDataSource* controls, neither of which works on a SharePoint site but which are included in the toolbox for ASP.NET site scenarios. There is also a *GridView* control that can bind to different data sources, including SharePoint lists and the *SiteMapDataSource* data source (which you used in Chapter 6.

- **Validation.** Controls in this section validate the data of other controls before that data is posted to a bound data source.

- **Navigation.** Controls in this section allow access to the structure of the site for use in navigation of the Web site. In addition to the *Menu* control that you used in Chapter 6, there is a *TreeView* control and a *SiteMapPath* (bread crumb) control.

- **Login.** Controls in this section let you insert user name and password controls for use with *forms-based authentication*, which means that when people browse to your Web application, they are redirected to a page containing user name and password boxes allowing them to log in to the Web site.

- **WebParts.** These controls also cannot be used in SharePoint sites. In this case, a message is displayed in the task pane indicating this.

See Also For more information about the specifics of ASP.NET control markup, see *Microsoft ASP.NET 3.5 Step by Step*, by George Shepherd (Microsoft Press, 2008).

In this exercise, you will insert a data source control of a list in your Web site, bind it to an ASP.NET list control on the page, and then create a filter in a data view based on the value returned by the *AutoPostBack* operation of the control.

BE SURE TO display the blog site in SharePoint Designer before beginning this exercise.

1. Press Ctrl + N to create a new page.

2. On the **View** menu, point to **Page**, and then click **Design**.

   The page is shown in Design view.

3. On the **Insert** menu, point to **ASP.NET Controls**.

   An initial set of ASP.NET controls is displayed.

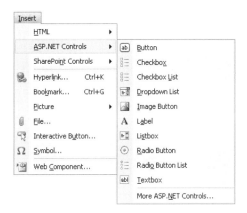

4. Click **More ASP.NET Controls**.

5. Scroll the task pane until you see the **DropDownList** control in the **Standard** group.

6. Right-click the **DropDownList** control, and then click **Insert**.

The *DropDownList* control is added to your page.

7. Click to place the cursor below this control.

8. On the **Task Panes** menu, click **Data Source Library**.

The Data Source Library opens or acquires focus.

9. Click the **Categories** list, and then click **Insert Data Source Control**.

An *SPDataSource* control is inserted into the page.

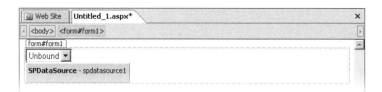

10. Select the *DropDownList* control and click the OOUI to open the **Common DropDownList Tasks** panel.

11. Select the **Enable AutoPostBack** check box.

12. Click **Choose Data Source**.

The Data Source Configuration Wizard opens.

13. For **Select a data source**, click **spdatasource1**.

14. For **Select a data field to display in the DropDownList**, click **Title**.

15. For **Select a data field for the value of the DropDownList**, click **Title**.

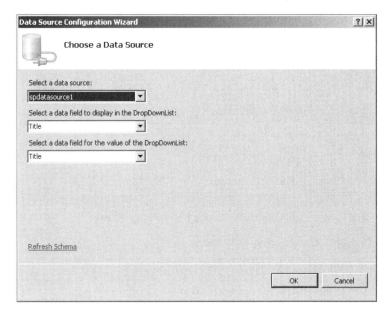

> **Tip** The *DropDownList* control displays the category name here because *Title* is the default name of the field in the category list that contains the category name data values. When you are binding data to an ASP.NET data source, it is important to remember the internal names of the fields, which might be different from their display names.

16. Click **OK**.

17. Click the page below the *SPDataSource* control.

18. From the **Data Source Library** task pane, drag the Posts list onto the page below the *SPDataSource* control.

A data view of the Posts list is inserted on the page.

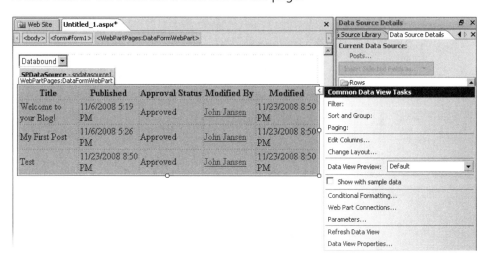

19. On the **Common Data View Tasks** menu, click **Filter**.

The Filter Criteria dialog box opens.

20. In the **Field Name** list, click **Category**.

21. In the **Comparison** list, click **Equals**.

22. In the **Value** list, click **Create a new parameter**.

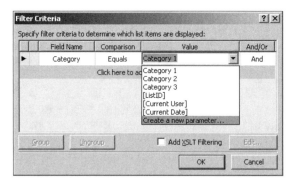

The Data View Parameters dialog box opens.

23. Click **Param1**, and then change the name to **CatName**.

24. In the **Parameter Source** list, click the arrow to see the choices.

The source for parameters in a data view can come from one of six locations. Each location serves a different purpose. Each location is described in further detail in Chapter 10, "Using Parameters in a Data View."

25. In the **Parameter Source** list, click **Control**.

26. In the **Control ID** list, click **DropDownList1**.

> **Tip** You might be tempted to select *SPDataSource1* here, but remember that *DropDownList* is being populated from *SPDataSource1*, so it is the value of *DropDownList* that matters.

27. In the **Default Value** box, type **Category 1**.

The Data View Parameters dialog box now has all of the information necessary to insert a data view parameter into your view and then filter that view by the default value.

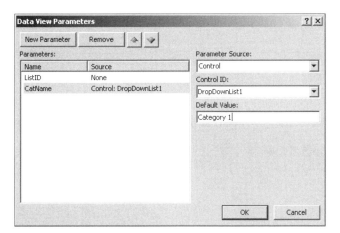

28. Click **OK** twice.

29. Save this page as **aspParameter.aspx**.

30. On the **File** menu, click **Preview in Browser** to see the page in action.

31. Change the value of the *DropDownList* control in the browser.

The page is refreshed when the value changes, and the data view is filtered to show items from the category you selected in the *DropDownList* control.

Formatting Values in a Data View as ASP.NET and SharePoint Controls

In the previous exercise, you inserted an ASP.NET control into your page, bound that control to an *SPDataSource* data source, and then filtered a data view based on that control's value. However, there are also times when you will want to leverage the power of ASP.NET from inside a data view by inserting a control directly into the XSLT for the view. For example, you might have a view of your products list on a page and want to be able to bulk edit the items in this view. In addition, you might want to be able to *see* the current status and *update* that status at the same time.

In this exercise, you will create a new list to store product names and insert a view of this new list onto your dashboard page. Then you will insert ASP.NET and SharePoint controls into the view to allow you to bulk edit the view.

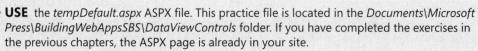

USE the *tempDefault.aspx* ASPX file. This practice file is located in the *Documents\Microsoft Press\BuildingWebAppsSBS\DataViewControls* folder. If you have completed the exercises in the previous chapters, the ASPX page is already in your site.

BE SURE TO display the blog site in SharePoint Designer before beginning this exercise.

1. Create a new list by pointing to **New** on the **File** menu, clicking **SharePoint Content**, clicking **Custom List**, and giving this custom list the name **Products**.

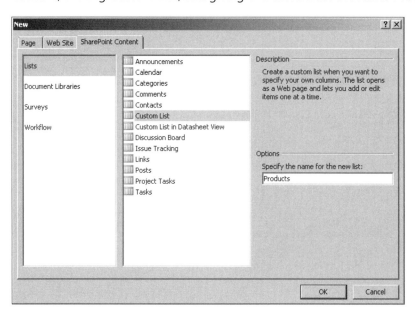

2. Click **OK** to create the list.

The list appears in the Folder List task pane.

3. In the **Folder List** task pane, select **Products**. Then press F12 to preview the list in the browser.

Your default browser renders the *allitems.aspx* page for the Products list.

4. Click **Settings**, and then click **List Settings**.

The Customize Products page renders in the browser.

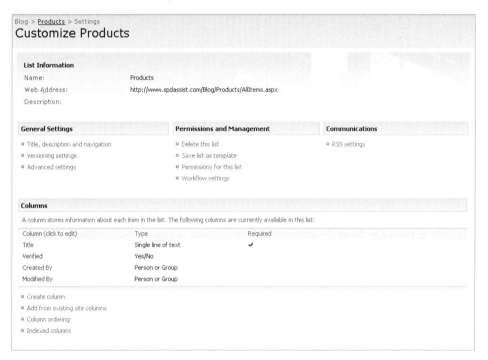

5. In the **Columns** section of the page, click **Create column**.

6. In the **Column Name** column, type **Verified**; in the **Type** column, click **Yes/No (Check box)**; change the default value to **No**, and then click **OK** to create this column.

The Customize Products page is displayed.

7. Click **Create Column**. Name the new column **Size**, and in the **Type** list, click **Choice**. In the **Type each choice** list, type **Small**, **Medium**, and **Large**, and then click **OK** to create this column.

8. In the bread crumb navigation controls near the top of the page, click **Products**.

9. On the toolbar in the middle of the page, click **New**, and then click **New Item.** Type **Product One** for the **Title**, select the check box to indicate that the item is verified, set the **Size** to **Small**, and click **OK**.

10. Again, on the toolbar in the middle of the page, click **New**, and then click **New Item.** Type **Product Two** for the **Title**, leave the check box cleared to indicate that the item is not verified, set the **Size** to **Large**, and click **OK**.

11. Switch back to SharePoint Designer, open *tempDefault.aspx* in Design view, and click on the page to place the cursor below the view of **Customers.**

12. On the **Insert** menu, point to **SharePoint Controls**, and then click **Web Part Zone**.

A Web Part zone is inserted below the view already on the page.

13. On the **Task Panes** menu, click **Data Source Library.** Click the **Products** list, and then click **Show Data**.

The Data Source Details task pane opens.

14. Select the **Title**, **Verified**, and **Size** fields, click **Insert Selected Fields as**, and then click **Multiple Item View**.

A view of the three fields in this new list is inserted into the Web Part zone.

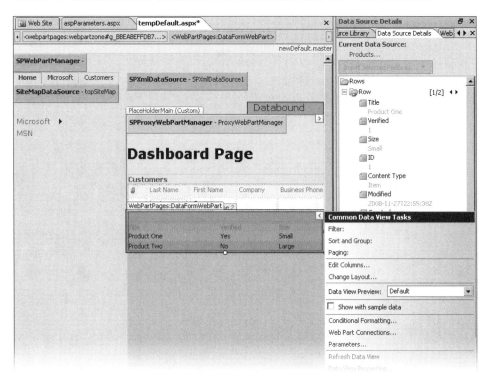

> **Tip** Notice that the Data Source Details task pane shows the number 1 for the verified value rather than Yes. This mismatch is because the data is stored in the database as a 1. To display the value as Yes or No, the data view has inserted some conditional formatting.

15. Right-click the view, and then click **Web Part Properties**.

The Products dialog box opens.

16. Click the **+** (plus) sign to expand the **Appearance** group, type **Products** for the title, and then click **OK**.

17. Right-click the *Yes* data value in the view, and on the menu that appears, point to **Format item as**.

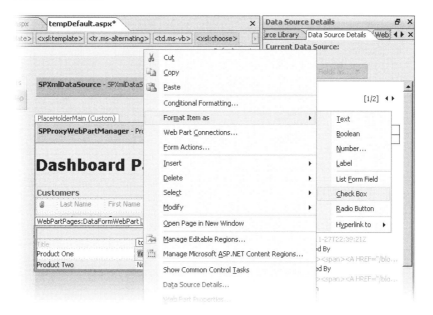

18. Click **Check Box**.

The data value is now formatted as an *asp:CheckBox* control.

19. In the data view, select the *Small* data value, and click the OOUI to display the **Common xsl:value-of Tasks** panel. Then select **List Form Field** in the **Format as** list of choices.

> **Tip** By using a List Form Field here, you can leverage some code from the SharePoint platform. With SharePoint, you can format list data values as List Form Fields, which causes the control to render according to the schema of the list. With standard ASP.NET controls, that might not be the case. For example, for fields that are links, SharePoint controls render two boxes: one for the URL and one for the description, but ASP.NET hyperlink controls do not.

20. On the **Data View** menu, click **Change Layout**.

The Data View Properties dialog box opens.

21. On the **General** tab, select the **Show view footer** check box.

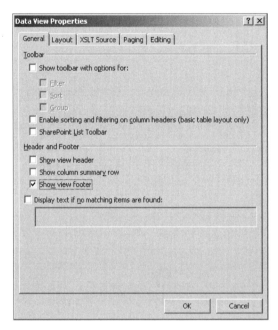

22. Click **OK**.

A view footer is added to the view. Inside that view footer is a *count* of the items in that view.

23. Delete the count text in the view footer.

24. On the **Task Panes** menu, click **Toolbox**.

The Toolbox task pane acquires focus.

25. Scroll down in the **Toolbox** until you see the **SharePoint Controls** section, and expand the **Data View Controls** subsection.

26. Double-click the **Form Actions Button** control to insert it into the view footer.

The Form Actions dialog box opens so that you can set the action this button will perform.

27. Click **Add** to add the **Commit** action, and then click **OK** to attach this action to the button.

28. Double-click the **Form Action** button, change the **Value/Label** value to **Save**, and then click **OK**.

29. Save the page, and then press ⌷F12⌷ to preview this page in the browser.

30. Make a change to the view, and click **Save** to see the changes committed back to the SharePoint list.

Using an ASP.NET Control in a Data View

In addition to formatting data values as ASP.NET and SharePoint controls so that they can write back to a data source, you can also format data values to *prevent* them from writing back to the data source. When you insert a set of data values as a Multiple Item Form in SharePoint, every field that *can* write back to the data source is formatted as either an ASP.NET control or a SharePoint control; however, there are cases in which you will want to write back only one field, and prevent users from being able to write back to the other fields in the data source. For example, you might have a SharePoint list such as the one in the previous exercise, in which you can write back the Title, Verified, and Size fields, but you might want to create a view that allows users to write only to the Verified and Size fields, with the Title field as a read-only field.

In the exercise in this section, you will explore the various templates available for editing the data view. Because the data view uses XSLT templates to show data, some of the templates are unavailable for editing in Design view. For example, when there are no items to show in the view, a template that says, "There are no items to show in this view" is displayed. To edit that template when there are items in the view, you must either cause the view to render at design time without any items in it or use the data view Preview commands to force the data view to show that template so that you can edit it. The templates available for editing are:

- **Hide All Filters.** If you have set some filters in such a way that no items are displayed by default, use this selection to force the data view to ignore the filter and display the list items.

- **Limit To 1 Item.** There are times when you only need to see one item from the data source in order to do all of your design work. For design performance, this is a good selection if you really don't need to see all of the live data.

● **Limit To 5 Items.** When you are doing conditional formatting or alternating-row formatting, it is helpful to see a representative number of items. Five items is a good choice to balance design performance and viewing live data.

● **Limit To 10 Items.** Most views are limited to 10 items by default, so this option allows you to see how those 10 items will render and how they might affect the rendering of the rest of your page. (This template is usually used to see whether 10 items will require a scroll bar.)

● **'No Matching Items' Template.** As mentioned earlier, this template allows you to modify the way that the text looks when there are no items returned to the view.

● **Edit Template.** Editing this template allows you to control how the view renders when users click the Edit link. This is the template you will edit in this exercise.

● **New Template.** This option will not be available for this view, because you will choose only the Edit template in this exercise. However, if you enable the New template by selecting Show Insert Item Link as well as Show Edit Item Links, this option would allow you to edit the way the view looks when users click the Insert link to create new items.

In this exercise, you will insert a view of the Products list from the previous exercise, enable inline editing of the view, and then modify the edit form to make the Title field read-only.

> **BE SURE TO** display the blog site in SharePoint Designer before beginning this exercise.

1. Create a new page by pressing `Ctrl`+`N`.
2. Click the **View** menu, point to **Page,** and then click **Design** to place the page in Design view.
3. On the **Task Panes** menu, click **Data Source Library**.

   The Data Source Library task pane acquires focus.
4. Click the Products list you created in the previous exercise, and then click **Show data**.

   The Data Source Details task pane appears, with the Products list data displayed as a tree.
5. In the Products list, select the **Title**, **Verified**, and **Size** fields.
6. Click **Insert Selected Fields as**, and then click **Multiple Item View**.

   A multiple-item view is inserted into the design surface of the new page.
7. On the **Data View** menu, click **Change Layout**.

The Data View Properties dialog box opens.

8. On the **Editing** tab, select the **Show edit item links** check box.

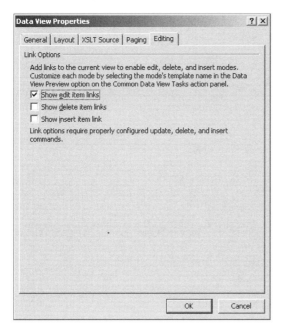

9. Click **OK**.

10. Click the OOUI for the data view to show the **Common Data View Tasks** panel.

11. Click the **Data View Preview** list to display the different preview options for the data view.

12. Click **Edit Template**.

The view renders as if the user has clicked the Edit link in the main data view with SharePoint Form Field controls rendering at design time.

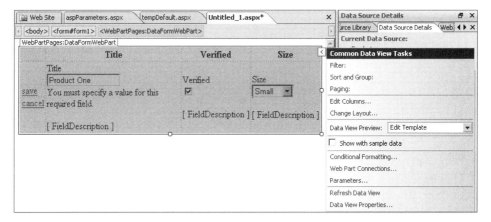

13. Click to select the **Title** SharePoint control.

14. Click the OOUI to show the **Common FormField Tasks** panel.

15. In the **Format as** list, click **Label**.

The SharePoint control changes to an *ASP:Label* control, which means it is no longer editable when users click the Edit link.

16. Save the page as **Products.aspx**.

17. On the **Format** menu, point to **Master Page**, and then click **Attach Master Page**.

The Select A Master Page dialog box is displayed.

18. Click **OK** to accept the default master page.

The Match Content Regions dialog box is displayed.

19. Click **OK** to accept the default settings, which places the body of the current page inside the *PlaceHolderMain* content region in the master page.

20. Save the page again, and then press [F12] to preview the page in your default browser.

The *products.aspx* page loads in your browser.

21. Click **Edit**.

The page renders showing the Edit template with the *Title* data value rendering in a read-only state.

Key Points

- You can use the SharePoint Designer tools to modify SharePoint controls and ASP.NET controls so that they render in ways that meet your application's needs.

- Binding data sources to ASP.NET controls is as simple as working through a wizard to map the fields of the data source.

- After an ASP.NET control is bound to a data source, it can be used to filter another data view on the page.

- You can format data values as ASP.NET and SharePoint controls to enable rich views for editing data sources.

- You can modify XSLT templates in a data view by leveraging template editing functionality to enable easy formatting of ASP.NET controls.

- Even though SharePoint prohibits designers from writing code behind their pages, designers can still create rich data access scenarios.

Chapter at a Glance

Create a parameter inside a data view, **page 214**

Display the value of a parameter in a data view, **page 220**

Use a math expression with a parameter for conditional formatting, **page 223**

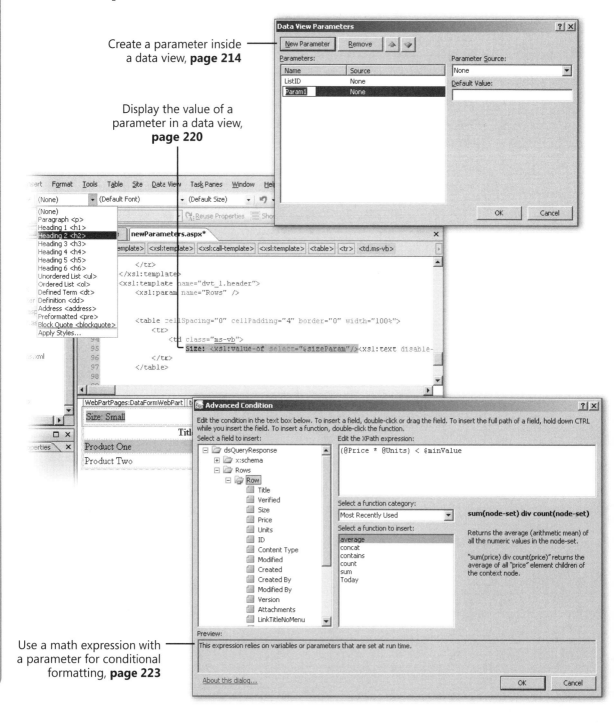

10 Using Parameters in a Data View

In this chapter, you will learn to

✔ Create a parameter inside a data source.

✔ Create a parameter inside a data view.

✔ Display the value of a parameter in a data view.

✔ Use a math expression with a parameter for conditional formatting.

Parameters are the driving force behind dynamic Web applications. Essentially, parameters are placeholders for values that can be used inside a view of data to cause that view to render in a way that is both useful and eye-catching. They are stored in the data view as name/value pairs. The value side of the pair is given a default setting, but actions by an end user can change that default value to something else, which causes the data view in turn to render differently. With Microsoft Office SharePoint Designer 2007, you can create new parameters by using a single dialog box in which you indicate the source of the parameter as well as the default value.

For example, in Chapter 9, "Using ASP.NET and SharePoint Controls in Data Views," you built a view that relied on the parameter value passed in from an ASP.NET *DropDownList* control. When users change the selection in the *DropDownList* control, an *autopostback* operation occurs and passes a new parameter value into the data view to filter that view. In addition to using parameters for simple filtering, you can use parameters to display server variables or user names, build complex filters by using XPath expressions, and even perform mathematical functions and set up conditional formatting based on the returned parameter value.

As demonstrated in Chapter 8, "Creating Data Views," data views are built from two separate components: the data source and the XSLT rendering of that data source. Parameters can be used on either layer. When you use them on the data source layer, they can be part of a filter and thereby make the data source query more robust (that is, they can cause the query to return only the records that are included in the parameterized filter). On the XSLT layer, you can use parameters to filter the data values that were already returned to the view (not giving you the performance benefit but allowing more complex filters than can be set at the source layer), or they can simply be displayed in the view. They can also be used in XPath expressions. In this chapter, you will see each of these in practice when you create parameters from several sources inside data views.

Important Before you can use the practice files in this chapter, you need to install them from the book's companion CD to their default location. For more information, see "Using the Companion CD" at the beginning of this book.

Creating a Parameter Inside a Data Source

Parameters can be used in several types of data sources. For example, when you created the Simple Object Access Protocol (SOAP) data source in Chapter 7, "Creating Data Sources in SharePoint," the dialog box used to pass in the query had a section that allowed you to include parameters. When you insert a view of list data, the data source contains a parameter for the *ListID* value. The *asp:SQLdatasourcecontrol* implements a method for passing parameters directly into a SQL query. Even XML data sources, for which you might not have access to the schema for that data, allow the XML file name to be passed into the source.

In this exercise, you will create a SOAP data source that will be used to pass the *ListID* parameter into a view of list data.

USE the blog site you created and modified in earlier chapters. If you did not create the blog site, you can still perform these exercises by creating a new blog site, following the steps in Chapter 1; however, the screen shots in some examples will not match the ones shown here.

BE SURE TO display the blog site in SharePoint Designer before beginning this exercise.

1. Create a new ASPX page by pressing Ctrl + N on your keyboard.
2. On the **Task Panes** menu, click **Data Source Library**.

3. In the Data Source Library, click the + (plus) sign to expand the **XML Web Services** group.

4. Click **Connect to a web service**.

The Data Source Properties dialog box opens. In this dialog box, you can insert the location of the Web service and create a new data source.

5. In the **Service description location** box, type **http://<*servername*>/blog/_vti_bin/ lists.asmx**, where <*servername*> is the name of the server you are using.

6. Click **Connect now**.

The Data Source Properties dialog box connects to the Web service and parses the Web Service Description Language (WSDL), which is a model for describing Web services. By parsing this data returned by the server, SharePoint Designer is able to show the different ports available and individual operations for those ports.

7. In the **Port** list, click **ListsSoap12**.

8. In the **Operation** list, click **GetListCollection**.

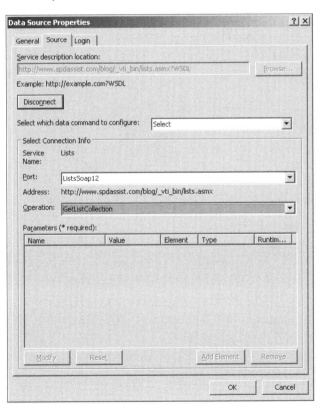

The Parameters section of the dialog box is unavailable because this SOAP method returns the list of lists, including their GUIDs (Globally Unique Identifiers), and does not take any parameters. In this exercise, you use this data source to populate the parameter value of another data view. It is the GUID that you are going to pass to the other view.

9. Click the **General** tab, give this data source the name **listCollection**, and then click **OK**.

10. In the **Data Source Library,** click **listCollection,** and then click **Show Data**.

The data from the SOAP data source is displayed in the Data Source Details task pane.

11. Select the **Title** and **ID** fields of the list.

12. Click **Insert Selected Fields as**, and then click **Multiple Item view**.

A new view of the list of lists on the blog site is inserted into the page.

Title	ID
Categories	{FB19D083-5BD1-4A28-B993-B4C787014185}
Comments	{31E12415-3569-460E-8F88-2D8436D28AFE}
Custom List	{A633845C-0A7F-419E-9B3A-354A1F67B2F9}
Customers	{757AE800-166E-4B6C-9878-3B09FBDAE554}
CustomerType	{D7001111-C8AE-4B4B-801C-6520C65F561E}
Documents	{E958A198-39E8-4421-A4C2-5DC397CC05C8}
fpdatasources	{044A210A-5C35-4083-9578-933029522BA4}
Links	{E3BC48B9-5C5D-4464-ABE7-707D2BF06095}
Master Page Gallery	{F117AD9A-451B-4EC6-A7FC-1EBACF222ECE}
Other Blogs	{DFB6A6E5-81F4-47DE-8FFA-5BCED4B16601}
Photos	{87B7DE97-5AF1-4CA0-9CAC-EF7847BB5268}
Posts	{6214F1C3-5DF8-4F08-B5A0-0540FEFB6348}
Products	{720552B9-C423-4FAC-A82A-517B24E06A1E}

13. Click to place the cursor below this data view.

14. On the **Task Panes** menu, click **Data Source Library**.

15. Drag the **Categories** list from the **Data Source Library** onto the page below the view of the SOAP data source.

A view of the Categories list is inserted below the view of the SOAP data source.

16. Right-click the view of the SOAP data source, and then click **Web Part Connections**.

The Web Part Connections Wizard opens, which enables you to pass the parameter from the SOAP data source into the view of the specific list.

17. In the **Choose the action** list, leave the default selection of **send a row of data to**, and then click **Next**.

18. Leave the default selection of **Connect to a web part on this page**, and then click **Next**.

19. In the **Target action** list, click **Get Parameters from**, and then click **Next**.

20. In the first cell under the **Columns in <untitled Web Part>** header, select **ID**.

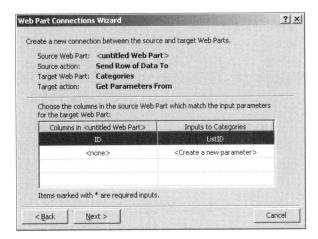

21. Click **Next**.

22. Click **Create a hyperlink on the Title**.

23. Click **Next**.

24. Click **Finish**.

25. Save the page as **listId.aspx**. Then press F12 to preview this page in the default browser.

26. Click any of the list names in the view.

The data view of list data changes to show the Title, Modified By, and Modified columns for each item in each list.

Creating a Parameter Inside a Data View

The small Web application you created in the previous exercise enabled you to pass the *ListID* parameter into the data source for the list so that the view of the fields that are shared across all of the lists is populated by the data query itself. In other words, each time you click a list name, you pass the *ListID* parameter into the data source and display the values from the list name that you click. However, sometimes you'll want to return all of the items of a data source and then perform a parameterized function on the view itself. For example, you might want to use a parameter in an XML data source (which by default only has two parameters at the source: the file name and the file path). Or you might want the view to read a parameter value and perform conditional formatting based on that parameter.

In the exercise in this section, you will use the Data View Parameters dialog box. This dialog box allows you to select from a list of six available parameter sources for parameter values. Each of these sources serves a different purpose, so select the source carefully based on what you want to accomplish. The sources are:

- **None.** If you select this option, the parameter will be populated by a Web Part connection. This restriction means that you can only populate this parameter when connecting one Web Part to another, but if that is the scenario you are trying to accomplish, this is usually more robust than using parameters from other sources.

- **Control.** As discussed in Chapter 9, controls are ASP.NET or SharePoint controls that can post to the page with the data view. This parameter source is usually used by leveraging a *DropDownList* control, or even a *CheckBox* or *TextBox* control on the page.

- **Cookie.** If the server writes cookies to the client computers, this can be a very effective source. It allows you to read from a cookie on the client's computer so that you can use the cookie's value to control your view. You could use this source, for example, to show data that the user has never seen before by storing a cookie on their computer that stores the data they have already seen.

● **Form.** The form source works in a way that is very similar to the way controls work, in that any form field on a page can be used as the source for a parameter value. Because of the way that SharePoint works with ASP.NET, you will almost always want to use controls instead of form fields for parameter sources, because using form fields requires you to either write custom JavaScript to parse the field's value or write custom forms pages that perform a *get* or a *post* operation to another page.

● **Query string.** One of the most popular parameter sources used on the Internet today, the query string parameter source can be used from other Web Parts or from hyperlinks to your page. If you control the hyperlink so that you can put the correct parameter in the URL, this source is a very versatile choice. It is the parameter source you will use in this exercise.

● **Server variable.** Microsoft Internet Information Services (IIS) has a collection of variables that you can access from within a data view's parameter collection. For example, by using this source, you can read information about the currently logged on user or the header response.

> **See also** For more information about server variables, read the MSDN article at *http://msdn.microsoft.com/en-us/library/ms524602.aspx.*

In this exercise, you will create a view of the Products list created in Chapter 9, and then create a parameter in the view that will read a value from the query string and conditionally format the view based on that value.

USE the *products.stp* template. This practice file is located in the *Documents\Microsoft Press\BuildingWebAppsSBS\Parameters* folder. If you have completed the exercises in the previous chapters, the Products list is already a data source in the Data Source Library.

BE SURE TO display the blog site in SharePoint Designer before beginning this exercise.

1. Press ⌃+N to create a new page.

2. On the **View** menu, point to **Page**, and then click **Design** to put the new page into Design view.

3. On the **Task Panes** menu, click **Data Source Library**.

4. Click the **Products** list in the **Data Source Library**, and then click **Show Data**.

The data for the Products list is displayed in a tree view in the Data Source Details task pane.

5. Select the **Title** and **Size** values.

6. At the top of the **Data Source Details** task pane, click **Insert Selected Fields as**, and then click **Multiple Item View**.

A data view of the Products list is inserted into the page.

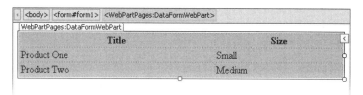

7. On the **Data View** menu, click **Parameters**.

The Data View Parameters dialog box is displayed. In this dialog box you can create new parameters, delete parameters that are already in the parameters collection, move parameters up and down in the collection, and set properties for parameters.

8. In the dialog box, click **New Parameter**.

A new parameter is created with a name of *Param1* and a parameter source set to None (which actually means that the parameter will be populated from Web Part connections). The source is the most important property, but it is also a good idea to change the name so that you can keep track of the parameter later.

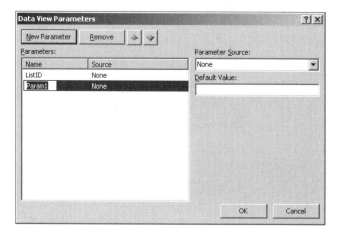

9. Change the name to **sizeParam**.

10. Click the **Parameter Source** arrow.

11. Click **Query String**.

The dialog box changes to display a box for the query string variable. Depending on the source chosen in this step, this middle box becomes either a box or a list of choices. In the case of controls, for example, a list of the controls on the page is generated and presented to you so you don't need to remember the control ID you want to use.

12. In the **Query String Variable** box, type **size**.

The query string can contain any number of variables. This value indicates which one of the query string variables should be used to populate the *sizeParam* parameter.

13. In the **Default Value** box, type **Small**.

14. Click **OK**.

The Data View Parameters dialog box closes and a new parameter is added to the data view.

15. Save this page as **newParameters.aspx**.

16. On the **View** menu, point to **Page**, and then click **Code**.

The new parameter can be seen in Code view, both within the parameters collection, where the *Location* attribute indicates the parameter source, and also in the XSLT itself as part of the root style sheet. It is placed there to ensure that it is in scope and can be referenced throughout the XSL style sheet.

```
     <body>  <form#form1>  <WebPartPages:DataFormWebPart>
16    <WebPartPages:DataFormWebPart runat="server" IsIncluded="True" FrameType="None" NoDefaultStyle="TRUE"
17    <DataSources>
18        <SharePoint:SPDataSource runat="server" DataSourceMode="List" UseInternalName="true" selectcomman
19    </DataSources>
20    <ParameterBindings>
21        <ParameterBinding Name="dvt_apos" Location="Postback;Connection"/>
22        <ParameterBinding Name="UserID" Location="CAMLVariable" DefaultValue="CurrentUserName"/>
23        <ParameterBinding Name="Today" Location="CAMLVariable" DefaultValue="CurrentDate"/>
24        <ParameterBinding Name="ListID" Location="None" DefaultValue="720552B9-C423-4FAC-A82A-517B24E06A1E
25        <ParameterBinding Name="sizeParam" Location="QueryString(size)" DefaultValue="Small"/>
26    </ParameterBindings>
27    <datafields>@Title,Title;@Verified,Verified;@Size,Size;@ID,ID;@ContentType,Content Type;@Modified,Mod
28    <XSL>
29 <xsl:stylesheet xmlns:x="http://www.w3.org/2001/XMLSchema" xmlns:d="http://schemas.microsoft.com/sharepoi
30    <xsl:output method="html" indent="no"/>
31    <xsl:decimal-format NaN=""/>
32    <xsl:param name="dvt_apos">'</xsl:param>
33    <xsl:param name="ListID">720552B9-C423-4FAC-A82A-517B24E06A1E</xsl:param>
34    <xsl:param name="sizeParam">Small</xsl:param>
35    <xsl:variable name="dvt_1_automode">0</xsl:variable>
36
```

17. On the **View** menu, point to **Page**, and then click **Design**.

18. In Design view, click inside the table cell to place the cursor next to the **Product One** text.

19. On the **Table** menu, point to **Select**, and then click **Row**.

The repeating table row is selected. To indicate that the formatting that is applied to the selected row will be repeated in every row in the data view (in technical terms, the XSLT in the data view will run a for-each loop over the data and write a new table row for each item of data), the other row in the data view is a light salmon color.

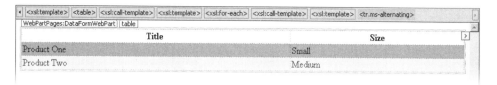

20. On the **Data View** menu, click **Conditional Formatting**.

The Conditional Formatting task pane opens and displays the conditional formatting that has already been applied to the view. In this task pane, you can create new conditions or modify conditions created previously. In addition, because some conditions might cause all of the data to disappear from a view (for example, if a condition shows all items whose ID is less than 1), you can change the visibility of conditions so that you can continue to modify your view.

21. Click **Create**, and then click **Apply Formatting**.

The Condition Criteria dialog box opens.

22. In the **Field Name** column, click **Size**.

23. In the **Comparison** column, click **Equals**.

24. In the **Value** column, click **[sizeParam]**, and leave the **And/Or** selection set to the default **And**.

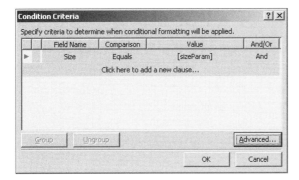

25. Click **OK**.

The Modify Style dialog box opens so you can set a style for the selected object in the data view, which in this case is the table row.

26. In the **Category** group, click **Background**, and then change the **background-color** value to **Gray**.

27. Click **OK**.

The Modify Style dialog box closes, and the first row in the data view turns gray because the default value for the parameter is *Small*. The condition you set creates an *xsl:if* statement that changes the background to gray for each table cell in the row where the *Size* field is equal to the value of the parameter.

28. Save the page again. Then press [F12] to preview it in the default browser.

29. Modify the URL to change *aspParameters.aspx* to **aspParameters.aspx?size=Medium**.

The background color for the row that meets the specific criterion turns gray.

30. Modify the URL again to change *aspParameters.aspx?size=Medium* to **aspParameters.aspx?size=Large**.

With each change, the background color for that specific row turns gray, unless the parameter value does not match any criteria in the view, in which case no rows turn gray.

Displaying the Value of a Parameter in a Data View

In the previous exercise, you created a query string parameter that enabled you to change the row color based on a value in the URL. However, you might have noticed one big drawback: the data view does not indicate which parameter value is being passed in, it merely changes the row background color based on that parameter. In other words, if you change the value to *small* with a lowercase *s*, no row color would change (because XSLT is case sensitive), and you would have a very difficult time understanding what was happening.

To not only help the people who are using your Web application but also help yourself in debugging the Web application, it is sometimes necessary to display the parameter values themselves in the data view. Unfortunately, there is no way to add parameters into a data view by using the user interface, so you must add the parameter by using Code view.

In this exercise, you will modify the view you created in the previous exercise to add a header row to the table and insert the parameter value inside that header.

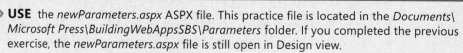

USE the *newParameters.aspx* ASPX file. This practice file is located in the *Documents\ Microsoft Press\BuildingWebAppsSBS\Parameters* folder. If you completed the previous exercise, the *newParameters.aspx* file is still open in Design view.

BE SURE TO display the blog site in SharePoint Designer before beginning this exercise.

1. Click inside the data view.

2. On the **Data View** menu, click **Change Layout**.

    The Data View Properties dialog box opens. This dialog box allows you to modify the data view by changing view styles, adding paging, or editing controls, as well as adding view headers and footers.

3. On the **General** tab, select the **Show View Header** check box.

4. Click **OK**.

    The Data View Properties dialog box closes and the data view is rendered with a new table row inserted at the top of the view.

5. Click to place the cursor inside this new table row.

6. On the **View** menu, point to **Page**, and then click **Split**.

The page is displayed in Split view, with the cursor flashing inside the table cell next to an *xsl:text* command. This technique is very useful for navigating through the XSLT. When you place the cursor in the data view first and then switch to Split or Code view, the cursor appears in the code panel within the XSLT that is causing that HTML to render.

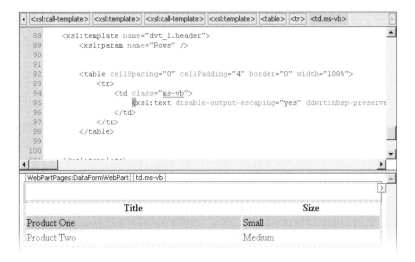

7. In the code panel, click to the left of the *xsl:text* tag that is selected in step 6.

8. Type **Size:** followed by **<xsl:value-of select=**.

> **Tip** When you type the code, the AutoComplete feature is activated. Typing XSLT code can be tedious, so leveraging the AutoComplete feature makes this task much easier. When you type the = (equal sign), for example, the necessary quotation marks are added automatically and the IntelliSense menu appears, showing all of the valid XSLT axes, formatting functions, and XPaths.

9. Type **$** to the right of = (the equal sign).

The IntelliSense menu scrolls down to the parameters that are in scope.

10. Click **sizeParam**, press ⎡Tab⎤, and then close the tag by typing **/>**.

> **Important** In addition to the *select* attribute, the *xsl:value-of* tag has a second attribute that you might have seen in the AutoComplete menu: *disable-output-escaping*. When this attribute is set to *Yes*, the parameter value will not be output escaped. This means that malicious users can place script into the URL of the page and create a cross-site scripting attack on your Web application. Never use the *disable-output-escaping* attribute unless you absolutely trust the data being passed into that parameter, as when the data comes from Web Part connections and you trust the data in the provider Web Part. When using a query string, however, you can never trust your data because anyone can create a hyperlink to your site and send it to anyone else. For more information on cross-site scripting attacks, see the MSDN article at *http://msdn.microsoft.com/en-us/library/ms998274.aspx*.

11. Click in the design panel.

The default value for *sizeParam* is displayed in the header row for this data view.

12. Select the text in the header row.

13. On the **Formatting** toolbar in the **Style** list, click **Heading 2 <h2>**.

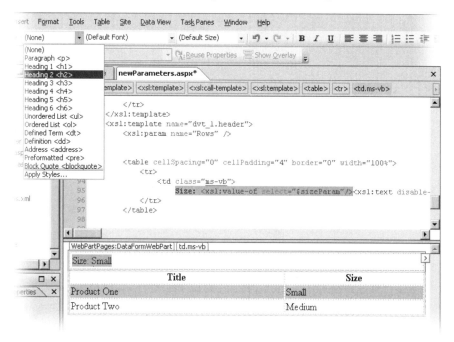

The value for the *Size* parameter is now displayed and formatted with the Heading 2 style in the header of the view.

Using a Math Expression with a Parameter for Conditional Formatting

In addition to enabling you to display parameters, use conditional formatting, and modify ASP.NET controls, the power of XSLT also provides another layer of data functionality: When you have numerical values in your data, you can use XPath expressions to perform mathematical functions on those numbers. For example, you can add a summary row to a data view and create a Totals column or calculate the average price of your products.

In this exercise, you will insert a new column into a data view and then create a mathematical expression in XPath that will be used for conditional formatting.

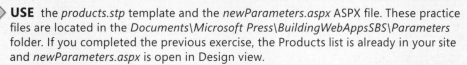

USE the *products.stp* template and the *newParameters.aspx* ASPX file. These practice files are located in the *Documents\Microsoft Press\BuildingWebAppsSBS\Parameters* folder. If you completed the previous exercise, the Products list is already in your site and *newParameters.aspx* is open in Design view.

BE SURE TO display the blog site in your default browser before beginning this exercise.

1. In the *allitems.aspx* page for the Products list, click **Settings** at the top of the page, and then click **Create Column**.

The *Create Column: Products* page is displayed. This page allows you to create new columns for the list.

2. In the **Column name** box, type **Price**, and for the column type, click **Currency**.

3. Click **OK**.

   The Products list's *allitems.aspx* page shows the new Price column.

4. Click **Settings** at the top of the page, and then click **Create Column**.

5. In the **Create Column: Products** page, type **Units** in the **Column name** box and click **Number** for the column type, then click **OK**.

   The Products list's *allitems.aspx* page shows the new Units column.

6. Point to the **Product One** title. In the Edit Control Block (ECB) that appears, click **Edit Item**.

   The *editform.aspx* page is displayed, filtered to show only the first list item. (This filter is performed with a query string parameter that provides the ID value.)

7. In the **Price** box, type **12.50**, and in the **Units** box, type **20**. Then click **OK** to save the changes.

8. Display the ECB for **Product Two**, and then click **Edit Item**.

9. In the **Price** box, type **25.00**, and in the **Units** box, type **7**. Then click **OK** to save the changes.

10. Switch to SharePoint Designer and open *newParameters.aspx*.

11. Place the cursor inside the data view on that page. Then [F5] to refresh the view.

When the view refreshes, the Data Source Details task pane also refreshes, showing the Price and Units data nodes in the tree.

12. On the **Data View** menu, click **Edit Columns**.

The Edit Columns dialog box opens. This dialog box displays the current fields in the Displayed Columns list on the right and the available fields returned from the data query on the left.

13. In the **Available Fields** list, hold down [Ctrl] and click to select **Price**, **Units**, and **Add Formula Column**, and then click **Add**.

The XPath Expression Builder dialog box opens.

14. In the tree control under **Select a field to insert**, double-click the **Price** field.

15. Click in the **Edit the XPath expression** box, press [Space], type * (asterisk), and then press [Space] again.

16. In the tree control under **Select a field to insert**, double-click the **Units** field.

A new expression is displayed in the Edit The XPath Expression box, and the results of that expression are displayed in the Preview section of the dialog box.

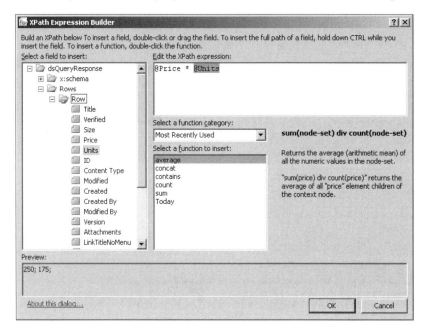

17. Click **OK**.

The XPath Expression Builder dialog box closes, and the Edit Columns dialog box again has focus, showing the three fields added to the displayed fields column.

18. Click **OK**.

The data view now includes the three new fields.

19. On the **Data View** menu, click **Parameters**.

The Data View Parameters dialog box opens.

20. Click **New Parameter**.

21. In the **Name** column, type **minValue**; in the **Parameter Source** list, click **Query String**; in the **Query String Variable** box, type **min**; and in the **Default Value** box, type **200**.

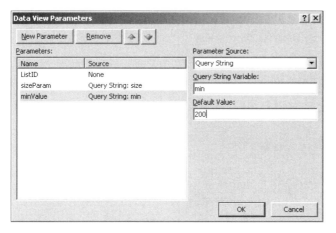

22. Click **OK** to create this new parameter.

23. In the data view, in the first row below the **@Price * @Unit** column heading, select the data value **250**, and on the **Data View** menu, click **Conditional Formatting**.

    The Conditional Formatting task pane opens.

24. At the top of the **Conditional Formatting** task pane, click **Create**, click **Apply Formatting**, and then click **Advanced**.

    The Advanced Condition dialog box opens. This dialog box is identical to the dialog box used in steps 19 through 22.

25. In the **Edit the XPath expression** box, type (@Price * @Units) < $minValue.

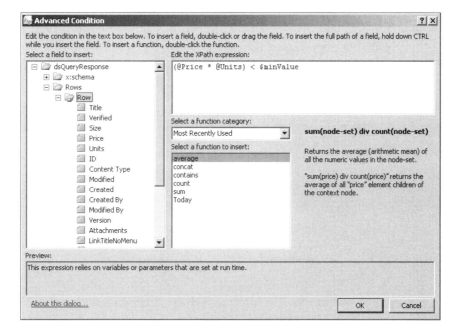

26. Click **OK** to close the **Advanced Condition** dialog box, and then click **OK** to close the **Condition Criteria** dialog box.

The Modify Style dialog box opens.

27. Change the **color** value to red.

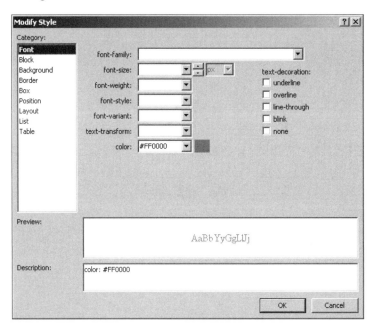

28. Click **OK**.

The data view renders with a column that shows the total value for each product in the Products list, and displays in red any product that has a value less than the value of the *minValue* parameter. In this case, the default *minValue* value is set to *200*, so the value for Product Two (175) is in red type.

29. Apply the default master page to this page by pointing to **Master Page** on the **Format** menu and clicking **Attach Master page**, then clicking **OK** twice to accept the default settings.

30. Save the page, preview it in the default browser by pressing [F12], and then modify the URL to **newParameters.aspx?size=Small&min=300**.

The size parameter value is displayed in the head of the view, and the conditional formatting displays the Price value of any product whose total value is less than 300 in red type. (In this case, both rows of data are less than 300, so both of these values turn red.)

Size: Small				
Title	Size	Price	Units	@Price * @Units
Product One	Small	12.50	20.00	250
Product Two	Medium	25.00	7.00	175

Key Points

- Parameters drive Web applications and help Web application designers create an interactive experience for end users.
- Web application designers can leverage parameters on both the data source and data view layers.
- Creating new data view parameters is as simple as typing into a dialog box.
- The SharePoint Designer tools and user interface display parameters and allow users to interact with them for filtering, conditional formatting, and performing mathematical functions.

Chapter at a Glance

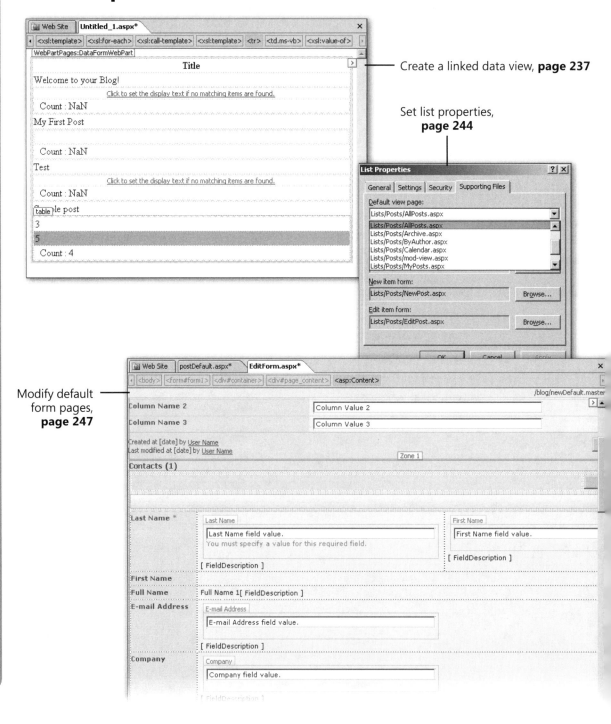

Create a linked data view, **page 237**

Set list properties,
page 244

Modify default
form pages,
page 247

11 Customizing List Forms and Pages

In this chapter, you will learn to

✔ Create a linked data source.

✔ Create a linked data view.

✔ Set list properties.

✔ Modify default form pages.

When you create a list in Microsoft Windows SharePoint Services 3.0, several ASPX pages are also created to support standard list operations. All lists create the same four base pages: *AllItems.aspx*, *DispForm.aspx*, *EditForm.aspx*, and *NewForm.aspx*. Each of these pages enables functionality that is well described by the page name: *Show All Items*, *Display Individual Items*, *Edit Individual Items*, and *Create New Items*, respectively. In addition to these pages, some lists include additional pages; for example, the Picture Library list has a *Slide Shows* page (*slideshow.aspx*) and an upload page (*upload.aspx*).

When creating a custom Web application, you need to be able to create your own stylized forms for inputting data into that application. From the end user's standpoint, it can be quite jarring to be viewing a highly customized default page and then see a "typical SharePoint page" used for data input. In fact, it isn't uncommon for people in that situation to feel as if they have left the application because the pages look so different.

In addition to the pure usability consideration, there are also times when you want to include fields that are different from those included in the list forms by default and, in fact, you might want to make some fields read-only. With the default form pages that come with lists, it is very difficult for a developer to provide a richly customized page for the end user. When these pages are open in Microsoft Office SharePoint Designer 2007, for example, the List Form Web Parts render as *atomic entities*, which means that you cannot place the cursor inside them, and when you attempt to make an edit, the entire Web Part is selected. This limitation means that you are able to modify only Web Part properties and Web Part zone properties, but that is the extent of functionality available. To provide a richly customized experience, you need to insert custom data views or custom list forms into pages and then set list properties so the lists can be redirected to these pages.

In this chapter, you will accomplish all of these things, from creating custom views to setting list properties, all the way through to modifying the layout of default form pages.

> **Important**   The exercises in this chapter require only the blog site you created and modified in earlier chapters. No practice files are supplied on the companion CD. For more information about practice files, see "Using the Companion CD" at the beginning of this book.

Creating a Linked Data Source

The *allitems.aspx* page that comes with each list displays the default fields for the list in a table. This page also has some very useful functions. For example, it allows sorting and filtering on column headers, and it has a toolbar that you can use to modify list settings and add new items. However, if you want to make the view more interesting, your choices are limited. You can add a sort, filter, or grouping to the view; change the paging; and change the fields that are displayed. But when it comes to rich customization of the view itself, or of the data in the view, you do not have many options available.

In SharePoint Designer, however, you can create rich views from scratch that can become the default pages for your lists. For example, by leveraging the linked data source feature discussed in Chapter 7, "Creating Data Sources in SharePoint," you can create a data view that shows data from two lists and demonstrates how those lists are relevant to each other. You can also set conditional formatting within a view, or use custom XPath expressions to render information that the end user will find useful.

In this exercise, you will create a new column to store a ratings value in the Comments list for the blog site you created in an earlier chapter, and then you will create a sample post and two comments, including ratings, for the post. After that, you will create a linked data source between the Posts list and the Comments list.

> **USE** the blog site you created and modified in earlier chapters. If you did not create the blog site, you can still perform these exercises by creating a new blog site, following the steps in Chapter 1; however, the screen shots in some examples will not match the ones shown here.
>
> **BE SURE TO** display the blog site in SharePoint Designer before beginning this exercise.

1. In the **Folder List**, expand the **Lists** folder, and then select **Comments**.

2. Press F12 to preview this list in the default browser.

   The *allitems.aspx* page for the Comments list loads in the browser.

3. On the **Comments** page, click **Settings**, and then click **Create Column**.

   The Create Column: Comments page loads in the browser.

4. In the **Column name** box, type **Rating** and, for the column type, click **Choice (menu to choose from)**.

5. In the **Type each choice on a separate line** box, type 1, and press Enter. Then type 2, 3, 4, and 5, pressing Enter after each number.

6. In the **Display choices using** list, click **Radio Buttons**.

7. Scroll down and click **OK** to create this column.

   The browser is redirected to the *allitems.aspx* page, and the column is added to the view. However, you shouldn't add items directly to this list. Because this is the Comments list, the only way to add meaningful content is to make a post and then comment on that post.

8. Browse to the *default.aspx* page for the blog site.

9. Click **Create a post**.

   The New Post page renders in the browser. A warning appears at the top of the page, telling you that this list requires content approval. If you have permission, you can either publish the post or save it as a draft; if you do not have approval permissions, you will only be allowed to save the post as a draft.

10. In the **Title** box, type **Sample post**.

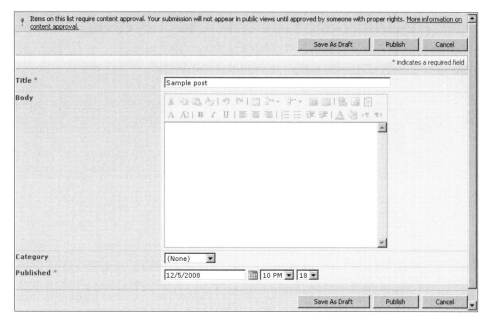

11. Click **Publish**.

The browser is redirected to the *default.aspx* page, and the sample post is displayed at the top of the page.

12. Click **Comments (0)**.

The new form for entering comments to the sample post is displayed.

13. In the **Body** box, type **Sample post comment.**, and for the rating, click **3**.

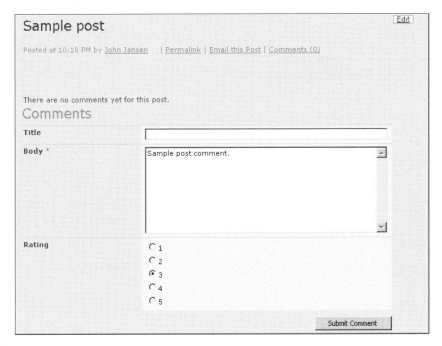

14. Click **Submit Comment**.

The page is refreshed, the new comment appears under the sample post, and an Add Comment form is displayed beneath the new comment.

15. Click **Comments (1)** and then, in the **Body** box, type **Sample post comment 2.**, and for the rating, click **5**.

16. Click **Submit Comment**.

The page reloads again and this time shows the sample post with two comments. These two comments give the sample post an average rating of 4.

17. Click over to SharePoint Designer.

18. On the **Task Panes** menu, click **Data Source Library**.

The Data Source Library opens, displaying the list of data sources in this Web site.

19. Click **Create a new Linked Source**.

The Data Source Properties dialog box opens.

20. Click **Configure Linked Source**.

The Link Data Sources Wizard opens.

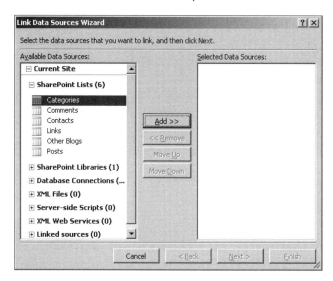

21. Double-click **Posts**, and then double-click **Comments** to add them both to the **Selected Data Sources** list.

22. Click **Next**.

23. Click **Join the contents of the data sources by using the Data Source Details to insert data views and joined subviews**.

24. Click **Finish**.

The Link Data Sources Wizard closes, and the Data Source Properties dialog box opens.

25. On the **General** tab, in the **Name** box, type **BlogRating**.

26. Click **OK** to close the **Data Source Properties** dialog box and create the new **BlogRating** data source in the **Data Source Library**.

27. Click **BlogRating** in the **Data Source Library**, and then click **Show Data**.

The Data Source Details task pane opens with the data for the linked data source displayed in the tree. In the Data Source Details task pane, you can see the Posts node, and if you scroll down you can see the Comments node.

Creating a Linked Data View

By completing the preceding exercise, you have created a data source in your site that combines the Posts list with the Comments list. However, the two lists do not have an explicit relationship; they have an implicit one. When creating a view that includes some data from one list and some data from a linked list, you should always insert the view in two steps: First insert the "parent" data values, and then select the "child" values and insert them as a subview. Trying to create the view in one step causes the subview to render incorrectly.

In this exercise, you will create a view of the Posts list and then insert a subview of the Comments list. You will then use the XPath Expression Builder dialog box to show the average comment rating for each post in the view.

BE SURE TO display the blog site in SharePoint Designer, with the Data Source Details task pane open and displaying the contents of the linked data source, before beginning this exercise.

1. Press `Ctrl`+`N` to create a new page in Design view.

2. On the **Insert** menu, point to **SharePoint Controls**, and then click **Web Part Zone**.

A new Web Part zone is inserted into the page.

3. Under the **dsQueryResponse/Posts/Rows/Row** node in the data source, click the **Title** data value to select it.

> **Tip** You can see the *dsQueryResponse/Posts/Rows/Row* node inside the Data Source Details task pane because the task pane reveals the full XPath necessary in the XSLT to make the data values show up in the HTML of the page, and it also serves as a way to distinguish one of the linked data sources from the other.

4. Click **Insert Selected Fields as**.

5. Click **Multiple Item View**.

   A view of the Title data value is inserted on the page.

6. Right-click the "**Welcome to your Blog!**" data value, point to **Insert**, and then click **Row below**.

   A new row is inserted below each repeating row in the data view.

> **Tip** Remember from Chapter 8, "Creating Data Views," that the XSLT generates each row of the data view by running a for-each loop over the data source, so that for each value in the data source, the XSLT generates a table row and the necessary table cells to display that data. When you do anything to one row, the same thing happens for each row in the table; therefore, a new table row is inserted after each row of the view.

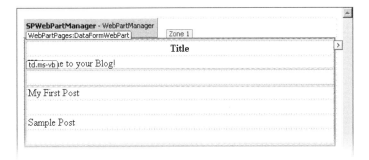

7. Click to place the cursor inside one of the new table cells that was inserted into the view.

8. Scroll down in the **Data Source Library** until you can see the **Comments/Rows/Row** section of the data source.

9. Click to select the **Rating** node.

10. Click **Insert Selected Fields as**.

11. Click **Joined Subview**.

The Join Subview dialog box opens.

12. In the **Row** list on the left, select **ID**, and in the **Row** list on the right, select **PostID**, and then click **OK**.

The Join Subview dialog box closes, and a subview is inserted into the parent view, showing each comment in which the comment's PostID is equal to the ID of the post.

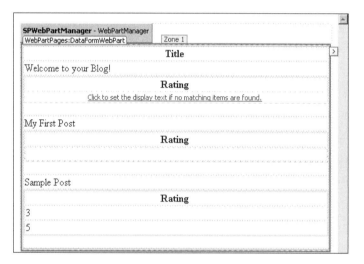

13. Click inside the subview that was just inserted.

14. On the **Data View** menu, click **Change Layout**.

The Data View Properties dialog box opens.

15. On the **General** tab, select the **Show column summary row** check box.

> **Tip** The Toolbar section of the dialog box is disabled, because you cannot add a toolbar to the subview, only to the parent view.

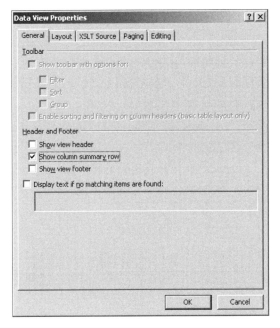

16. Click **OK**.

    The Data View Properties dialog box closes, and a new row that includes the count of responses for each blog post is added to the subview.

17. Right-click the value for the count in the first subview, and click **Edit formula**.

    The Insert Formula dialog box is displayed, with *count($Rows)* displayed in the Edit The XPath Expression box. This currently shows the number of comments made to each post, but you will change it to show the average value for the rating of each post in the comment (the sum of the ratings divided by the count of the ratings).

18. Change the value in the **Edit the XPath expression** box to:

    ```
    sum(../../../Comments/Rows/Row[@PostID=current()/@ID]/@Rating) div
    count(../../../Comments/Rows/Row[@PostID=current()/@ID]/@Rating)
    ```

19. Click **OK**.

The data view now shows the average rating for each blog post. In the next steps, you will modify the view so that it displays only the averages, not the values themselves.

20. In the header of the subview, select **Rating**.

21. On the **Table** menu, point to **Delete**, and then click **Delete Rows** to delete the row that contains the name of the column.

22. In the table cell in the subview, select **5,** and on the **Table** menu, point to **Select,** and then click **Row**.

The table row with the data value of 5 is selected in Design view.

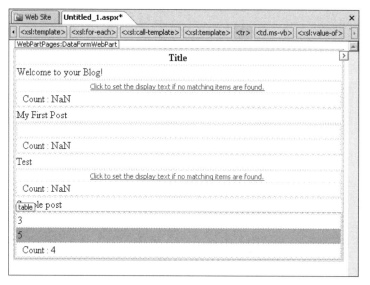

23. On the **Data View** menu, click **Conditional Formatting**.

The Conditional Formatting task pane opens.

24. In the **Conditional Formatting** task pane, click **Create**, and then click **Show content**.

The Condition Criteria dialog box opens.

25. Click **Advanced**.

The Advanced Condition dialog box opens.

26. In the **Edit the XPath expression** box, type **@Rating < '1'**.

27. Click **OK** to close the **Advanced Condition** dialog box, and then click **OK** again to close the **Condition Criteria** dialog box.

The view now renders without showing any of the data values for the subview. The condition you set above indicates that the repeating table row should be displayed only when the Rating value is less than 1. Because that can never be true, the table row never appears in the view.

28. In the view, select **Count**, and replace it with **Average Rating**.

29. Select **Sample Post** and, on the **Insert** menu, click **Hyperlink**.

The Insert Hyperlink dialog box opens.

30. In the **Address** box, type the following:
/Blog/Lists/Posts/Post.aspx?ID={@ID}#Comments

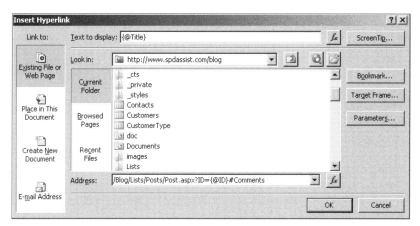

31. Click **OK**.

The Insert Hyperlink dialog box is dismissed, and the view now renders with a link to the *post.aspx* page, on which you can post new comments to any of the posts by clicking the post's title.

32. Save the page as **postDefault.aspx**.

Setting List Properties

The view from the previous exercise would make an excellent default view for the Posts list in the blog site. Unfortunately, because of the way that the SharePoint platform determines what pages can be used for default list pages, there is more work that needs to be done to that page to make it work with a list. The page that is registered as the default view for lists is important because it is the page that will render when users browse directly to the list, or when they click to submit or edit list items in the browser.

Before a page can be set as the default view page for a list, it must contain a view of the list inside a Web Part zone. In the previous exercise, you inserted a view of a *linked data source* (not a view of the list) into the Web Part zone on the page, so that page does not meet the criterion necessary to be set as the default view page. In fact, if you tried to set it as the default view, it would not even be listed as a choice in the SharePoint Designer user interface.

In this exercise, you will modify the *postDefault.aspx* page created in the previous exercise so that it contains the necessary information to allow it to be set as the default view for the list. After that, you will set the list property to make this page the default view page for the Posts list; finally, you will attach the page to the master page so that the branding of the page matches that of your Web application.

USE the blog site you modified in the previous exercise.

BE SURE TO have the *postDefault.aspx* page open for editing before beginning this exercise.

1. Click to place the cursor below the current data view on the page.

2. On the **Insert** menu, point to **SharePoint Controls**, and then click **Web Part Zone**.

   A Web Part zone is inserted below the data view, with a Click To Insert A Web Part link.

3. Click **Click to insert a Web Part**.

The Web Parts task pane opens, with the Team Site Gallery showing a list of the Web Parts you can insert into this zone.

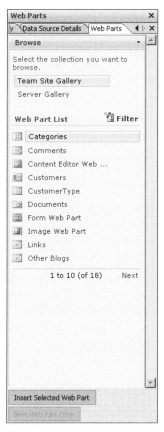

4. Click **Next** in the task pane until the **Posts** Web Part appears.

5. Click to select the **Posts** Web Part, and then click **Insert Selected Web Part** at the bottom of the task pane.

A List View Web Part is inserted inside the zone on this page. This page now meets the minimum criteria to be set as the default view for the list.

6. Save the page.

7. In the **Folder List** task pane, expand the **Lists** folder.

8. Right-click the **Posts** list, and then click **Properties**.

The List Properties dialog box opens.

9. On the **Supporting Files** tab, click the **Default view page** arrow.

The Default View Page list is displayed, showing the pages in the current Web site that have a view of the Posts list inside a Web Part zone. Because the *postDefault.aspx* page now contains a view of the Posts list inside a Web Part zone, it is available in this list. Due to the potentially large number of pages that have views inside zones, you might have to scroll down in the list to see the page you want.

10. Select **postDefault.aspx**, and then click **OK** to close the dialog box.

11. Right-click the List View Web Part you inserted in step 5, and click **Web Part Properties**.

The Posts dialog box opens.

> **Tip** This is the same Web Part properties information that is displayed in the browser when you click Web Part Properties. In fact, it is hosted in a browser window, even though it looks like a SharePoint Designer dialog box.

12. Expand the **Layout** section.

13. Select the **Hidden** check box, and then click **OK**.

The Web Part continues to be rendered in the SharePoint Designer design surface, but the title now indicates that it is hidden. As mentioned at the beginning of this section, the page must have this Web Part in a zone to be set as the default page for the list; however, the Web Part does not need to be visible on the page for this setting to work. Because showing it on the page would be confusing, you have set it to be hidden when the user browses to the page.

14. On the **Format** menu, point to **Master Page**, and then click **Attach Master Page**.

The Select A Master Page dialog box opens.

15. Click **OK** to apply the Default Master Page.

The Match Content Regions dialog box opens.

16. Click **OK** to accept the default mapping of content to content placeholder.

All of the content on *postDefault.aspx* renders in the PlaceHolderMain content region.

 BE SURE TO save your work.

Modifying Default Form Pages

In addition to modifying the default view page for a list, it is sometimes important to also modify the input and edit forms for that list. List forms allow you to insert data into the fields in the list, but the fields that allow this always appear stacked top to bottom. There are times when a different layout would make more sense. For example, if the user were filling out the Contacts list, it would be simpler to place the last name to the left of the first name, rather than above it.

Customizing the default forms for lists is challenging. A form is rendered via a List Form Web Part, which means that there is no way to drag and drop fields to make the form appear the way you want it to. Even in SharePoint Designer 2007, the amount of customization you can do to a List Form Web Part is very limited. To provide a rich customization experience, you will insert a different Web Part on the *EditForm.aspx* page.

In this exercise, you will create a new Contacts list, open the *EditForm.aspx* page for this list, and insert a custom list form into this page. Next, you will make a field read-only. Finally, you will place one field next to another field to change the layout of the form.

BE SURE TO display the blog site in SharePoint Designer before beginning this exercise.

1. On the **File** menu, point to **New**, and then click **SharePoint content**.

The New dialog box opens, showing the SharePoint Content tab with the Lists category selected.

2. In the list of available templates, click **Contacts**, and then click **OK** to create a list called *Contacts* in the blog Web site.

> **Tip** The list is not created in the lists folder, but rather shows up at the bottom of the Folder List task pane.

3. Expand the *Contacts* folder, and double click *EditForm.aspx* to open it for editing. Then on the **View** menu, point to **Page**, and click **Design**.

The page is opened in Design view, giving you enough room to insert content below the current list form.

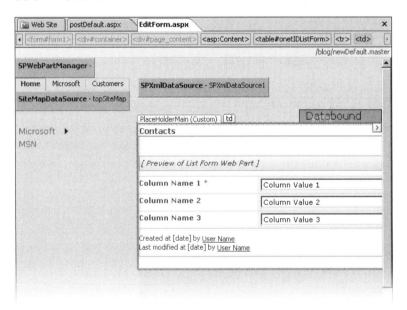

4. Place the cursor below the list form on the page.

A one-pixel-high image that spans the width of the entire content area is selected.

5. Press the ⟵ key to move the insertion point immediately to the left of the image, and then, on the **Insert** menu, point to **SharePoint Controls** and click **Web Part Zone**.

A Web Part zone is inserted immediately above the image selected in step 4.

6. On the **Insert** menu, point to **SharePoint Controls**, and then click **Custom List Form**.

The List Or Document Library Form dialog box opens.

With this dialog box, you can insert a customizable list form for any of the lists or document libraries in the current site. In addition, you can use the Content Type To Use For Form list to specify the content type for the list that the form will be used for, and you can choose the kind of form to create (either a new item form, an edit item form, or a display item form). Finally, you can choose to show the default toolbar at the top of the form.

7. In the **List or document library to use for form** list, click **Contacts**.

The Content Type To Use For Form list changes to display any of the content types that are enabled for the list chosen in this step. In the case of the Contacts list, there is only one content type: Contact.

See Also For more information about creating new content types for SharePoint lists, refer to the article on the Microsoft Developer Network (MSDN) site at *msdn.microsoft.com/en-us/library/ms472236.aspx*.

8. Under **Type of form to create**, click **Edit item form**, and then click **OK**.

The custom edit form is inserted into the Web Part zone you inserted in step 7. Because you have not created any items in this list yet, no edit form fields are displayed. To see the form controls on the page, you must set the form to show sample data.

9. On the On Object User Interface (OOUI) panel, select the **Show with sample data** check box.

The custom list form refreshes, showing each form control on the page.

10. Close the task panes on the right side of the SharePoint Designer application, expanding Design view so you can see the entire form.

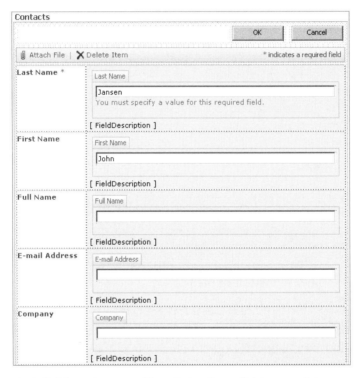

Each field renders as a SharePoint form field control; however, because this is a custom list form, the fields can be converted into other control types.

11. Select the **Full Name** form field control, and click the arrow that appears when you select the control to display the OOUI panel for this control.

12. Click the **Format as** arrow to show the list of choices available for this control.

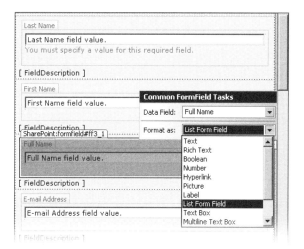

13. Select **Label**.

This field is now read-only; when the user browses to this page, the field will render as an *asp:label* control displaying the text value for the field, not a form control for the field.

14. Place the cursor to the right of the [**FieldDescription**] control in the **Last Name** row.

15. On the **Table** menu, point to **Modify**, and then click **Split Cells**.

The Split Cells dialog box opens.

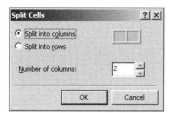

16. Click **OK** to split the current cell into two columns.

17. Drag the **First Name** form field control into the new table cell that was just created.

18. Drag the **[Field Description]** for the **First Name** field below the form field control.

> **Tip** Sometimes it can be difficult to drag and drop something to the exact destination you want, so it might be helpful to add some space first by putting the cursor into the table cell and pressing Enter.

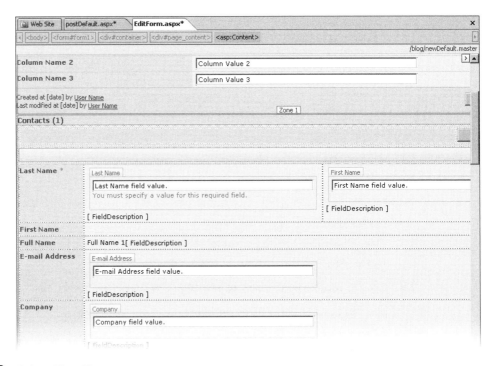

19. Select **First Name**.

20. On the **Table** menu, point to **Select**, and click **Row**. Then on the **Table** menu, point to **Delete**, and click **Delete Rows**.

The row that used to contain the First Name form field and Field Description controls is deleted.

21. Select **Last Name** * and delete it. Then replace it with **Name (Last, First)**.

The form now renders with the Last Name and First Name form field controls in the same row, and the text indicating what form fields they are has changed to indicate the order of the fields. The last thing to do is to modify the controls so they are narrower by default.

> **Important** To determine the correct class to apply to the form field control, you would perform the same steps you did in Chapter 3, "Accessing the Styles Behind SharePoint Pages," by browsing to the page to capture the run-time HTML and then viewing that HTML in SharePoint Designer. In this case, the class is *.ms-long*, but as you customize other controls, you will need to find out their individual classes.

22. On the **View** menu, point to **Page**, and then click **Code**.

The page changes to Code view.

23. Scroll up to the top of the page until you see the following line of code:

```
<asp:Content ContentPlaceHolderId="PlaceHolderMain" runat="server">
```

24. Immediately after this line of code, add the following style block:

```
<style>.ms-long{width:150px;}</style>
```

25. On the **View** menu, point to **Page**, and then click **Design**.

The page changes to Design view, where the form field controls now render with widths of 150 pixels.

26. Right-click the old List Form Web Part, and then click **Web Part Properties**.

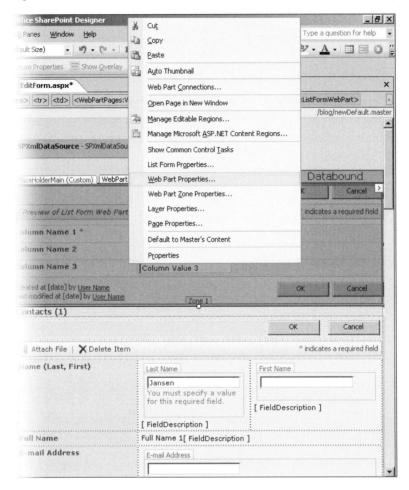

The Web Part Properties dialog box opens.

27. Expand the **Layout** section of the **Web Part Properties** dialog box, select **Hidden**, and then click **OK**.

28. Save your work, and then browse to the **Contacts** list and add a new contact to the list.

29. On the *allitems.aspx* page, point to the last name for that new contact, click the arrow, and then click **Edit**.

The *EditForm.aspx* page renders in the browser with the new custom list form.

Key Points

- Creating new list pages enables you to create rich applications.
- When creating views of lists in SharePoint Designer, you can use subviews to show related data.
- After creating forms and view pages for lists, you can set those pages as the default list pages in SharePoint Designer.
- Modifying the out-of-the-box list pages enables you to create read-only fields and display fields in the layout that is most useful for your Web application.

Chapter at a Glance

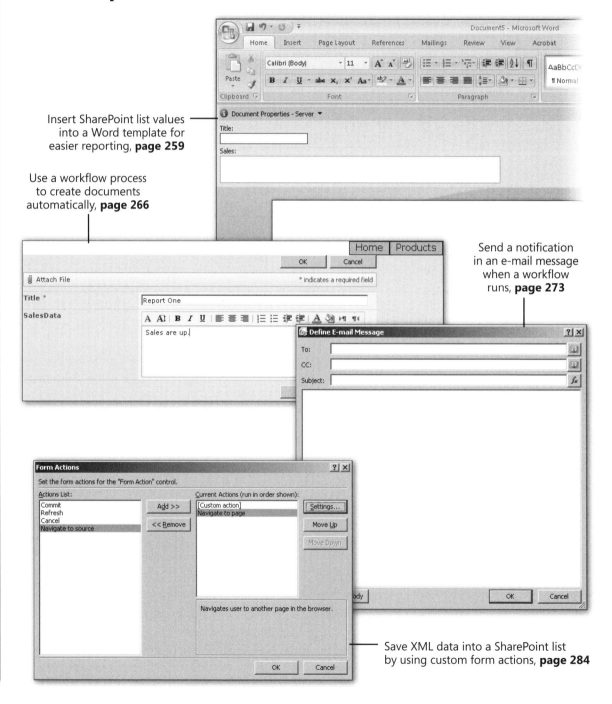

Insert SharePoint list values into a Word template for easier reporting, **page 259**

Use a workflow process to create documents automatically, **page 266**

Send a notification in an e-mail message when a workflow runs, **page 273**

Save XML data into a SharePoint list by using custom form actions, **page 284**

12 Using the Windows Workflow Foundation

In this chapter, you will learn to

✔ Insert SharePoint list values into a Word template for easier reporting.

✔ Use a workflow process to create documents automatically.

✔ Send a notification in an e-mail message when a workflow runs.

✔ Add workflow data to an e-mail message.

✔ Create a logical branch in a workflow step to control the flow of a workflow process.

✔ Save XML data into a SharePoint list by using custom form actions.

Workflow is a generic term that refers to a predictable series of tasks performed to produce a specific outcome. For example, a task can be assigned to someone, then completed and assigned to someone else for evaluation, and then reviewed and marked as satisfactory. In the context of Microsoft Office SharePoint, however, the definition is more specifically discussed as a way to automate the movement of documents or list items through a series of tasks. On the first layer, *workflow* refers to the Windows Workflow Foundation, the platform upon which all workflow actions are based. The next layer of workflow is its specific implementation for use on SharePoint sites. This level refers to such implementations as an *approval workflow* or a *document routing workflow*, both of which are available out of the box when you create a document library. The third layer is really just an extension of the second in that it is specific to SharePoint, but it requires Microsoft Office SharePoint Designer 2007. It focuses on building complex activities on SharePoint that run redundant business processes.

It is common practice in many different kinds of organizations for one person to create a Microsoft Office Word document and send it to others in an e-mail message for input and approval. As soon as a copy of that document is sent off, however, the sender and other contributors have no way of knowing when it has been modified or approved. This issue can be addressed by using workflow methods and automating the process by using SharePoint Designer.

Another example of a fairly standard workflow process is when an organization needs a way to change the status of a contact and then use that change to trigger an action on someone's part. Suppose, for instance, that your company has a list of customers and potential customers. You might want customers designated as *Cold* to receive a phone call, those designated as *Warm* to get an e-mail message, and those designated as *Confirmed* to be moved to another list so that they receive regular updates on your products or services. This relatively straightforward process has numerous possible points of failure: how can you make sure that everyone on the team knows the status of each customer, that everyone knows who should be getting called that day, and that the e-mail messages are generated correctly? Each of these potential pitfalls can be avoided by using SharePoint Designer and workflow, which reduces the overall risk to customer tracking.

In this chapter, you will use the Workflow Designer in SharePoint Designer to create a few different processes that allow you to automate tasks that are otherwise tedious, not only making your team more productive, but establishing clear tracking mechanisms as well. First you will create a Word document containing list data, for use as a template for a document library; then you will create a process whereby items added to a list in the SharePoint site will populate field values in the document library so that the Word document contains those values. After that, you will create a workflow that includes a logical process, so that when a workflow on the list is triggered and a field equals a certain value, a new document is created and a formatted e-mail message is sent. Finally, you will create a custom form action that takes data from an XML data source and pushes that data into a SharePoint list.

> **Tip** In addition to the out-of-the-box workflow actions that ship with SharePoint Server, you can also use Microsoft Visual Studio to create new actions to meet your needs. To make these actions available to SharePoint Designer, you must have permission to access the server's file system and to place DLLs and XML data directly onto the SharePoint server. As mentioned at the beginning of this chapter, *workflow* is one word describing three concepts; because one of the layers of workflow is the basic platform, writing on top of that platform is an important consideration. However, creating new workflow actions on the server is beyond the scope of this book.

See Also For more information about creating custom actions in Visual Studio, I recommend starting with the following article on the Microsoft Developer Network: *http://msdn.microsoft.com/en-us/library/cc627284.aspx.*

> **Important** The exercises in this chapter require only the blog site created and modified in earlier chapters. No practice files are supplied on the companion CD. For more information about practice files, see "Using the Companion CD" at the beginning of this book.

Inserting SharePoint List Values into a Word Template for Easier Reporting

It is common for members of a team to send weekly status reports to the team's manager, and then for that manager to roll those reports into a teamwide status mail. In this process, several people are involved in sending e-mail messages every week and then verifying that they were sent and understood; every week, one person then has to shuffle through the messages to determine which ones matter, and then copy and paste from those e-mail messages; every week, each team member receives an update in his or her inbox to read and track. There should be an easier way to perform these redundant tasks. Workflow in SharePoint Designer is that easier way.

In this exercise, you will create a new Word document to serve as the template for a document library. This template will contain fields that will hold SharePoint list data when new documents are created.

> **Important** If you do not have Microsoft Office Word 2007 installed on your computer, you will not be able to complete this exercise.

USE the blog site you created and modified in earlier chapters. If you did not create the blog site, you can still perform these exercises by creating a new blog site, following the steps in Chapter 1; however, the screen shots in some examples will not match the ones shown here.

BE SURE TO display the blog site in your default browser before beginning this exercise.

1. Browse to the */blog/_layouts/create.aspx* page for the blog site.

The Create page is loaded in the browser and displays the five different categories of SharePoint content that you can create.

2. In the **Libraries** category, click **Document Library**.

The New page is loaded in the browser.

3. In the **Name** box, type **TeamStatus**.

4. In the **Document Template** list, click **Microsoft Office Word document**.

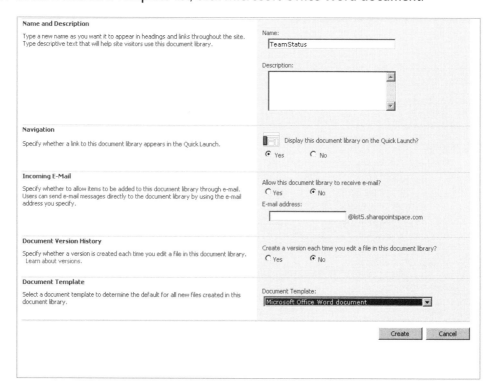

5. Click **Create**.

A new document library is created, and the *allitems.aspx* page for the TeamStatus document library is rendered in the browser.

6. On the *allitems.aspx* page, click **Settings**, and then click **Create Column**.

The Create Column: Status page is displayed in the browser.

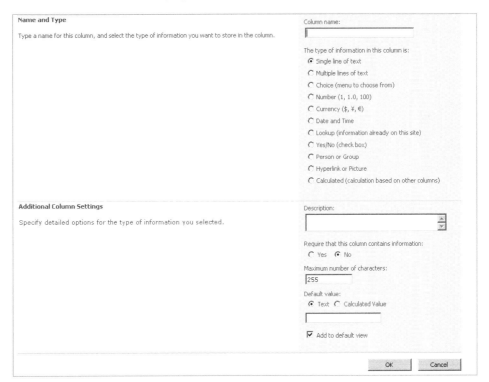

7. In the **Column name** box, type **Sales**.

8. In the **The type of information in this column is** list, click **Multiple lines of text**.

9. Click **OK**.

The new column, Sales, is created and added to the default view. It can be seen in the list view on the *allitems.aspx* page. By creating this field, you have added it as a property on the documents in this document library. This means that every document created in this document library can have a Sales property, and that the property can be inserted into the text of the document itself and updates automatically when the property in the document is modified.

10. Open this site in SharePoint Designer.

11. Expand the **Folder List** task pane so that it is full size.

12. In the **Folder List** task pane, expand the **TeamStatus** document library.

The Forms folder for the document library is shown.

13. Expand the **Forms** folder.

All of the supporting files for the document library are shown, including a file called *template.dotx*.

14. Right-click *template.dotx,* point to **Open With**, and then click **Microsoft Office Word**.

Microsoft Office Word 2007 opens and displays a blank document. This document is the template for the TeamStatus document library.

15. On the document page, type **Team Status for:**.

16. Press ⎡Enter⎤ to create a new line in the document.

17. Type **Sales Team:** onto the page, and press ⎡Enter⎤.

18. On the **Insert** tab, in the **Text** group, click **Quick Parts**, point to **Document Property**, and then click **Sales**.

The template is now set up so that when a new document is created in this document library, the document will automatically be populated with the text from the Sales field.

```
Team Status for:

Sales Team:

[Sales]
```

19. Press ⎡Ctrl⎤+⎡S⎤ to save the page to the document library, and exit Microsoft Office Word.

20. Browse to the *allitems.aspx* page for this document library, and click **New**.

A warning dialog box opens, indicating that some files can harm your computer.

21. Click **OK**.

Microsoft Office Word opens and displays a new document based on the template you saved to the server in step 19. In addition, the Title and Sales properties load in the Document Properties window. Even though you did not add the Title field to the template, SharePoint added it for you because it is the default field for every document library and is a required field.

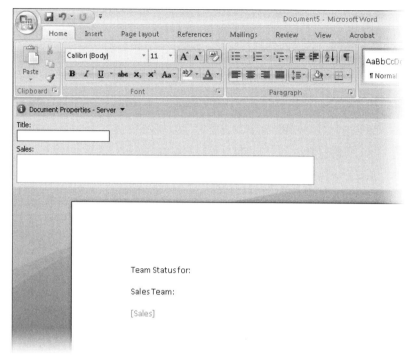

22. In the **Document Properties** window, in the **Title** field, type **TeamStatusDocument**.

23. In the **Sales** field, type **Sales are up in every category**.

This text is displayed in the body of the document, because the document property was inserted into the document itself in step 18.

24. Place the cursor to the right of the **Team Status for:** text in the document.

25. On the **Insert** tab, in the **Text** group, click **Date & Time**.

The Date And Time dialog box opens.

26. Select a date format from the list of available formats.

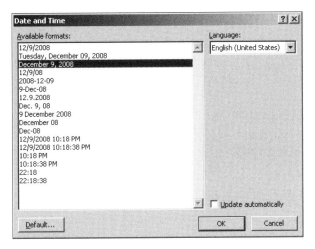

27. Click **OK**.

The current date is inserted onto the page.

28. Press ⌈Ctrl⌉+⌈S⌉ to save the page to the **TeamStatus** document library.

> **Important** When prompted for the save location, type the full URL for your blog site, including the name of the document library. For example, I typed *http://www.spdassist.com/blog/TeamStatus/TeamStatusDocument.docx.*

29. When the page has been saved, browse to the *allitems.aspx* page and click the new document to open it in Microsoft Office Word.

The document opens, displaying the information you added in this exercise. By repeating these steps, you can create a new property for each contributor to the weekly status report, quickly building a Word template that allows everyone to share one template, and never again have to e-mail a series of reports to one person who then has to compile the reports manually.

Using a Workflow Process to Create Documents Automatically

In the previous exercise, you created a field in a document library and then placed that field in a Word document. Techniques like this make creating and editing weekly reports and other such documents much more straightforward than e-mailing the myriad subsections around and then compiling them into a new document. The new process works well, but it does not allow the document's owner to approve the sections before they go live.

In most cases, one person is in charge of documents like this, and that person usually wants to own the quality of the information as well as the quality of the layout. With Microsoft Office SharePoint Server 2007 (MOSS) and Microsoft Windows SharePoint Services 3.0, there are several different ways to maintain this kind of document version control: you can create a document approval workflow; you can require contributors to check out the document; you can use the Publishing feature specific to MOSS; or you can create a SharePoint list, connected to the document and the document library through workflow, into which contributors enter their data. In this final approach, each person who owns a section of the document can fill in a field in a list, and then when the person in charge of the overall summary selects a check box, a new document is created in the document library that contains all of the data from that list item.

In the exercise in this section, you will use a feature of SharePoint Designer called the *Workflow Designer*. I am reluctant to call this feature a dialog box or a wizard, because it contains such a rich set of functionality that it really could be considered a full extension of the SharePoint Designer user interface.

Name and association   Initiation options   Help information

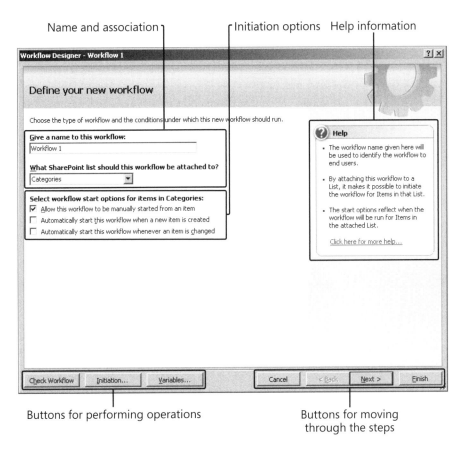

Buttons for performing operations

Buttons for moving
through the steps

The functionality available in this designer is extensive and complex. On the initial screen, for example, there are five basic sections:

- **Name and association.** Here you give the workflow a name. It is helpful to use descriptive names, because this will drive the user interface, including the folder names in the Web site.

- **Help information.** Here you can read high-level help information about the user interface, as well as link to further help topics.

● **Initiation options.** The choices here allow you to set a workflow to start manually or to start when items are created or edited (or any combination of these three choices).

● **Buttons for performing operations.** These three buttons allow you to check for errors as you are building the workflow (which can be very helpful when you are building complex processes), create initiation variables that the user will be required to fill out before a workflow begins, or create standard variables that can be used during the workflow as the process progresses.

● **Buttons for moving through the steps.** After setting the name, initiation options, and variables, you can use these buttons at the bottom of the Workflow Designer to advance to the next step.

In this exercise, you will create a SharePoint list that contains a field in which the Sales team members can enter their status, and then you will fill out a list item to populate that field with data. Next, you will create a workflow that will be started manually from that list item. The workflow will generate a new document that will contain the sales information from this new list.

> **USE** the blog site you modified and the *TeamStatus* document library you created in the previous exercise.
>
> **BE SURE TO** display to the blog site in your default browser before beginning this exercise.

1. Browse to the */blog/_layouts/create.aspx* page for the blog site.

The Create page loads in the browser and displays the five SharePoint content categories.

2. In the **Custom Lists** category, click **Custom List**.

The New page loads in the browser.

3. In the **Name** field, type **Weekly Status**, and then click **Create**.

A new list is created, and the browser renders the *allitems.aspx* page for that list.

4. On the Web Part toolbar, in the **Settings** list, click **Create Column**.

The Create Column: Weekly Status page loads in the browser.

5. In the **Column name** field, type **SalesData**, in the **The type of information in this column is** list, select **Multiple lines of text**, and then click **OK**.

The browser returns to the *allitems.aspx* page for the Weekly Status list.

6. On the Web Part toolbar, click **New**.

The *newform.aspx* page renders in the browser.

7. In the **Title** field, type **Report One**, and in the **SalesData** field, type **Sales are up.**.

> **Tip** The reason you designated this field with the Multiple Lines Of Text type in step 5 was to allow a wide array of formatting to be included in this field. In addition to simple text, you can add bulleted lists, bold characters, and other formatting options.

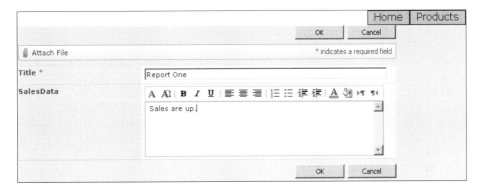

8. Click **OK** to create this new list item.

9. Open the blog site in SharePoint Designer. Then on the **File** menu, point to **New**, and click **Workflow**.

The Workflow Designer opens.

10. In the **Give a name to this workflow** box, type **StatusReport**, in the **What SharePoint list should this workflow be attached to?** list, select **Weekly Status**, and then click **Next**.

The Workflow Designer Step Creation page opens. You can use the options on the right side of this page to add new steps to the workflow process, and then for each new step create conditions and actions for that step.

11. In the **Step Name** box, delete the default value of **Step 1** and type **Create New Report**.

12. Click the **Actions** button, and then click **More Actions**.

The Workflow Actions dialog box opens, showing all of the actions that are available from the server. Items in this list allow you to build dynamic strings (to concatenate two data values into one, for example), to pause until a specific date (ensuring that the step in the workflow will not execute until a specific date is reached), to send an e-mail message, and much more.

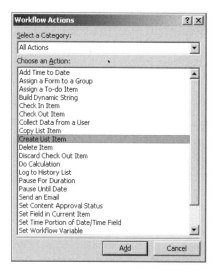

13. Click **Create List Item**, and then click **Add**.

> **Tip** Remember, document libraries are treated by the SharePoint platform essentially the same way that lists are, even though they are based on different content types. When you want to run a workflow that creates a new document in a document library, you select the Create List Item action.

A new dynamic string (one that contains links and information) is created next to the Actions button:

Create item in this list (Output to Variable: create)

This string allows you to click *this list* to select the list in which you want an item to be created, and it also tells you that this action will output data to a workflow variable called *create*.

14. Click **this list**.

The Create New List Item dialog box opens.

15. In the **List** list, click **WeeklyStatus**.

The list of fields in the dialog box is populated with a list of the required fields.

16. Select **Name (for use in forms)**, and then click **Modify**.

The Value Assignment dialog box opens.

17. Click the **Fx (Insert Function)** button to the right of the **To this value** box.

The Define Workflow Lookup dialog box opens.

18. Leave the **Source** selection set to the **Current Item** default value, and in the **Field** list, select **Title**.

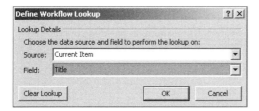

19. Click **OK** to return to the **Value Assignment** dialog box, and then click **OK** again to return to the **Create New List Item** dialog box.

20. Click **Add**.

Again, the Value Assignment dialog box opens.

21. In the **Set this Field** list, click **Sales**.

22. Click the **Fx** button next to the **To this value** box.

The Define Workflow Lookup dialog box opens.

23. Leave the **Source** value set to **Current Item.** In the **Field** list, select **SalesData**, and click **OK** to return to the **Value Assignment** dialog box, and then click **OK** again to return to the **Create New List Item** dialog box.

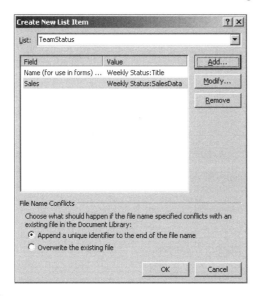

24. Click **OK**.

The Create New List Item dialog box closes.

25. Click **Finish**.

> **Important** After you click Finish, the workflow is compiled and saved to the server. During this process, if any errors occur, the workflow displays an error dialog box explaining that the compilation failed. It is essential that you immediately correct any errors you see during the save and processing of the workflow. If you do not, the workflow will not run.

This workflow, when executed, creates a new item in the TeamStatus document library. The item's name is set to the title for the WeeklyStatus list item, and the one field that is available for reporting (Sales) is set to the data entered in the WeeklyStatus list item.

26. Browse to the *allitems.aspx* page for the **Weekly Status** list you created in step 3.

27. Refresh the page to make sure that the workflow you just created is available, point to **Report One**, and click to display the menu for this item.

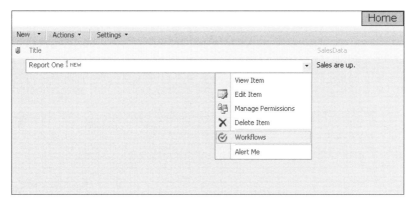

28. Click **Workflows**.

The Workflows: Report One page opens in the browser.

29. Click **StatusReport**.

The StatusReport workflow start page opens in the browser.

30. Click **Start**.

The workflow runs and creates a new document in the document library with the Sales status field filled in with the correct data.

Sending a Notification in an E-Mail Message When a Workflow Runs

In addition to creating documents (or list items) as you did in the previous exercise, you can also use workflows to perform many other actions, as indicated in the Workflow Actions list in the Workflow Designer. One of the most common actions is to send an e-mail message when an event occurs. For example, if a task is added to a task list and assigned to someone, that person can receive an e-mail notification. However, using the Workflow Designer to create an e-mail message with a richly formatted body is challenging. Doing so requires you to include HTML code directly in the body of the e-mail message that is generated by the workflow.

In this exercise, you will modify the workflow you created in the previous exercise so that it sends an e-mail message with richly formatted text, which you will design by using the HTML editor in SharePoint Designer.

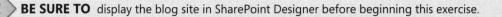

BE SURE TO   display the blog site in SharePoint Designer before beginning this exercise.

1. Press [Ctrl]+[N] to create a new page.

2. Verify that the page is in Design view by pointing to **Page** on the **View** menu and clicking **Design**.

3. On the **Edit** menu, click **Select All**.

4. Press [Del].

   The form that is inserted in the ASPX document by default is removed from the page.

5. Type **Weekly Status** on the page.

6. Select the **Weekly Status** text you just typed. On the **Formatting** toolbar, select **Heading 2 <h2>** from the **Style** list.

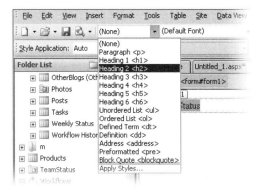

7. Click on the design surface below **Weekly Status**, and then type **Summary:**.

8. Select the **Summary:** text you just typed. On the **Formatting** toolbar, select **Heading 3 <h3>** from the **Style** list.

9. Click on the design surface below **Summary:**, and on the **Insert** menu, click **Hyperlink**.

The Insert Hyperlink dialog box opens.

10. In the **Text to display** box, type **Full Report**.

11. In the **Address** box, type **PLACEHOLDER**.

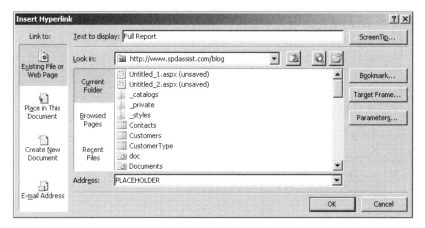

12. Click **OK** to insert a hyperlink into the document.

13. On the **View** menu, point to **Page**, and then click **Code**.

14. Select all of the code between the opening and closing *<body>* tags.

15. On the **Edit** menu, click **Copy**.

16. On the **File** menu, click **Open Workflow**.

The Open Workflow dialog box opens.

17. Select **StatusReport**, and then click **OK.**

The Workflow Designer opens, displaying the step you added in the previous exercise that generates a document based on the WeeklyStatus list items.

18. Click **Initiation**.

The Workflow Initiation Parameters dialog box opens.

19. Click **Add**.

The Add Field dialog box opens.

20. In the **Field name** box, type **Summary**.

21. In the **Information type** list, click **Multiple lines of text**.

22. Click **Next**.

23. Leave the **Default value** text field blank, and click **Finish** to create this field. Then click **OK**.

A new workflow initiation variable has now been created. When the workflow is started, this variable will need to be populated by the person who starts this workflow.

24. In the same row with the **Create item in WeeklyStatus (Output to Variable: create)** string, click **Actions**, and then select **Send an Email**.

A new line is added that says:

then Email this message

25. Click **this message**.

The Define E-mail Message dialog box opens.

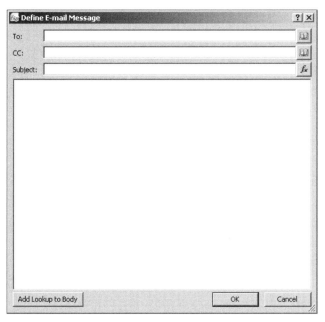

Address Book

26. Click the address book button to the right of the **To** box.

The Select Users dialog box opens. In this dialog box, you can select members of the SharePoint site, individuals or groups from the address book, or specific users.

27. In the **Or select from existing Users and Groups** list, click **Team Site Members** (which is one of the default groups in SharePoint).

> **Important** You do not need to have a particular e-mail program installed on your computer to send the e-mail message, but the server does need to be configured by the server administrator to send e-mail.

28. Click **Add** to add the group to the **Selected Users** list, and then click **OK**.

The Team Site Members group is added to the To line of the e-mail message.

29. In the **Subject** box, type **Team Weekly Summary**, and then click in the body area. Press Ctrl + V to paste in the HTML code you copied in step 15.

The e-mail message now contains all of the formatted HTML code so that the message will be nicely formatted.

30. Click **OK** to close the **Define E-mail Message** dialog box, and then click **Finish** in the **Workflow Designer**.

The workflow is compiled and is now ready to be tested. When you run the *statusreport* workflow, an e-mail message will be generated and sent to everyone in the Team Site Members group.

Adding Workflow Data to an E-Mail Message

In the exercise in the previous section, you created an e-mail message that will be sent whenever the workflow runs. You might have noticed, however, that the message does not contain any meaningful information for the people who receive it. To make the message meaningful, you should include dynamic content populated from the workflow itself. Using the Windows Workflow Foundation and SharePoint Designer, you can include workflow variables in any field of the e-mail message.

> **Tip** When you include workflow variables in the subject of the message, those variables must make up the entire subject line; when you include workflow variables in the body of the message, they can be placed inline with other static text that you type.

In this exercise, you will modify the e-mail message you created in the previous exercise to include workflow data so that the content of the message is dynamic, includes an initiation variable, and includes a link to the document that is created.

 BE SURE TO complete the previous exercise before beginning this exercise.

1. On the **File** menu, click **Open Workflow**.

The Open Workflow dialog box opens.

2. Select **StatusReport**, and then click **OK**.

The Workflow Designer opens, displaying the step you added in the previous exercise that generates a document based on the WeeklyStatus list items and sends an e-mail message to the team.

3. Place the cursor to the right of the closing **</h3>** tag.

4. At the bottom of the dialog box, click **Add Lookup to Body**.

The Define Workflow Lookup dialog box opens.

5. In the **Source** list, click **Workflow Data**.

6. In the **Field** list, click **Initiation: Summary**.

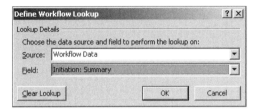

7. Click **OK**.

The Define Workflow Lookup dialog box closes, and the variable is inserted into the message body.

8. In the HTML code, select **PLACEHOLDER**. Then press [Del].

9. Type the full path for the **TeamStatus** document library. For example, in my case, I would type **http://www.spdassist.com/Blog/TeamStatus/**.

10. With the cursor to the right of the final slash in that URL, click **Add Lookup to Body**.

The Define Workflow Lookup dialog box opens.

11. Leave the **Source** value set to **Current Item**.

12. In the **Field** list, click **Title**, and then click **OK**.

13. With the cursor flashing to the right of the new workflow variable that you just added, type **.docx**.

The code in the body of the e-mail message now looks like this:

```
<h2>Weekly Status</h2>
<h3>Summary:</h3>[%Initiation: Summary%]
<p><a href="http://www.spdassist.com/blog/TeamStatus/[%Weekly_Status:
Title%].docx">Full Report</a></p>
```

14. Click **OK** to dismiss the **Define E-mail Message** dialog box, and then click **Finish** in the Workflow Designer.

15. Browse to the **Weekly Status** list and create a new item.

16. Point to this new item, click to open the menu for the item, and then click **Workflows**.

The Workflows page for that item opens in the browser.

17. Click **StatusReport**.

The Initiation form for the StatusReport workflow renders in the browser, displaying a multiple-line box for text entry.

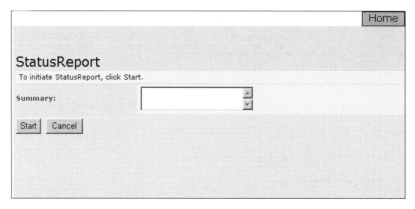

18. Type **This is a test** into the box, and then click **Start**.

The workflow runs on the server. When it is finished, you will receive an e-mail message containing the information included in step 13.

Creating a Logical Branch in a Workflow Step to Control the Flow of a Workflow Process

Not only can you use the workflow platform to send e-mail messages, create documents, build strings, and set field values, you can also use it with *conditional branches*. With conditional branches, you can create *if/then* statements to control the flow of workflow logic. For example, if you want a certain step in a workflow to run only when a particular field value is true, you would create a condition in the Workflow Designer that contains that statement. The list of conditions available in SharePoint Designer allows you to work with a variable such as the size of a file (which is useful when you are creating workflow actions associated with a document library), *Title Contains* keywords, and many other choices. These options allow you to create a rich set of conditions with which you can control when specific workflow actions take place.

In this exercise, you will modify the action created in the three preceding exercises so that the document is created and the e-mail message sent only when a field in the list is set to *Yes*. When that field is not *Yes* (in other words, when it is either not filled in or is set to *No*), no document is created and no e-mail message is sent; instead, a task to review the status report is assigned to a user.

> **BE SURE TO** display the blog site in SharePoint Designer, and ensure that the StatusReport workflow is in the blog site, before beginning this exercise.

1. In the **Folder List** task pane, select the **Weekly Status** list. Then press [F12] to preview the list in the browser.

   The *allitems.aspx* page opens in the browser.

2. On the Web Part toolbar, in the **Settings** list, click **Create Column**.

3. In the **Column name** box, type **Reviewed**.

4. In the **The type of information in this column is** list, click **Yes/No (check box)**.

5. For the **Default value** setting, select **No**.

6. Click **OK**.

   The Reviewed column is added to the default view of the list.

7. Add a new list item with a title of **Logical Test**, and select the check box so that **Reviewed** is equal to **Yes**.

8. Display this site in SharePoint Designer.

9. On the **File** menu, click **Open Workflow**.

   The Open Workflow dialog box opens.

10. Select **StatusReport**, and then click **OK**.

    The Workflow Designer opens with the workflow created in the previous three exercises displayed.

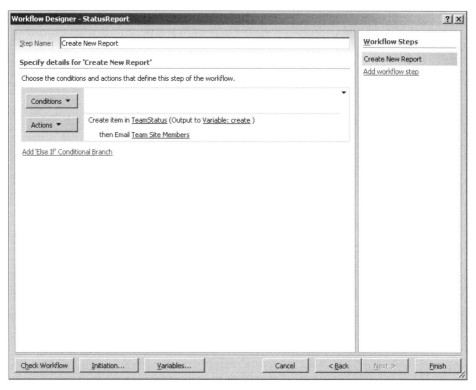

11. Click **Conditions**, and then select **Compare Weekly Status field**.

A new line is added to the workflow:

if field equals value

12. Click **field**, and then select **Reviewed**.

13. For the comparison, leave the value set to **equals**.

14. Click **value**, and then select **Yes**.

A new condition is now in the workflow. This condition controls when the actions below it will occur. In this case, the actions will occur when the *Reviewed* field is set to *Yes*.

15. Below the current action, click **Add 'Else If' Conditional Branch**.

The Workflow Designer changes to show the branching of logic.

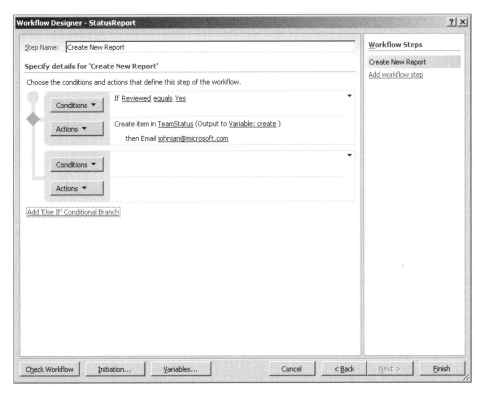

16. Click **Actions** in the new branch.

17. Click **Assign a To-do Item**.

A new string is added:

Assign a to-do item to these users

18. Click **a to-do item**.

The Custom Task Wizard opens.

19. Click **Next**.

20. In the **Name** box, delete **New Task** and type **Review Weekly Status list**.

21. Click **Finish**.

The Custom Task Wizard finishes.

22. Click **these users**.

The Select Users dialog box opens.

23. Type the e-mail address of the person who is to review the Weekly Status messages—for example, **john@spdassist.com**.

24. Click **OK**, and then click **Finish**.

The workflow recompiles on the server and now contains a new set of logic: when the *Reviewed* field is set to *Yes*, the workflow creates the document and sends an e-mail message; when the *Reviewed* field is not *Yes*, it assigns a task to *john@spdassist.com* to review the Weekly Status list item.

25. Browse to the *allitems.aspx* page for **Weekly Status,** and point to the **Logical Test** item you created in step 7.

26. Click the arrow, and select **Workflows**.

27. Click **StatusReport**.

The Initiation form renders in the browser, displaying a multiple-line box for entering the summary of the weekly reports.

28. Type **This is the summary text** into the **Summary** box.

29. Click **Start**.

When the workflow for this item is done, there will be a new document in the TeamStatus document library that contains the summary for the Sales team. If you repeat steps 25 through 28 for any list item that does not have a value for the *Reviewed* field or that has a value of *No*, the Tasks list for this site will create a Review Weekly Status list task and assign it to *john@spdassist.com*.

Saving XML Data into a SharePoint List by Using Custom Form Actions

So far in this chapter, the workflows you have created all work against list data. However, SharePoint Designer also allows you to grab strings from inside a data view and insert that data into a list. This means that rather than creating a workflow based on list data, you can create a custom form action by using the Workflow Designer user interface. For example, if your data is streaming in from an RSS feed or a SQL database, you can write a custom form action so that when a user clicks a button on your Web page, the data is copied into a SharePoint list. It can then trigger additional workflows you create, or otherwise participate in all the other benefits that lists can leverage on SharePoint (such as the permissions model, list forms pages, and exposure through Web services). The exercise in this section uses a simple XML file, but you can use the same functionality for any data source that can be viewed in a data view and then formatted.

The exercise in this section uses the Form Actions dialog box, which by default provides five actions and the ability to create custom actions:

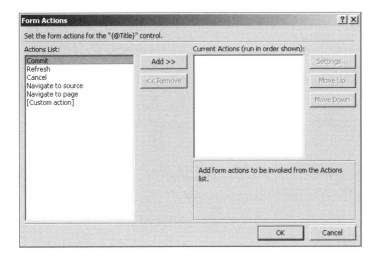

- **Commit.** This command creates an action that posts the current data values to a data source. When the data values in a data view are formatted as form field controls, this command creates an action that posts the current data values to the data source in the same way that a Save command works with list data.

- **Refresh.** This command allows the page to be refreshed without doing an actual browser refresh. Occasionally, when a browser is refreshed, a warning appears stating that the page must resubmit the data; this command prevents that warning from appearing.

- **Cancel.** This command cancels any ongoing form action.

- **Navigate to source.** When there is a source parameter in the URL for a page, this command will cause the browser to redirect to that URL. SharePoint uses this function to track where to return users to when they click on site settings pages.

● **Navigate to page.** This command behaves like a hyperlink. It is included in the list of form actions so that you can perform another action first, and then navigate to a specific URL.

● **[Custom action].** This command allows you to create a workflow that will run when the button is clicked.

In this exercise, you will create a simple XML file and then create a data view from that file. Inside that data view, you will format the data so that it can be used in a custom form action, and then you will create a custom form action that copies that data value into a new SharePoint list.

 BE SURE TO display the blog site in SharePoint Designer before beginning this exercise.

1. On the **File** menu, point to **New**, and then click **SharePoint Content**.

The New dialog box opens with the Lists category on the SharePoint Content tab selected.

2. Click **Custom List** and, in the **Specify the name for the new list** box, type **XMLData**. Then click **OK** to create the list.

3. Create a new XML file in SharePoint Designer with the following code:

```
<products>
  <product id="1" name="Soda" category="Beverages" />
  <product id="2" name="Beer" category="Beverages" />
  <product id="3" name="Wine" category="Beverages" />
  <product id="4" name="Bread" category="Food" />
  <product id="5" name="Meat" category="Food" />
</products>
```

4. Press Ctrl+S, type **productList** into the **File Name** box, and then click **Save** to save this file as **productList.xml**.

5. Press Ctrl+N to create a new page, and place it in Design view by pointing to **Page** on the **View** menu and clicking **Design**.

6. In the **Folder List** task pane, select the *productList.xml* file, drag it into the design panel for this new page, and drop it onto the surface of the page.

A data view of that XML file is inserted into the page.

id	name	category
1	Soda	Beverages
2	Beer	Beverages
3	Wine	Beverages
4	Bread	Food
5	Meat	Food

7. Select the **Soda** data value in the **name** column.

8. Click the On Object User Interface (OOUI) arrow to show the **Common Label Tasks** panel.

9. Change the **Format as** value from **Text** to **Label**.

In Design view in SharePoint Designer, nothing looks different. However, the data value that was being displayed with an XSLT *value-of* command is now being rendered as the text attribute value of an *asp:label* control. Doing this enables the data value to be available to the workflow process, which has the logic to read Microsoft ASP.NET control values, but not XSLT values.

10. In the data view, right-click above the **1** data value in the **id** column, and then point to **Insert**.

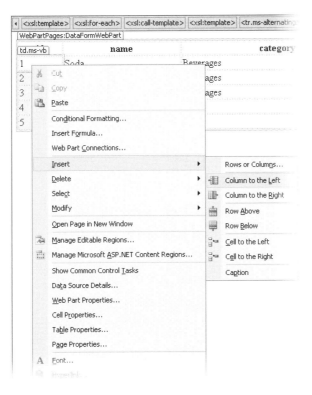

11. Click **Column to the Left**.

A new column is added to the left of the ID column.

12. On the **Task Panes** menu, click **Toolbox**. Then scroll down in the **Toolbox** to the **SharePoint Controls** category, expand the **SharePoint Controls** category, and expand the **Data View Controls** subcategory.

13. Click the **Form Action Button** control.

14. Drag the control from the **Toolbox** into the first column (the one you inserted in step 11) of the second row of the data view.

The Form Actions dialog box opens.

15. Select **[Custom Action]**, and then click **Add**.

The custom action is added to the Current Actions list.

> **Tip** As noted in the user interface, the *current actions* run in the order in which they occur in the list. This is very important, because if you happen to add a Navigate To Page action before a Commit action (for example), the Navigate action will occur before the Commit action, so the Commit will never happen.

16. Click **Settings**.

The Workflow Designer opens. This dialog box looks very much like the Workflow Designer from the previous exercise; however, there is no back button and no way to associate this workflow with a list.

17. Click the **Actions** button, and then select **Create List Item**.

A string appears:

Create item in this list (Output to Variable: create)

18. Click **this list**.

19. In the **List** list, click **XMLData**.

The Field list is populated with the one default field created in the custom list: Title.

20. Select **Title(*)**, and then click **Modify**.

The Value Assignment dialog box opens.

21. Click the **Fx** button next to the **To this value** box.

The Define Workflow Lookup dialog box opens.

22. Leave the **Source** set to **Form Fields**, and click in the **Field** list to select **Form Fields: ff1 (@name)**.

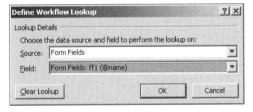

23. Click **OK** to close the **Define Workflow Lookup** dialog box, click **OK** again to close the **Value Assignment** dialog box, and click **OK** a third time to close the **Create New List Item** dialog box.

24. In the Workflow Designer **Step Name** field, type **Save XML**, and then click **Finish** to compile the workflow.

The Workflow Designer is closed, and the Form Actions dialog box opens again.

25. In the **Actions** list, select **Navigate to Page**, and then click **Add**.

The Navigate To Page action is added to the list of current actions under [Custom Action].

26. Click **Settings** to open the **Form Actions Settings** dialog box, and then click **Browse** to open the **Edit Hyperlink** dialog box.

27. In the **Edit Hyperlink** dialog box, double-click the **XMLData** folder and select *Allitems.aspx*, and then click **OK** to close this dialog box.

The Edit Hyperlink dialog box is closed, and the Form Action Settings dialog box now contains the path for the XMLData list's *allitems.aspx* page in the Target Page box.

28. Click **OK**.

The Form Actions dialog box now has two current actions set to run: [Custom Action] and Navigate To Page.

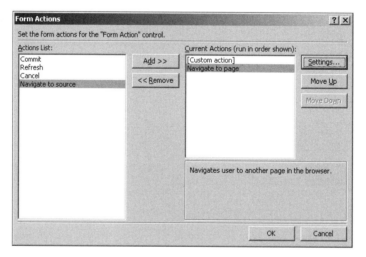

29. Click **OK**.

The Form Action button is inserted into each row of the data view. This button's properties can be modified just like those of any other button inserted on the SharePoint Designer design surface.

30. Save this page as **formActions.aspx**, press [F12] to preview this page in the default browser, and then click **Form Action** next to any of the data values.

You are redirected to the *xmlData/allitems.aspx* page. A list item appears for the item for which you clicked Submit Data in the *formActions.aspx* page.

Key Points

- At one layer, workflow is a platform upon which you can build processes to automate redundant tasks. On SharePoint, workflow is about document and task automation and management. When accessed through SharePoint Designer, workflow can be used to automate a wide breadth of automatable tasks.

- You can use workflow to create documents or lists in addition to many other out-of-the-box actions.

- You can also use workflow to link SharePoint list data to Word documents.

- Logical branches help control when certain workflow actions can occur in a process.

- When you include workflow data in an e-mail message generated by a workflow process, you enable rich content in otherwise static text.

- With custom form actions, you can create workflow for any data view.

Index

A

AccessDataSource control, 192
actions, form, 284-290
Add Code Snippet dialog box, 27-28
Add Field dialog box, 276
Add File To Import List dialog box, xv
Add Web Parts To Full Page dialog box, 14
Advanced Condition dialog box, 227-228
Advanced Grouping dialog box, 167
Advanced Sort dialog box, 165-167
aligning text, 77
allitems.aspx, 231
  customizing, 232
  overview of, 232
anchor tags. *See also* hyperlinks
  default styles for, 56
applications, Web. *See* Web applications
Apply Styles task pane
  functions in, 47
  overview of, 46
  in SharePoint Designer, 21
asp:Checkbox control, 201
asp:Content tags, 103
asp:ContentPlaceHolder tags
  creating to account for *asp:Content* tags on
    external pages, 103
  filling in, 92
  overview of, 85
asp:menu controls
  appearance of, 116
  customizing, 112-118
  editing menu items, 114-115, 118
  formatting, 120
  inserting, 113
  navigating with, 116
  properties, viewing, 120
  rendering incorrectly, 122
  schemes, applying, 119
  style properties, modifying, 116-122

ASP.NET
  internal field names, 195
  overview of, 187
ASP.NET controls. *See also* controls
  AutoPostBack operation, 192-197
  binding data to, 188-192
  data, 192
  data source, selecting, 117
  filtering views by, 192-197
  formatting, modifying, 116-122
  inserting, 193
  login, 193
  navigation, 193
  passing data to page, 192-197
  populating parameters with, 214
  rendering incorrectly, 122
  standard, 192
  testing, 191
  validation, 192
  viewing all, 192
  views, changing, 118
ASP.NET templates, 118
ASP.NET v2.0.50727 status, setting, 4
ASPX pages
  creating, 210
  creating from master pages, 88, 93-96
Attach Style Sheet dialog box, 47
authentication
  Kerberos, 145
  single sign-on (SSO), 145
AutoComplete, 221
AutoFormat dialog box, 117-118
AutoPostBack operation, 192

B

background colors, changing, 74-75
blog posts
  average rating, displaying, 241
  creating, 10
  as data sources, 236

X

About the Author

John Jansen is a Lead Software Design Engineer in Test at Microsoft, working in the Microsoft Office SharePoint Designer product group. He has been with Microsoft for more than nine years, working as a Microsoft Office FrontPage support technician before moving over to a test position in 2001 in the FrontPage product group. He has been testing the SharePoint Designer implementation of XSLT and Microsoft ASP.NET controls for the last few years, and leads a team of six engineers. He also focuses his energy on security throughout the SharePoint platform, as well as blogging with the community and researching new Web application design techniques. Before coming to Microsoft, John taught online English courses at North Seattle Community College and worked with a small team of real estate agents as a database administrator and marketing specialist. When not working full time at Microsoft or writing books about SharePoint Designer, John maintains his wife's business Web site (which was built on SharePoint Team Services and then migrated to Microsoft Windows SharePoint Services). In addition, he likes to hang out with his 4-year-old daughter, Ryan, and his wife, Christa, in Seattle, Washington.

Acknowledgements

I would like to thank my wife and daughter for allowing me the time and solitude to work late into the night and early in the morning to complete this book. I'd also like to thank Bob Hogan for the technical review (even amid horrible ice storms and power outages), Kathy Krause for building a reasonable schedule for me that I could actually meet (as well as the rest of the OTSI team for all their hard work), and Juliana Aldous and Sandra Haynes for getting this book rolling at Microsoft Press. I must also give thanks to Jerome Thiebaud, Mike Navarro, and Ron Harper for giving me the inspiration and ability to complete this book.

What do you think of this book?

We want to hear from you!

Your feedback will help us continually improve our books and learning resources for you. To participate in a brief online survey, please visit:

microsoft.com/learning/booksurvey

...and enter this book's ISBN-10 or ISBN-13 number (appears above barcode on back cover). As a thank-you to survey participants in the U.S. and Canada, each month we'll randomly select five respondents to win one of five $100 gift certificates from a leading online merchant. At the conclusion of the survey, you can enter the drawing by providing your e-mail address, which will be used for prize notification only.*

Thank you in advance for your input!

Where to find the ISBN on back cover

Example only. Each book has unique ISBN.

Stay in touch!

To subscribe to the *Microsoft Press* *Book Connection Newsletter*—for news on upcoming books, events, and special offers—please visit:

microsoft.com/learning/books/newsletter